Vintage Breslin

In 1963 a relatively unknown sportswriter by the name of James Breslin was hired as a columnist by the *New York Herald Tribune.* He was an instant breath of fresh air. Today Jimmy Breslin is considered the greatest journalist to come along since Ring Lardner and Damon Runyon.

Here, for the first time, is a collection of the best of Breslin. You will meet Jimmy's friends—Fat Thomas, who weighs in at about four hundred pounds on a clear day; Mutchie, the occasionally genial boniface of Mutchie's-by-the-Sea on the East River; Marvin the Torch, the affable arsonist. Then there is Breslin reporting the major events of our decade—the Harlem and Rochester riots; Selma; Vietnam, where he was deeply affected by what he saw; Churchill's death; and there is Breslin's classic piece on the Kennedy assassination, "A Death in Emergency Room One."

"It is simply not enough to let this go by saying this is a fine, funny-sad book. It is that, to be sure, and more; it is the literature of a journalist who is among the very best at his trade. He just may be the best. Beautiful."

—Cleveland Press

THE WORLD OF JIMMY BRESLIN

By Jimmy Breslin

Annotated by James G. Bellows
and Richard C. Wald

BALLANTINE BOOKS • NEW YORK

Library of Congress catalog card number: 66-19161

This edition published by arrangement with
The Viking Press.

First Printing: July, 1969

Printed in the United States of America

BALLANTINE BOOKS, INC.
101 Fifth Avenue, New York, New York 10003

Contents

THE WORLD OF JIMMY BRESLIN

1

How He Is Cared for and Fed

Jimmy Breslin is too fat. He drinks too much, he smokes too much, and if he makes it past his fortieth birthday a lot of clockers and watchers are going to be surprised.

But he is not entirely uncaring about this. As he puts his cigarette down on the edge of the bar at Gallagher's on West 52nd Street and sips from his half-empty beer glass, he complains that he isn't feeling well. Most often he says that his circulation is going bad on him the way it went on Whitey Ford, and if you think pitchers need their arms, you should just know that a writer also needs his fingers. If the circulation isn't that troublesome for the moment, he can work up a pretty good case for the fact that his column isn't going as well as it should or that the Governor is avoiding him or that his wife, Rosemary, is upset with him again. And with every complaint comes a flow of reminiscence and anecdote that is almost uninterruptedly funny. It takes a happy man to sing a worried song that way.

Breslin is a walking contradiction who happens to be Irish and a little ambivalent about it. He is sometimes seen in the process of inventing himself, a luxury permitted only to the intelligent few, but he is inventing something pretty close to a kid who grew up in a rough section of Queens and never really left. When he is caught off-guard, he uses perfectly clear and well-articulated English because his mother is an English teacher in high school and that's the way she taught him to speak.

He is thirty-seven, which is on the borderline of not being young any more. His early days were spent in the parochial and then public schools of Queens. He likes the fact that few of the kids he grew up with ever get divorced, not because the Church is against divorce, but because so many of them came from broken homes that most of them determined to keep what they have together.

Facts on his education are hazy because he lies so much about it. He has claimed he has a doctorate from Cambridge. He also has said he attended Elmira Reformatory. There is a valid question as to whether he graduated from high school, which he attended for five years. He enrolled somehow in a college in 1948, but he was already working on a Long Island newspaper and he used his college status to impress editors with the idea that he was trying to improve himself. His only real interest was sports writing, which he did for practically no pay and on the worst shift. His scholastic career soon faded while he wrote about Sandlot football games.

What made him a writer instead of just a sports reporter was sheer, scrambling necessity. The twins were born a year after he and Rosemary Dattolico were married fourteen years ago. They were premature; nobody in the family had any money; the cost of incubators for a month's stay in the hospital is high, and you can't pay it with choirboy looks when the bill comes around. So he got out and began to sell the only thing he could make real money at—stories for magazines.

It was a curious progress. He moved from the Newhouse papers to Scripps-Howard to Hearst, each time a step up the journalistic ladder, each time almost getting a column, each move made on the strength of the magazine articles he had to write to stay in the newspaper business. And he began to discover that Breslin was his most salable commodity. You take in the sights that other people see and you turn them out through the lens that makes you an individual, and suddenly other people see them better. That's why he always writes about Breslin and why people go on reading about Breslin and why he keeps on living like Breslin. The bars and the drinking and the ever-present cigarette are part of a slapdash poetry that irritates the hell out of a lot of people and charms others. Breslin is just trying to capture the essence of his own life and turn it into words. He also happens to be lucky that people will pay to watch.

He has a furious energy to find out what happens in the city because he identifies himself with it, or at least with a sidelong view of it. When he works for a newspaper he is never long out of touch with the City Desk. He gets furious if something happens and no one calls him. He constantly betrays his pose of ignorance by calling the shots for better coverage of the city. He is always frantically scheming how to get the best story out of any news event. And this is the way he writes about himself.

Measles

Fat Thomas, the bookmaker, his 415 pounds encased in a plaid sports jacket, stood in the doorway of the bedroom. He would not come any closer.

"How are you, baby?" he said.

"Terrible," I said.

"What are you going to tell people?" he said.

"I'm sick," I said. "What the hell can I say?"

"Yeah, but you can't tell people you got the measles," Fat Thomas said. "Everybody will be sending you baby food."

"I feel so lousy I don't care."

"I'll tell them you got a nervous breakdown, baby," Fat Thomas said. "I can't mention the measles. It'll break everybody up."

I pulled the covers up over my eyes and said I didn't care. This was on a wet Thursday morning a couple of weeks ago. At thirty-four, and with a wife and children, and with enough debts to qualify as an adult any place in the world, I had the measles. Not just a touch of the measles. I had the measles from face to foot, and a fever and sore throat to go with them. The doctor was on his way, but his decision was going to be academic. When I had awakened an hour before, Kevin Breslin, aged nine, wandered into the bedroom and said hello, then looked at me carefully and let out a yell.

"You got something," he said. "You got the measles."

"I got *what?*"

"Jamesy, come here and look at Daddy," he yelled. His twin brother came in. The two of them, the bills of their baseball caps poking me in the eyes, inspected my face close up.

"Open your shirt," James said.

"See? He's got them all over his chest," James announced.

"Does your throat hurt?" Kevin asked.

It did. It hurt like hell.

"Uh-huh." Kevin nodded. "You got them all right. You have to stay in bed."

Then, with the experience of his years, he bent over, pulling down both the window shades, and announced that the room would have to stay dark. Then he and his brother left to go downstairs for breakfast.

"Too bad," James said as he left the room. "But you got them all right."

They went downstairs to announce, over Shredded Wheat, that their father had the measles. Their mother let out a scream, ran up the stairs, took one look, then went downstairs and was in tears when Fat Thomas arrived.

"Don't get upset," he told her. "It's only a kid thing. It can't be bad."

"I don't care about the measles," she said. "I just don't want him in the house all day."

The kids went to school. The doctor came and left. And now Fat Thomas, still standing in the doorway and coming no closer, said he had to leave and book his bets for the day, and when he disappeared from the doorway I was left to face probably the worst morning of my life.

I've had bad mornings in my time. Once I had a hangover that was so bad I couldn't make it out of the house and had to hire a private ambulance to get to work. It cost 45 hard dollars and the attendants came and carried me out on a stretcher and threw me into the ambulance and I slept all the way to work. Then I was single and living with my friend Max in an apartment on the West Side. We had a policy of paying nobody and the bill collectors got so bad that one morning we woke up with the finance-company guy sitting at the kitchen table. It was unnerving, but we grabbed the bum and threw him into the shower and Max held him in while I turned on the cold water. It fixed the finance-company guy, but it was a tough way to start off the day.

But no morning could come close to this one. Measles, like toy guns, are supposed to be for children. Adults are supposed to have sicknesses of their own. We have infectious hepatitis, bad virus, gout, old war wounds, recurrent malaria and, for the more sophisticated, unbreakable appointments with analysts and nervous exhaustion. But I had measles. I had measles just like Stevie Kirschenbaum next door and Danny Koch around the corner and Ramona Bartlett up the block, and let me see you try and tell me how you can pick up the phone and call your office and tell them, "No I won't have a column today; I caught the measles from Danny Koch and I have to stay in bed and keep the window shades down." You try that. Pick up the telephone and call Pennsylvania 6-4000 and ask for Mr. John Hay Whitney and say, "Jock, how are you, I got some bad news. No, not a libel suit. Not today, anyway. It's measles. I can't do any work for you today because I got the measles." When you're finished with him, start dialing again and call off all your appointments. Call the Waldorf-Astoria barbershop and tell the girl to get you a customer named Mr. Frank Costello. When he gets on tell him, "Frank, I can't meet you for lunch at Moore's. I'm home with the measles. Frank, stop it, this isn't a gag. Listen. Do you hear the noise? That's me slapping myself. You're not supposed to scratch, remember?"

Then, when you're finished with him, call Mutchie and tell him you can't meet him at the racetrack later in the day and tell him why.

"Oh, I know what the measles are," Mutchie said. He was the only one to sound sympathetic.

"I'm glad you do," I told him.

"Yeah," he said. "Once they held me for four days with them."

"Where?"

"At Ellis Island. I had them when I got off the boat from Palermo. I was sick."

I hung up on him. Then I got down under the covers again and lay there, a big speckled lump. It was no joke. I felt about as sick as I've ever felt. A kids' disease, when caught by an adult, can be hell, the doctor said. He was right. I had a throat that was closed tight, a mouth that hurt so much I couldn't eat for three days, and a fever that nailed down my whole body. I was left with only a temper. This is the one luxury I have when I'm sick. Anger. Good, deep, vicious anger. Sometimes it's almost worth getting sick for, this anger you get when you're sick in bed.

At noon little Rosemary came home from first grade in tears and it was great.

"Ritchie took my Beatles button when I was up reading and he won't give it back," she wailed.

"Didn't you tell the teacher?" I called down.

"I did, but Ritchie told her it was his button, and she believed him. He lied, and she believed him."

"Ritchie, hah?" I yelled. "That's my *stick* today. I'm going to fix that Ritchie."

I got out of the bed and went to the typewriter. I typed out a note to my daughter's teacher. It read:

Dear Mrs. Stirt:
My daughter came home in tears because one of the future commercial criminals in your class stole her Beatles button and then lied about it. Which is about what I'd expect of the people here. They teach their children shoplifting, not honesty. I demand that Ritchie give back that Beatles button. If he doesn't, I'm going to have somebody come around tonight and set his father's car afire. I'd do it myself, but I am sick in bed with the measles.

Thank you,
Mr. Breslin

I called little Rosemary up to the room. "Don't say a word to anybody," I told her. "You put this note in your coat pocket and give it to the teacher. Remember, don't tell anybody." She nodded and skipped off to school, the note in her pocket. I fell asleep. I almost felt good.

Some time later I could hear, dimly, the phone ringing and my wife downstairs talking on it and saying, "Oh, Lord," and, "Oh, I don't know what to say," and then she hung up and came storming up the stairs.

"You," she screamed. "Do you know what's the matter with you? You're crazy. You've got that woman at the school all upset. You belong in an institution, that's where you belong. I never heard of an adult doing something like this in my life."

"I'm going to have Ritchie killed if he doesn't give back the Beatles button," I said. Then I went back to sleep.

This one morning now became four mornings and afternoons all in one, because I was asleep and half asleep during all this time, and I would wake up sporadically and do a few things by myself and then go to sleep again. It all became one long morning with the measles. The things I would do when I woke up were all little things. Talking to people mostly.

On Friday morning the *Herald Tribune* carried a little line in the space where my column usually runs. It said: "Jimmy Breslin's column will not appear today. Mr. Breslin says he has the measles. (Honest.)" Right away, a fellow I know called me up.

"I just saw the paper," he said. "I'm sorry to hear you're sick. . . ."

"Smart guy," I said. "I'm going to call up your wife and tell her about the night I saw you having dinner with that broad."

I hung up on him and went back to sleep. I felt satisfied. When I woke up the next time, I did another thing. I fixed the Dugan's man.

"How much bread do you want today?" he called through the front door.

"Two loaves of white," my wife said from the kitchen.

"Fine. Mrs. Breslin, would you want to pay me now or should I come back tomorrow?"

"Oh, I'm in the middle of cooking and my hands are all greasy. Would you mind coming back tomorrow?"

"Wait a minute!" I shouted. I threw off the covers and hit the floor with both feet flying.

"So you like pressuring people, do you?" I yelled while I was coming down the stairs. "Who the hell are you to come around here like a shylock? I'm going to bite your nose right off your face."

By the time I got to the door, Dugan's was out in the truck.

"Look at him," I said. "He's yellow. Put the bull on these tough guys and they all bend in half."

My wife said a word she is not supposed to know. Then she said another word. Then she called me an entire string of names.

"You're going to the hospital," she said finally. "You're going to the hospital and you're not coming out until I see the reports myself."

I went back to bed. I felt a little better now. I had fixed that Dugan's real good. So I turned on the television and spent the rest of the afternoon watching Ajax commercials. These are the commercials where an armored knight on a white horse charges at people with a lance and turns their dirty clothes to white. It is the ultimate testimonial to the tastelessness and nonsense which runs through most of the help in the advertising field. But I loved this Ajax commercial. It let me dream. I lay in bed and watched that knight come with his horse and lance and I dreamed of him running the lance right through that jerk in the dirty T-shirt.

And so it went. Stripped of manly pride and forced to admit that I had the measles, I stayed in bed and got back at the world. I turned on the radio loud. WABC was my favorite station. It plays Beatles songs all day and it drives everybody crazy and it's wonderful. You can lie in bed and just by a twist of the knob you can make the Beatles louder and get the grown-ups so mad that they shout at you. That's when it's really good—when you get the grown-ups mad.

Then, just as they came, the measles left. And on a morning five days later I was standing in front of the house waiting for a cab to go to work. A now familiar car was parked across the street in front of Lederman's house. It was the doctor's car.

"What's the matter over there?" I asked my wife.

"Stephen Lederman has the measles," my wife said. Stephen Lederman is three.

"Oh," I said. I didn't say anything else to her. But I felt good. I felt power surging through my hands.

"That'll teach that Stevie Lederman to fool around with me," I said to myself.

The cab came. I glanced over at Stevie Lederman's house and sneered. Then I got in and went back to work for a living.

The Sign in Jimmy Breslin's Front Yard

The wife of a new neighbor from up on the corner came down and walked up to my wife and started acting nice, which must have exhausted her.

This woman is one of the people I have to live with. Four years ago, in the true style of an amateur, I "moved out a bit." I moved onto a block with a lot of other people who live side by side in houses. Now, people are all right. Get them alone and they're pretty good. But put five of them together and they start conforming and after that all they are is trouble. Put sixteen families on the same block, the way it is on mine, and they become unbelievable. They are not people any more. They are enemies. On my block they sweep the lawn and have the waxer polish the front walk and all of them ring doorbells about kid fights and if everything isn't the same, and everybody doesn't worry about things that show, they bother you as an occupation. Anybody who has his own mind and moves out of a beautiful, anonymous Manhattan apartment and goes to a house on a block is crazy.

For four years now, so many of the neighbors have come to the door, or had their kids run up like stool pigeons to report some crime my kids committed, that now I sit at the front window and watch one of them come down the block and as he walks I dream of a big black car pulling up and three guys in big hats jumping out and breaking both my neighbor's legs.

It is this bad to live with these people, and this woman could get first on the whole block.

"I haven't gotten a chance to see you since the baby," the new one said. "How nice. This is, uh, your . . . ?"

She knew the number, she knows everything. She knew my take-home pay by the end of the first week she was on the block.

"Fifth," my wife said.

"How wonderful," she said. "And did you plan this one?"

"Oh, yes," my wife said sweetly. "Why, everybody I know plans their fifth baby."

The woman got mad and walked away. Which was great. And I was going to say something to her that she could tell her husband for me, but I didn't have the time. I had to stay on Walter, from the Dazzle Sign

Painting Company, who was on my lawn and acting like a coward.

"Put it up, Walter," I told him.

"Not in the daylight," Walter said.

Walter had two big wooden posts and a lot of tools in his arms.

"An argument is an argument, but if you do this it lets everybody know that you're crazy," my wife says.

"Put it up, Walter," I said. "I want these people to read my sign right now."

Walter shook his head. Then he dropped everything and began jamming one of the posts into the lawn. My wife ran inside the house. She is the former Rosemary Dattolico and she is very Italian. She likes knives on black nights, not big posters in broad daylight.

"Let's go, Walter," I said, and Walter, from the Dazzle Sign Painting Company, put in both the stakes and tacked the sign on, and when he was finished, right there on the lawn was the most beautiful sign you ever saw.

It was about three feet high and five feet wide and it was in three bright colors and it read real good. On the top, in two lines of big red upper-case letters, the sign said:

SORRY TO MAKE YOU LOOK AT THIS BECAUSE I KNOW HOW TIRED YOU PEOPLE GET MOVING YOUR LIPS WHEN YOU READ

Underneath this, in smaller, but still real big blue letters, was a line which said: PEOPLE I'M NOT TALKING TO THIS YEAR.

The line was centered. Right under it, in neat columns, like a service honor roll, was the name of everybody who lives on my block. Everybody. All the couples, all the mothers-in-law, and all the kids. Every single person alive on my block had his name printed on that sign by Walter, from the Dazzle Sign Painting Company. And at the end of the list of names, I had Walter put "Dugan" for the bread man and "Stylon" for the dry-cleaning guy and "Borden's" for the fat milkman I don't like.

The best was at the bottom. In clear orange italics, the little passage said: *"I also am announcing a special service for people who ring my bell to tell me what my children did. This service includes a man who answers the doorbell. Why don't you come and ring my bell and see what happens to you?"*

Walter and I stepped back to look at the sign. The white pasteboard looked nice in the sunlight. It was the greatest sign I ever saw.

"Nobody ever had a sign like this," Walter said. "Nobody. I paint 'Fire Sale' and 'Prices Slashed' and for gin mills I do 'Under New Management' or 'Sunday Cocktail Hour,' but I never in my life done a sign like this."

"Beautiful," I said. I stood back and admired it. This was my message, my own personal message to everybody on the block. How could you find a better way to put it across? For a year now, my wife has been hissing at the neighbors, "He's writing a novel about the block and you're in it because he hid a tape recorder under your kitchen table." But this sign of mine beat any book. And even those Burma Shave signs—"She went wild/When he went woolly"—they never read as good as my personal sign.

"The sign costs $27.50," Walter said.

"Walter, it's worth $100," I said. "Look at that." I grabbed his arm. "Look at that woman up the block, Walter. She just saw the sign. She's dying to come up here and see it, I bet. Look at her, Walter. She's dying. Wait'll she comes up here and sees what it says. Can you imagine the face on her when she does that, Walter? Boy, this takes care of them. Why don't you stay around so we can both look out the window and watch?"

"I think you're sick," Walter said.

"No, I'm not, I just hate those people."

I hate them all. In the whole area where we live, I hate them all. Once I thought we got a break. A big gangster from Brooklyn moved out and tried to live quietly with his two Cadillacs parked in front of the house and his pearl-gray hat stuck on his head even when he came out for the milk. But the guy was in the neighborhood only three months and then he got arrested and he was all over the papers. People began detouring two blocks so they wouldn't go near his house, and the fellow stayed holed up so much that you never could meet him. He finally moved, and left me with all the garbage. One thing you can bet, I wouldn't have had Walter, from the Dazzle, put the gangster's name on my sign.

After I had watched my sign for a while, and Walter left with his truck from the Dazzle, I went into the kitchen and had coffee and waited until this friend of mine called Bad Eddie showed up. Bad Eddie is called this because he doesn't do anything nice, and I had things I wanted him to do to my neighbors that aren't nice.

"There's a lot of people out on the block," Bad Eddie said.

"That's good, we're going to get rid of them all," I said.

"Oh, dear Lord, look at this," my wife said. "They're coming from the other block, too."

"They could get hurt, too, and I wouldn't complain," I said.

Then I got down to business with Bad Eddie. "Now look," I said, "we're going to do this big-time. We'll get white mice and put them in someone's house. That'll fix them. Now, look out the window. See that guy up there in his back yard? Walking around the bushes? We don't even mess with him. He goes."

"What do you mean, he goes?" Bad Eddie said.

"Any way you want to do it," I said. "But he goes. We're going to do this right, just like Capone. We'll use mice, threats, beatings, anything we want."

Bad Eddie did not look up from his coffee.

"Don't that joint of his give him any vacation?" he asked my wife. "He needs a rest." Nobody answered.

"It's going to be crowded out there," my wife said. "Almost like the day Jason Robards and Lauren Bacall were across the street."

That was the biggest day in the history of the block and the people did just what you'd expect them to do. They acted like jerks. They walked back and forth, then back and forth again, or they stood on the sidewalk and gaped at Mr. Robards and his wife. They were visiting their accountant, who lives across the street and doesn't talk to me, but they should have charged admission for coming out in front of the house.

When they left, the block went back to normal. Which means all that ever happens is some grown man, pushed out by his wife with an adolescent's mind, comes up the door and tells you, "Your Jimmy tried to strangle my son the other day." And you tell him, "I'm awfully sorry. I'm awfully sorry Jimmy messed up the job and didn't kill your kid."

Now, for the rest of this day, I sat over coffee with Eddie and plotted doing things to people, and, outside, the people stopped to look at the sign and they stumbled through the reading and then went on. And in one day everybody got my personal message.

They never did get Bad Eddie's message because he spent the whole day sitting at the kitchen table and shaking his head and when he left he only said one thing. "Get yourself a good rest," Bad Eddie said.

Since then the sign has come down, but it's in the garage and it can go up any time, just like a flag. That is, if there is a garage left. As a precaution against a slow real-estate market when we find something in town and put the house up for sale, I had Marvin the Torch over one day. He is a man who burns down things for a living.

He went out in the front and dug a fingernail into the wood and looked around.

"Not too good," he said. "The wood is green. Too green. To do this sure, I might have to load it up, and that would mean taking out half the block."

"Don't let that stand in your way," I told him. The new one was right up the block looking at us.

Breslin's life was like this even when he wasn't employed on newspapers. There was an interlude of three years, starting with an unamiable row with the old New York *Journal-American* in 1960, when he managed to break the tie completely and get away from daily journalism for the world of magazines and books. It was in this period that he wrote a book about the New York Mets called *Can't Anybody Here Play This Game?* The answer was a little foggy but the book wasn't. It was serious and funny and very informative about a club that was beginning to take the place of the Dodgers, a manager named Casey Stengel, who might have been invented by Breslin, and an owner named Mrs. Charles S. Payson, who was not only Breslin's ideal of what a woman should be but also John Hay Whitney's sister.

Like his sister, Mr. Whitney believed in backing something exciting. Together, they were owners of Greentree Stables. On his own, Mr. Whitney had had several successful careers. The first was in show business (he was David O. Selznick's partner in producing *Gone with the Wind,* for instance); the second was in the Air Force during World War II; a third was in the private venture capital business after the war; and by 1959, when he took over control of the New York *Herald Tribune*, he was regarded as one of this country's best ambassadors to Great Britain as well as a leading figure in Republican politics.

Mr. Whitney liked the book and asked the *Trib*'s sports editor, Hal Claassen, if he could get the serialization rights. The same day, Claassen got the same comment from Lawton Carver, a former assistant editor at the *Trib* who was soon to become a food columnist. Claassen figured that with recommendations like that from the galley and the bridge, he couldn't possibly go wrong. The book was available and the *Herald Tribune* began to print it.

At that time the *Trib* was run by four editors. The Editor was James G. Bellows. He was from out of town. The Managing Editor was Murray M. Weiss, who was not from out of town and had no idea how much he was going to learn from Breslin. The Foreign Editor was Seymour K. Freidin, whose natural habitat is the Balkans and who was the only person in the *Trib* City Room able to match Breslin pound for pound in spreading gloom and destruction. The National Editor was Richard C. Wald, who was exactly Breslin's age, from Breslin's kind of neighborhood, and just as reliable in a pinch.

All four editors liked the book and when the Mets launched themselves into a highly improbable four-game winning streak, Bellows and Weiss conned Breslin into writing a free news story for page 1, to go along with the chapters that were then running.

This is the story.

The Mets

On Wall Street yesterday, the stock market hit a new high for the year with a volume of 5,600,000 shares. On Madison Avenue, a large men's apparel division of Genesco shifted its big ad account to the Rockmore Company. On 55th Street, a literary agent was making a cocktail date to sell an unfinished novel for $350,000 to a producer of movies. And throughout the muggy day, box-office men at the 46th Street Theatre were saying, "No, you can't get a ticket for tonight to see *How to Succeed.*"

This was New York City as we know it. Millions were in town and they were conducting the big business of the only city in the world worth talking about.

Then, at 4:31 p.m. everything changed. It was just another Thursday, but it became one of our great days. The money in the stock market? Forget it. You can borrow money. The ad account? You could have it. Who cares about anything? For at 4:31 in the afternoon, Al Jackson ran across home plate at the Polo Grounds and we beat the Philadelphia Phillies, 3-2. It was our fourth win in a row, and someday soon we are going to absolutely murder the Giants and Dodgers.

We, of course, is the New York Mets. And the Mets are, right now, the biggest thing to happen to this town since we got rid of Walter O'Malley.

"We win again." You heard that any place you went yesterday. Only 3435 were at the Polo Grounds yesterday. Which was all right because we don't have unemployment here. The crime was, the game was not on television.

For some reason, which the New Frontier should handle promptly—the Mets are the New Frontier—the station did not telecast their game.

But everybody knew about it. Yesterday we came barging into eighth place in the National League standings. And on the subways, and on commuter trains pouring through tunnels out of the city, everybody felt just a little bit better at the end of the day.

Except for one traveler. Out at Idlewild Airport, Marvin Throneberry stepped on a plane that was going to take him to Atlanta, Georgia, and the minute he put up his money for the ticket all of New York was poorer for it. Marv had been optioned to Buffalo, which was playing in Atlanta last night.

For Marvelous Marvin Throneberry is the man who made the New York Mets what they are today. Without Throneberry we would all be lost. His brand of baseball, as displayed last season, made the Mets. He had to be your hero. Anybody a little late paying a loan could understand Marvelous Marv when he went for, then usually missed, a pop fly. Only the bucketshop operator, who specializes in old widows, didn't like Marvelous Marv.

Everybody else fell in love with him. He did so many things wrong you need a whole newspaper to recount them. But all of New York fell in love with him while he was messing up—just as we'll all do—and before anybody knew what was happening, the New York Mets became *our* team.

They shipped Throneberry out to the Buffalo team of the International League last night because he simply does not fit any more. Casey Stengel has kids like this Ed Kranepool, who went to James Monroe High—the same place that Hank Greenberg did. Kranepool and the ones like him are going to make the Mets a plausible baseball team before they are through.

But someday, when we're up there fighting for the pennant, let's all think of Marvelous Marvin Throneberry, the man who started it all.

Think of him? How could you forget him? Yesterday, he was supposed to go into Casey Stengel's office before the game to hear the bad news. People go in and out of Casey's office casually before a game. It's easy. Just open the door and walk in.

Marvelous Marv even had trouble here. He kept turning the doorknob the wrong way. Gil Hodges had to open it for him.

2

How His Column Grew

All this was happening in May, 1963, the month following what had been—up to that point—the most destructive newspaper strike in New York's history. The editors and Mr. Whitney were looking for a New York columnist, or maybe a sports columnist, or maybe something new. They knew exactly what they wanted but they just couldn't put it in words. They figured that Breslin might be it.

When he finished writing his Mets story, Breslin was asked to hang around for a while in the bar of the Artist and Writers Restaurant, next door to the *Trib* building. Since Breslin is fascinated with the sight of his name in print, he was more than happy to wait until the paper came up from the presses at 9 p.m. As soon as the edition was in, Mr. Whitney and Mr. Bellows went over to the bar, where they found Breslin and Lew King, a friend of his from the *Journal-American*.

First crack out of the box, Breslin announced to Mr. Whitney, "Hey, I got to hand it to your sister. She's one hell of a broad."

The story behind this is that while writing the Mets book Breslin had gone down to Pennsylvania Station to interview Mrs. Payson, who was on her way to Florida. As he told it, "I get there and I can't find her nowheres. So I ask this guy and he says, 'Sure, her train is over there in the corner.' God damn, she's got TWO private cars going to Florida, and there I was looking for her in the Pullman. How the hell was I supposed to know? So we get into this big goddamn drawing room with the servants in the other one and she offers me this drink and she has one and before I knew it, I was stiff. I mean stiff. They threw me out at Trenton. And she just took it all in like it was part of life. Beautiful. What a broad."

Mr. Whitney agreed with Mr. Breslin's appraisal of his sister. He tried to buy a drink, and Breslin was so mesmerized by the thought of buying one for a millionaire, he wouldn't allow it. Whitney then brought up the subject of a column.

Breslin said, "You ain't got enough money to make me work for a newspaper. I worked for Hearst, Newhouse, and Scripps-Howard and they all stink. There ain't enough money in the *world* to make me go back."

To which Mr. Whitney said, "Well, I think I can afford another writer on the staff," and Lew King said, "Hey, Breslin, this bum is fading you," and Breslin said, "Yeah," and a short time thereafter—although not without a great deal of sweat in dealing with one tough agent and one oddball writer—Breslin began writing sports columns with the expectation of eventually moving onto the split page (first page of the second section) of the *Trib*.

All-Time Champ

The place was two stories high and strangers with money were welcome. Jess Jacobs was the owner and he had billiard tables on the first floor and a bar and eight bowling alleys upstairs. His joint was old, and it sat between crumbling buildings on 12th and Wabash in Chicago. The people who hung around it could do a classic job on new money.

When you came in you were hit with Major White, who was the best pool player in Chicago. He was always asking newcomers to teach him to play. Then there was Mike Kovacs, a square-faced Hungarian guy who wore overalls and tried to talk like a farmer. "I think these tables are for dice games," he would say. He had been raised in a pool room in Trenton, New Jersey, and a cue in his hands was as good as a gun.

Upstairs, on the bowling alleys, the great Count Gengler bumbled around. He had a ladies' change purse in his hands and he wore a white suit and a Panama hat. He spoke in a thick German accent. When he bowled, he took only one step and then dumped the ball.

He had been chased out of New York after he broke everybody in town, so now he was in Jess Jacobs' and his line was the same:

"I giff you bets if we bowl against vun another."

The one woman in the place was named McDonald. She was big and heavy and acted like a mother. Anybody who bowled against her for money went home sick to his stomach.

This is where Willie Mosconi learned to be the greatest billiards player of all time. Willie was only nineteen when he got to Jess Jacobs' joint. The year was 1933 and the country was in the middle of a depression. But Willie could do things with a pool cue and in one big hurry he was making $15,000 a year.

Mosconi is forty-nine now, and his hair is gray. But the game has been good to him. Willie never hustled a sucker in his life. If you wanted to play him, you had to do the challenging and you had to know who he was before he made the deal. He is a dead honest, classy little guy who now is substantial, big business.

Because of a movie called *The Hustler*, pocket billiards, to give pool its proper name, has made a big comeback. Willie, who always had a fat Brunswick contract, now has Willie Mosconi Enterprises going for him too. He leases out these new carpeted billiard rooms they are throwing up every place.

But yesterday afternoon he was talking about the old days. Willie was walking across Main Street in Flushing to go into a place called Kings and Queens Billiards, where he was going to put on an exhibition.

The place is on the second floor and a kid was looking through the venetian blinds to see if Willie was coming.

"There's a sucker who can't wait for you," Willie was told.

"Those days are gone," Willie said. "People are too smart.

"I remember the first time I saw Mike Kovacs. He was in this place in Trenton and he had a real act. If you listened to him, you could almost hear the milk going into the pail. Then he'd let you win a couple of games. After that, it was a joke.

"You know what would happen today? First, they'd know who he was the minute he showed up. Then if he still tried the act, they wouldn't even bother to hit him on the head with a bottle. They'd just laugh."

Upstairs, a crowd of a hundred young kids stood around the clean, air-conditioned place and watched as Willie unpacked his cue, then played an exhibition match with this fellow in a sports shirt whose name was John.

Mosconi doesn't have time to play in competition any more, but he is something to watch. Those blue eyes flash as he walks around the table for his next shot, and he can do things on a table that are so good you have to laugh.

The kids enjoyed it. They were the same type of kids who always have been in pool rooms. The hair is worn a little longer and they all smoke. If you got a little fresh, they would know what to do about it.

They probably are the most maligned kids on earth, these ones watching Mosconi yesterday, and all the ones who have hung out in pool rooms throughout the years. A pool room always was a place which caused people to cluck their tongues upon mention. At the same time, a kid hanging out in one of them could get an education that lasted a lifetime. He also stood to get in a lot less trouble than he would in a car in the parking lot of a country club.

"Sure, bad fellows used to be in them," Willie was

saying between maneuvers yesterday. "But that kind would have been in trouble any place. They didn't need billiard rooms."

"This is a real nice place here," Willie was told.

"They're always nice," Willie said. "My father owned one of them in Philadelphia. These places have been good to me all my life."

Then he went back to play. Everybody watched him closely. He is the all-time champ of the pool rooms and Willie went over big with the kids in Flushing yesterday.

The Low Country

Rain dripped from the huge elm trees lining the stately driveway of the Westchester Country Club yesterday morning. In the lobby, a trim blonde in a pink suit, a big diamond on her hand gleaming in the lamplight, fussed over last-minute details of the inevitable women's buffet and card game. Down the hall, a gray-haired man in a checkered sports jacket watched his money move across a movie screen.

Out on the practice tee, Ben Hogan, now fifty but still commanding, still a chilling sight with a golf club in his hands, hit a two wood. A silent crowd watched. Hogan is here to play in the $100,000 Thunderbird Classic, which begins tomorrow. There are 130 other pros here with him.

All of this is George Low's country. There are golfers, and there are three barrooms, and, most important, people who have money are all over the place. So George was on the scene at Westchester yesterday, and the knowing held on to their wallets at all times.

George Low is a big tanned man who wears a blue plaid sports jacket and gray slacks and he is the oldest one on the professional golf tour in point of service. Not that George plays tournament golf. That's too much like work, and George doesn't go in for that.

"My game is playing with other people's money," he is proud to say.

Low is an institution, founded, supported, and loved by the sport of golf. Primarily what George does is to live good without paying for it. On the professional golf tour, he is known as America's Guest. The pros won't play unless Low is on the scene. He lives at the Eldorado in Palm Springs, California, or at the Desert Inn at Las Vegas. If the room is less than $75 a day, George won't stay.

He has a silo for a stomach and he eats a frightening amount of food. There is no sense saying how much beer George Low can drink because nobody would believe you if you told him. "I can drink any given quantity," George says.

He has played in one golf tournament in his life. That was in 1944 and he took first money at Memphis. This snapped a string of thirteen straight victories by Byron Nelson. Tournament officials would have made quite a fuss of it at the presentation ceremony, except George Low wasn't there for it. Somebody had to go into the bar to hand George his prize money. George cashed the check and promptly announced his retirement.

"What do I want with golf?" George was saying yesterday. "Here I got all them millionaires walking around and not knowing what to do with their money and you want me to waste time on a golf course? Get out of here. I mean that. I can't afford to. You've got to have a Dun & Bradstreet rating just to talk to me."

Oh, George has a good-will connection with a string of motels, the Ramada Inns, but he couldn't afford to sit on a bar stool one day a week at that.

Mainly he deals with rich people. Now and then, if it is somebody like Del Webb, George will even go out and play a round of golf with him. He probably is the most dangerous man on a putting green in America—he kicks it in with his foot better than most pros do with a club. Because of this, George always says,

"Give me a multimillionaire with a bad backswing and him and me will have a pleasant afternoon together."

In this league, what was perhaps George's finest day came when he accompanied the Duke of Windsor and the late Robert R. Young, the railroad man, for a round at the Seminole Club in Palm Beach, Florida.

George had a rather good day with his putter, as he always does when the company has money. At the end of the round, there was a matter of $50 concerning the Duke.

George stood by and sort of coughed.

"Oh," Young said, "His Royal Highness never pays money."

"His Royal Highness never does *what*?" George said. "Mr. Young, you take care of your railroads and I'll take care of my Dukes."

George got the money.

Yesterday at Westchester, George was around observing things, as he will be for the rest of the tournament. Late in the day he was at the first tee, watching Hogan start off on a practice round.

"He wouldn't be here unless he had it," George said. "This man won't let himself get embarrassed no way."

Then George turned and took a man in an expensive gray suit by the elbow and guided him toward the grill room. The gray suit looked like he had a lot of money.

The Numbers Game

The Attorney General of the United States, working in cahoots with local enforcement agencies, judges who issue warrants allowing wiretapping, and various firms which manufacture electronic spikes and other hearing aids not usually associated with the deaf, has succeeded this year in severely hampering the National Pastime, which is betting on games of baseball.

Whether everybody is to be commended for this depends upon what side you take. A bookmaker whose New York office once did $300,000 worth of volume each week on baseball was rather bitter about the whole thing yesterday.

"Money and me had a divorce over this thing," he said over the phone from Las Vegas. "They bet you baseball here, you got to take a 10 per cent federal tax right off the top," he said. "The whole oil industry couldn't stand 10 per cent. I'm wasting my time."

On the other hand, one of his former customers, currently experiencing the thrill of paying bills on time, was delighted.

"This is the first time I've ever gone past June 1 without having my car repossessed," he said yesterday. "You know when I give it up? When the bookmakers had to get off the streets and give up regular phones and they took to using telephone-answering services.

"I had this one number to use early in the season and I called it and left my name and home number with the answering service. All the time, the bookmaker is supposed to call his service every ten minutes, get your number, and call back. Well, you know what other kind of people use telephone-answering services. So what happens? I call from home to bet the St. Louis Cardinals in a ball game. The answering service screws up the message. And who calls me back? Some broad who said her name was Sonny. My wife is on the extension in the kitchen. You could forget the whole day."

However, because people in the garment center have to do something with the money they make, baseball betting is not a totally lost cause. Which is good, because baseball has a wearing effect on adults in July and August, and people betting the sport do much to uphold its interest.

The lowest bet accepted on a baseball game today is $25, a "five-time" bet, as it is called in gambling circles. Only large offices are left to handle the action, and they do not handle the $5 and $10 bettor. These smaller people are forced to spend their money at

Jones Beach, where they sit on sand and say mean things about Robert Kennedy.

For the five-time-and-up bettors, the big thing in baseball this week is what Mickey Mantle's absence has been doing to the price on New York Yankee games.

"Mantle," a bookmaker explained yesterday, "is a five-cent ballplayer. Now you say that to somebody who don't know what you're talking about and he thinks it's an insult. Well, it's the other way around. It means he is worth five cents on every dollar when you're handicapping a game.

"If the Yankees got Mantle in the line-up, you have to lay, say, $150 to win $100 if you bet the Yankees. Mantle is home in Dallas now. So the nickel comes off. Now you only got to lay $145 to win $100."

Mantle is one of the few non-pitchers who can affect the odds on a game. Baseball betting really is only betting on pitchers—more specifically, the value of a certain pitcher against a certain club. The earned-run average of a pitcher for the season, for example, could be 3.00. But to get this, he could be 4.00 against one club and 2.00 against another. You go broke more quickly if you don't know this.

To illustrate, the other day a fellow I know who walks the streets with a transistor radio pinned to his ear so he can keep up with the games, won himself $900 because he keeps up with this.

He won it on a pitcher for the New York Mets, Tracy Stallard, who is not Walter Johnson. In a game at the Polo Grounds a week earlier, Stallard had limited the Cincinnati Reds to only two runs. Anybody who gives up only two runs at the Polo Grounds, with the Mets arrayed behind him in the field, is a national hero, our man figured.

A week later Stallard was named to face Cincinnati at Crosley Field. The price on the game was 9–11. This meant you either bet the Mets and took 9–5 or bet the Reds and laid 11–5. There is, of course, a number in between here. This belongs to the bookmaker and he takes girls out to night clubs because of it.

Anyway, Stallard, as his record indicated he would, delivered handsomely against the Reds. Our man had a $500 bill going on it. He took down $900 and this is a lot better than Jones Beach.

The $900, it must be noted, represents only a partial payment to the bookmaker, and to his friend who loans money, because of previous wagering on Stallard.

In fact, Stallard and his ups and downs as a pitcher illustrate the reason why baseball betting is far and away the most popular form of chance-taking in this country, even with present restrictions.

"I had a couple of good days early in the season," our man was saying. "One day I got the Mets with Stallard against the Braves. The game is at Milwaukee. I got a 3–2 lead with two out in the ninth and all the Braves got is a man on first and Lee Maye up. He can't hit a little bit. The game was 2-12. That means I was getting 2–1 with the Mets. If you liked Milwaukee you had to lay 12–5.

"Well, I'm getting dressed to go out. I am tying my tie. I am going to break out all over town. The radio says Stallard throws a pitch. It says Maye hits it eight miles.

"I take off my tie and for the next several weeks I am one of the missing dead. That's why the game is so great. One swing of the bat can wreck your whole life."

By this time it was becoming apparent that the *Trib* had on its hands a man capable of arousing strong emotions. When Breslin finished writing a column, his desk was surrounded with stubs of pencils, discarded leads to stories (about four false starts for each piece and at least two rejected middle sections) and a pack and a half of destroyed cigarettes, all of which led the part of the staff that hated his prose to refer to him as "the animal," while another part saw him as a jolly overweight pixy. They were both wrong, but the readers also began to take sides. Letters to the editor like the following became fairly frequent.

To the *Herald Tribune:*

Jimmy Breslin's column, "At City Hall," might have left some readers believing that the school system's current program of integration was sprung suddenly on the public without prior communication. Nothing could be further from the truth.

Hundreds of meetings on the school integration proposals were held with parent, civic and community leaders for at least six months before the program was announced. . . . As was stated last spring in the school system's announcement of the measures: "Indeed it is unlikely that there has ever been in this city, on the part of a Board of Education, as determined an effort to explore the thinking of the community in order to decide upon programs of action."

Unfortunately, Breslin lacked the virtue of humility. He once said the nuns taught him it was unnecessary. Anyway, he began to answer the letter in his own way. For instance, he answered this one—from a city official with the following telegram:

ONCE BEFORE I FOUND YOU WASTING PUBLIC'S TIME AND MONEY WRITING LETTERS TO NEWSPAPERS ABOUT ME. THIS IS THE SECOND TIME YOU HAVE PLACED YOUR DEEP IGNORANCE IN PRINT CONCERNING ME. YOU NOW HAVE SOMEBODY WHO IS NOT GOING TO REST OR STOP UNTIL YOU ARE OUT IN THE STREET DOING NOTHING LIKE THE BUM YOU ARE. I START ON YOU NOW AND IF YOU HAVE ANY BRAINS YOU BETTER GET SOMEBODY TO BODYGUARD YOU. WHO THE HELL ARE YOU? SOME INCOMPETENT UNDER PUBLIC TEAT COMMENTING ON THE WORK OF A NEWSPAPERMAN? YOU GO.

JIMMY BRESLIN NEW YORK HERALD TRIBUNE

When he began to feel at home sufficiently to heckle the staff, Breslin moved on to his next and his favorite target, the editors. When he needed his copy read, he would put on the face he used when he was an altar boy. The minute it was processed, he would turn to the attack in memos like this, all in capital letters:

MR. BELLOWS, EDITOR:

PLEASE HAVE THESE SONSOFBITCHES PUT THIS STORY INTO NEXT SUNDAY'S MAGAZINE SO'S I CAN GET RID OF THIS LEVEL OF ANNOYANCE FROM MYSELF AND FROM SUCKERS WHO CLAIM THEY GET ROBBED WHEN I AM NOT IN THE NEWSPAPER ON SUNDAY. WHICH, OF COURSE, THEY DO. I APPRECIATE YOUR HELP AND UNDERSTANDING AND KINDNESS IN THIS MATTER. THANK YOU, AND PLEASE HAVE THESE SONSOFBITCHES PUT MY STORY INTO THE MAGAZINE.

J. Breslin

ALSO, MR. WALD, ANOTHER BIG EDITOR, FAILED TO SPECIFY ON HOW BIG HE WILL MAKE MY NAME IN THIS SUNDAY'S REGULAR SECTIONS, AND WHERE HE WILL DISPLAY THE STORY WITH MY NAME ON IT. I WISH I COULD RECEIVE SOME COMMUNICATION FROM MANAGEMENT ON THIS MATTER AS I FEEL MUCH BETTER WHEN I AM VERY BIG.

jb

He also joined in an intermittent battle with Art Buchwald, most of it fought out over the teletype wire between New York (Breslin turf) and Washington (Buchwald turf). The first time Breslin made a state visit south of the Mason-Dixon Line, Buchwald wanted a new clause in his contract saying Breslin could not come below Baltimore without permission. Breslin was accompanied on that first visit by Dick Wald and this exchange of messages came back on the wire:

NOTE TO DESK:

BUCHWALD WANTS ME TO SAY THAT WE HAVE A PACT THAT EITHER BOTH OF US APPEAR ON FIRST PAGE OR NONE OF US AND THAT YOU ARE TRYING TO BREAK US UP BY THIS ALTERNATING. HE SAYS THAT I'M SUPPOSED TO THREATEN YOU WITH A DUAL WALKOUT IF IT HAPPENS AGAIN. WELL, THE HELL WITH HIM. I HOPE YOU BURY THE SONOFABITCH. JUST TAKE CARE OF

ME. I THOUGHT YOUR USE OF TYPE ON PAGE ONE THIS MORNING WAS SO GREAT I WAS OVERCOME.

Breslin

I AM TURNING THE OTHER CHEEK. BRESLIN IS NOT A CHRISTIAN. BUT I LOVE HIM BECAUSE THERE IS TOO MUCH HATE IN THE WORLD. IF WE CAN LOVE BRESLIN WE CAN LOVE EVERYBODY. BLESS THE STAFF THAT MAKES UP THE PAPER.

Buchwald

I AM STAYING OUT.

Wald

At Christmas time, Buchwald struck back and almost gave Breslin apoplexy until he figured out how to reply (using, in this instance, the name of a real copy boy):

JIMMY BRESLIN
NEW YORK HERALD
DEAR JIMMY,

JUST RECEIVED MY $1000 BONUS CHECK FROM HERALD TRIBUNE. I FEEL IT'S LOW. IF YOU GOT MORE COULD YOU LET ME KNOW SO I COULD RAISE HELL IN NEW YORK.

REGARDS
Buchwald

P.S. DON'T MENTION THIS TO WASHINGTON REPORTERS AS THEY ONLY GOT $500.

MR. BUCHWALD
WASHINGTON BUREAU
DEAR MR. BUCHWALD:

MR. JIMMY BRESLIN IS NOT HERE. IF YOU NEED HIM HE CAN BE LOCATED AT MARTY ERLICHMANN'S MIDTOWN CUSTOM-BUILT CADILLAC AGENCY, BROADWAY AND SIXTYFIRST STREET. BRESLIN SAW WHITNEY EARLY TODAY AND RAN OUT OF HERE TO BUY A NEW CAR.

George Robinson Copy Boy

JIMMY BRESLIN
NEW YORK HERALD TRIBUNE
SORRY TO HAVE BOTHERED YOU. THE TWO BONUS CHECKS WERE STAPLED TOGETHER AND I ONLY SAW THE SMALLER ONE FOR A THOUSAND BUCKS. THE OTHER ONE WAS STUCK BEHIND IT. HOW STUPID OF ME TO GET EXCITED.

CHEERS
Buchwald

3

In Which Some of His Friends Are Mentioned

Breslin grew up with the same varied lot of kids that many New York neighborhoods can show. They were a little poorer than some, a little more Irish than others, a little closer to the racetrack than most. They wound up as cops and robbers in adult life. A few were bookies, and one was really an arsonist. The girls got married and had kids, as other girls did, and the boys got jobs as other boys did; only a large percentage of them never quite made it to the upper-middle-class brackets where too many writers spend their time. Fat Thomas was a kid Breslin went to school with who grew up to be a very, very fat bookmaker. He actually weighs 460 pounds now but he gets embarrassed about it, so he lies and says he weighs 410, which is just like anybody else, really. The girls who got stuck out in the suburbs hated it or loved it, and the ones who liked the Broadway life got trapped in various ways. It happens all the time. It's just that Breslin stayed a little bit where he came from, so the guys he went around with at Pepe's bar were not generally from the publishing companies or the corps of foreign correspondents. And when he wrote, he wrote about what he knew, or at least what he was told. The world is crazier than most people think, is all.

So when the column moved out onto the split page Breslin began writing about types, New York types who don't usually look so strange until you mention that they moved their household stuff on the subway. One nice thing about it all, aside from the fact that it gave many *Trib* readers a new look at the people you see through the train windows—Breslin's friends don't sue for libel.

Fat Thomas's Friends and Dale Carnegie

Among great education achievements of the year not commented upon by such as James B. Conant was the performance of Fat Thomas's brother in the Dale Carnegie course at Attica State Prison. Fat Thomas's brother was awarded the Dale Carnegie Gold Pencil for Achievement. He is doing a short bit in Attica for poor usage of a gun.

"They tell me he was beautiful," Fat Thomas says.

"He was a very good pupil," Harry Kindervatter, of the Dale Carnegie Staff in Buffalo, says. Kindervatter donates his time to Attica, just as the Peace Corps people do in Mesopotamia, and his is to be similarly applauded.

"We feel our course has tremendous value to these boys," Kindervatter says. "Few of them ever stood up before crowds and had to speak." This is understandable. Criminals who talk too much in public usually wind up among the missing dead. The last great public speaker we had around here was Abe Reles. They threw him out a hotel window.

"With this course of ours," Kindervatter says, "the boys get confidence."

"Confidence?" Fat Thomas yelled. "He's up there to get straightened out, not to become a confidence man."

According to the Dale Carnegie people, talking has become quite a rage in better prisons throughout the nation. Courses are given in nearly all New York institutions and one of the best in the land is conducted at Leavenworth.

There are, of course, severe problems attached to this great work. A guy named Cousin brought this up during a small party Fat Thomas threw in honor of his brother's achievement. Cousin is an expert on the subject. Some years ago he was subject to deep personal embarrassment when police found a machine gun in the trunk of his car. Cousin insisted he had no intention of using the gun, although, when discovered, it was not packed in cosmoline for storage. The judge, for some reason, did not listen to Cousin.

So one night he wound up filing into a room in the Trenton State Prison in New Jersey to attend his first Dale Carnegie course.

"It got you out of the cell for a couple of hours," Cousin was saying, "so if you had any brains you had to go for it. Besides, they gave you half a pack of cigarettes if you came.

"Well, you know how the Dale Carnegie course operates. They get you up and you talk about something in your past. It's easier talking about something you know about and you have lived with than it is to stand up there and read from a book or something.

"But for openers, the guy running the course tells us to stand up and say what kind of work you did before you got here. 'What is he, crazy?' I said to myself.

"Nobody would get up. So then he changed it. He said to talk about something from way back in your past. That was better. It gave you a chance to talk about some legitimate thing you did when you was a kid.

"So up pops this one old guy who came off the East Side. He can't wait to talk. 'When I was a kid,' the guy says, 'we stood up-a on the roof and wait for the cop to come by. Then we push-a the chimney over and the bricks, they fall five stories on the cop's head. Serve him right. He was-a always beat us on the shins.'

"I yell at him, 'Shut up, you jerk.' But he thinks I'm doing this heckling business that's part of the course.

He keeps going. He got the bit in his mouth and he won't let go. Before the instructor got him down, he tells the whole class, and an assistant warden sitting in the back, about two more homicides and a good stickup.

"I don't know what happened to the bum. I can tell you this. I cut the next two classes."

"I don't understand all this talking," one of the guys at Fat Thomas's table said. "I come up different. When I got grabbed by the FBI the last time I just sat down in the room and I says, 'Sir, I don't want to insult your intelligence with a lot of smart talk. So I'm not going to answer no questions.'

"And the guy says, 'Fine,' and that was it. Now what's the matter with that? How much more talkin' do you need to get by with?"

He was wrong. The Dale Carnegie people have found that few people with prison addresses are able to communicate with words efficiently. This gives them a tremendous problem. So to gain recognition, which was not available by word, they went out and pulled off some fine heists. And this search for recognition extends even to the prison yard.

"What are you in for?" a close friend asked a newcomer to the population at Danbury one day.

"Big bank robbery," the new guy said. "The cops busted in right in the middle of it. I was all set to shoot it out, but one of them nailed me from behind. You must of read it in the papers."

The next day an inmate-clerk made a small check of the newcomer's record. He was in for being what is known as a Slow Walker. This is a person who follows the mailman around and steals checks out of mailboxes. But at Danbury he felt he needed a more romantic background in order to gain that recognition.

"When I left the place," my friend recalls, "the Slow Walker still was telling about this big bank robbery."

Dale Carnegie people, and prison officials, feel they can combat this type of problem by teaching inmates how to get up and talk to others. It is a fine idea. And

Fat Thomas feels its usefulness goes far beyond even this.

"My brother don't need recognition," he said. "They run his picture page one when he got nailed. What he needs is a trade so he can be paroled. Now he got one. He is going to be an after-dinner speaker."

Marvin the Torch

Marvin the Torch never could keep his hands off somebody else's business, particularly if the business was losing money. Now this is accepted behavior in Marvin's profession, which is arson. But he has a bad habit of getting into places where he shouldn't be and promising too many favors. This is where all his trouble starts.

There was this one time a few winters ago when he listened to a hard-luck story from a guy who had a custard stand, located on the wrong side of a big amusement park, that was a bad loser and the owner had no way to get rid of it. Marvin the Torch should have kept his mouth shut, but he had a couple of drinks with the fellow, and sure enough, he wound up promising to do something about it. So a week later, gas cans at his feet, he stood in front of the guy's custard stand. The custard stand was just an old boarded-up place and it was an insult to bring Marvin the Torch anywhere near it. Marvin the Torch is a man who has burned in the best industries.

But here he was, stuck with another favor, so he picked up the gas cans and went to work. As long as he was at it, Marvin decided to put a little spectacle into the job. Marvin the Torch wanted to try to make the roof blow straight up into the air without bending the nails in it.

This would have been all right, except Marvin the Torch's fire caught a good south wind and the wind carried the fire straight over the amusement park and before the day was over, Marvin the Torch's favor job on the custard stand had also belted out most of a million-and-a-half-dollar amusement park.

He got into the restaurant business in Florida on one of these favors, and it nearly ruined him. Marvin was down there visiting restaurants which were not doing too well to see if he could drum up a few contracts. In one of the places he was eating at a table near the kitchen entrance when he noticed the chef hanging in the doorway with a disgusted look on his face during most of the meal.

"Business bad?" Marvin asked him.

"See for yourself," the chef said.

"Why don't you get yourself a cup of coffee and sit down with me," Marvin said.

Over coffee, Marvin carefully sold the chef on a deal to "build an empty lot," as Marvin refers to his trade, on the site of the chef's restaurant. The chef liked the idea. Then, during a succeeding conference, a hitch developed. The chef said that after collecting the insurance and then coming up with Marvin's fee, he wouldn't have enough left to buy the new place he had his eye on.

Right here Marvin went ahead and opened his mouth. Some of his friends say he gets such a kick out of burning places down that he'll do anything for a deal. Whatever it is, Marvin wound up agreeing to waive his fee and take a partnership in the new restaurant the chef was going to get when Marvin burned his old one down.

Two weeks later, on a dark night, and with the chef visiting relatives two states away for alibi purposes, Marvin the Torch arrived at the restaurant with his team, which consisted of Benjamin, the blanket man, and a fellow named Lou, who drove. Now, arson is a three-man job. Two men pour, then one of the pourers comes out and becomes the blanket man. He holds an old car blanket and throws it over anyone coming out whose clothes are on fire. The driver counts the gas cans to make sure none is missing. In short, people don't pay you if they find gas cans in the ruins of your accidental fire. The Torch, of course, does the actual igniting.

Following the usual delay, the chef received his insurance money and bought his new restaurant. Marvin returned and the venture was off to a bright start. After two weeks, the customers started finding out. After a month, Marvin the Torch found the place was costing him money and he was telling the chef good-by.

"I'll be back around next season and stop around to see you," Marvin said. "If you're doing any good by then, we'll square up."

Marvin the Torch came back, all right. He came back a year later at four one morning and he belted out the restaurant with so much juice that the kitchen pots melted. But this still didn't satisfy him. In the end, he had had to do two jobs for the price of one.

"Favors," Marvin the Torch says in disgust. "Favors are for pyromaniacs, not professionals."

Mutchie

All his life, my friend Mutchie has done the right thing. When somebody gets killed, he sends a big basket of flowers with a nice note saying, "I Am Very Sorry It Had to Come to This." When somebody gets married, Mutchie shows up with an envelope in his hand, even if everybody else stays away because the FBI is making Panavision movies of the invited guests. Mutchie is very good at christenings, twenty-fifth wedding anniversary dinners, and every other kind of swell occasion. But he is not very good at girls, and there is a lot of trouble over this.

Like any other man, Mutchie is sure he is seventeen years old. His idea of a lady companion is a young blonde who is built like a municipal statue and who is just smart enough to answer the telephone. He was certain he had that kind of girl when he began to take out Vivian. She is blond, she is built, and she says "Hello" into the telephone.

"She is a special friend of mine," Mutchie was saying one night.

Vivian was sitting at the bar. Her hair was piled a foot high on top of her head, she was chewing gum in time to the juke box, and she giggled and said, "Gee," when anybody talked. Most of the time she looked like a dope and kept daydreaming. She daydreamed about the pizzeria she and her boy friend, who is not Mutchie, wanted to open when they could get the money together.

One night Mutchie wanted to read something in the newspaper and he asked somebody to go upstairs and get a pair of glasses for him.

"You're wearing glasses," Vivian said.

"These are my social glasses," Mutchie said. "I can't see a thing except somebody's face with them. When I read anything, even a headline, I got to have my work glasses."

"Oh," Vivian said. She started daydreaming again. She daydreamed numbers.

A week later Vivian and Mutchie were out having cocktails. On the third martini, Vivian sort of looked at an afternoon paper which was on the bar.

"What do you think of this?" she said. She pointed to a big story about sex that was right on top of the one about Viet Nam.

"I can't see a thing," Mutchie said. "I left my other glasses back at the joint."

"Do you want to go to Roosevelt Raceway tonight?" Vivian said.

At the racetrack, Vivian led Mutchie to the bar. He couldn't see a thing with the glasses he had on. She had that going for her. But she had one other problem. At a racetrack the crowd always shouts the number of the winning horse when it crosses the line. "Six horse win it," they shout. If you can't see the winning horse, you still can hear it. There was only one way out of this.

"Let's drink doubles," Vivian said to Mutchie. "I want to get high with you tonight." She giggled like a dope and Mutchie smiled and began popping doubles into him and Vivian kept telling him to hurry up and order another one. She wanted Mutchie to drink himself deaf.

Which he did. He handed her $100 and bet on the daily double and she went around the corner and put the money into her purse. He had told her to play the 1–5 combination. The horse won the first race. Mutchie was at the bar talking to himself about something that happened in 1932 when the crowd shouted the number out.

"Who won?" he said.

"Number five," Vivian said.

She didn't even bother to use numbers after that. She just said, "You lost again."

Vivian and Mutchie became regulars at Roosevelt. And every morning Mutchie was looking for oxygen and Vivian was out with her boy friend looking at empty stores that might make a good pizzeria.

The other day she was in Mutchie's bar and somebody looked at her and said to Mutchie, "You know, I don't think Vivian is dumb like she makes it to be. I think Vivian is doing something to you."

"Never," Mutchie said. He was mad. "I been around all kinds of girls in my life. I know Vivian. She's kind. Do you know what she just done? She asked me if I knew of a cook who needed a job. She said she knew a place that could put him to work. How many girls do you know think like that?"

The Mechanic

The cigarettes tasted lousy. They were hot, and he couldn't stop smoking them. His eyes were puffy and the cigarette smoke put needles into them. His back ached and pain kept running across his shoulder blades. Once he could sit at a table and play cards for forty-eight hours and feel nothing. But now he is fifty-five and at 5 a.m., after only nine hours of playing, he was falling apart. And this Swede he was supposed to bust out still was pushing up his chips and lucking his way through the night.

The Swede is in shipping. He plays cards with friends twice a month in a midtown hotel room and for the last six months he has been taking everything. His friends got together and brought in the Mechanic to handle the Swede. It was an old story to the Mechanic. If propositioned quietly, nine out of every ten people in a card game will go with larceny, particularly if it is against old friends. There were five of the Swede's friends in the game on this night. One of them was thrilled to be the take-out guy. The take-out guy always wins. The Mechanic feeds him the cards. Then the Mechanic just plays along and gets nowhere for himself and attracts no attention.

At 11:30 the Mechanic gave the take-out guy a pair of kings. The Swede had queens. The pot was over $3000 and it looked like this was the start. They were going to put a torpedo into the Swede's wallet. But nobody is perfect. Not even the Mechanic, who is the Jimmy Brown of card cheats in New York. And on the last card the Swede lucked into another queen and he stood up, the way he always does, and said, "Olson calls," and he pushed his chips with both hands into the middle of the table. The Swede pushed his chips as if he were launching a freighter. He won the hand.

The Mechanic swore to himself. Then he sat forward and began to grind the money back out of the Swede. Now it was 5 a.m. and he was disgusted. Room service was shut down and the coffee on the table was cold. He didn't want any more whisky. He was punchy enough. He looked at the Swede, who was red-faced with concentration. "No wonder this bum owns big boats," he said to himself. "He's giving me a workout at my own game."

The Mechanic picked up the cards and went to work. He has long, soft fingers that handle cards as if they were pieces of broken glass. He has been through it all. He has made big scores in places like London and Honolulu. And he has been in trouble too. In San Francisco they stripped his take-out guy and hung him by his neck from the doorway, the feet just touching the floor. Then they put lighted cigarettes to the take-out guy's body.

Now his hands moved over the cards and he started dealing the hand. He was going to get the Swede this time if he had to kill him with an ax.

The Swede's hole card, the one that doesn't show, was a jack. The Mechanic gave the take-out guy a queen. They bet, and he started to go around again and it kept going and, who knows how these things happen, it gets late and the cigarettes bother you and you think a little slow, and the Swede had a jack showing and on the last card he came up with another jack. That gave him two jacks showing, and with one in the hole, and the take-out guy only had a queen showing and one in the hole and now he didn't know what to do. He looked at the Mechanic. He got a look back. "Go naked," the look said. "The hell with it," the Mechanic said to himself. "I use the ax."

The Swede stood up and pushed his chips into the middle of the table. "Olson bets five hundred," he said.

The take-out guy pushed his chips out. "I bet you five hundred and raise you a thousand," he said.

The Swede stood up again. "Boys, I might as well go all the way. I bet you two tousand and I raise you two tousand." His hands got behind his chips and he began that freighter-launching push of his. While the Swede pushed, the Mechanic's hand flicked out into the table right under the Swede's arms and then it flicked back.

"What have you got?" the take-out guy asked.

"Three yacks," the Swede said.

The Swede pushed the two jacks showing. Then he turned over his hole card. His mouth dropped open. The hole card was a seven of clubs now, not a jack.

The Swede let out a scream. "One of my yacks, he yumped away."

The Mechanic had the jack under his right thigh.

A few minutes later the game broke up and the Mechanic got up and walked out into the early-morning air. He met the take-out guy in a Riker's on 54th Street and they cut up $8500.

The Swede came back to the game two weeks later. He sat down and when they gave him his first hole card he reached into his pocket and took out a cardboard holder full of thumbtacks. He took one of the thumbtacks and pounded it into the hole card with his fist.

"Nothing yumps away this time," the Swede said.

Jerry the Booster

It was a beautiful thing to see. Here they came, spread out like the Army, the three stumpy guys from Providence, which is where the best thieves in the world come from, each one of them marching along an aisle, and here in the main aisle, walking straight down the middle of it, his white satin tie spotless, his white on white shirt glistening, his chin stuck out so he looked just like Mussolini, here came Jerry the Booster, the greatest department-store thief in the history of the world. And all of them, Jerry the Booster and the three stumpy guys from Providence, were heading straight for the Hickey Freeman 42 regulars hanging in neat, wonderful rows in the men's department of Goldwater's Department Store, Phoenix, Arizona. The salesman standing there right in front of the Hickey Freeman 42 regulars did not know why, but his nose began to twitch when he saw Jerry the Booster coming right at him and, out of the corners of his eyes, the three boys from Providence turning in from the flanks.

"Yes, sir?" the salesman said. He said it the way he

always says "Yes, sir?" to a customer. Only this time his nose was twitching.

"I would like a whole new wardrobe of clothes," Jerry the Booster said.

"I want a suit," a Providence boy called out from the right.

"Could I have a little service, please?" a Providence boy called out from the left.

"This looks nice," the third Providence boy, his hands all over a navy blue, said.

"Yes, sir?" the salesman said. But the salesman was not looking at Jerry the Booster when he said "Yes, sir?" The salesman, his nose twitching, was looking over Jerry the Booster's fat head. The salesman was trying to catch the attention of somebody who was someplace else in Goldwater's Department Store.

"The bum is trying to get a cop," Jerry the Booster said to himself.

Jerry the Booster pulled on the salesman's sleeve. "Say, mister," Jerry said to the salesman, "look at what I know how to do."

Jerry stuck his tongue out at the salesman. Then he swiveled his shoulders around. His fingers flicked at his belt line. And, in one motion, Jerry's jacket slid off his back, and his pants dropped to the floor.

"Nyaaaahhh," Jerry the Booster, tongue out, sang to the salesman.

Jerry stepped out of his pants and he turned around. He went back up the main aisle of Goldwater's Department Store. He skipped along in his underwear, and he went right up to three women who were hanging over the costume-jewelry counter.

"Look at me, look at me, I got no clothes on," Jerry the Booster sang out.

The salesman from in front of the Hickey Freeman 42 regulars deserted his post. He came running up the aisle after Jerry. The salesman was shouting. The women at the costume-jewelry counter were gasping. The saleslady was slapping her hand on the little bell by the cash register. From all sides of Goldwater's Department Store, people were running at Jerry the Booster. And Jerry the Booster skipped between counters and into a corner of the store, far away from the Hickey Freeman 42 regulars, and when the crowd of salesmen and store detectives came close, Jerry the Booster called out to a saleslady.

"Say, lady, watch what my mother taught me how to do. I know how to take off all my underwear."

He hooked his thumbs into the top of his shorts. The crowd of salesmen and store detectives made a rush at him.

Back in the men's department, a whole rack of Hickey Freeman 42 regulars was gone. The Providence boys had them. They had them, brown wooden hangers and all, shoved down the fronts of their suspender-held size 60 working trousers. Fifteen good suits, $155, $175, and $210 retail, never again would be on display in Goldwater's Department Store. And while the crowd scuffled to stop Jerry the Booster from going naked, the three boys from Providence, which delivers the best thieves in the world, went out of the store. They walked with wide strides, because the coat hangers kept slipping down and digging into the insides of their legs.

Jerry the Booster was whisked back to a dressing room. Under the supervision of two store detectives, he put on his clothes. Once he was dressed, the two store detectives escorted him toward the door.

"Nyaaaahhh," Jerry, his tongue out, sang in front of the tie counter. His left hand went for his beltline. The detectives grabbed at it and pushed Jerry the Booster out the door and he walked up to the car, his afternoon of department-store browsing, as he calls it, at an end. That night, in a suite at the Hotel Adams, the wise guys from downtown Phoenix attended a private sale of clothes with the labels ripped out. The receipts were $975. Cut four ways, this came to a bit less than the $250 a day Jerry the Booster wanted to make on his road trip from New York. But by eleven o'clock at night he was drunk, and he didn't care.

"One thing about that store," Jerry the Booster notes today. "We done it when Goldwater personally still owned the store. So I'm glad he didn't get in for President. He would've been rough on boosters."

A booster is a man who boosts things up off a counter or a rack in a store and goes out with the things. The crude term for this is shoplifting. But it is not a precise term. Anybody can shoplift. Housewives and children do it all the time. Boosting is a whole way of life. A booster is a full-time worker who puts in at least six hours a day touring department stores and taking things that belong to the store. He travels the country, and most times he is part of an experienced team which, with half a break, can clean out a counter in a matter of a few seconds. Nearly all the good boosters come from Providence. There is a historical reason for that. Providence is a factory town that has a history of not overpaying its workers. The factory workers, in turn, have compiled an impressive history of stealing some of the things they make. This stealing breeds ambition. From their factories in Providence, the thieves spread out and start hitting local department stores. Then they take trips to Boston. Pretty soon they are out around the country as qualified boosters. But none of them, not even the best Providence ever has sent out, comes close to being as good as Jerry the Booster, who lives in a hotel room on West 58th Street in New York.

Jerry is a jowly forty-five-year-old with wavy hair and big shifty eyes which look through black-rimmed glasses. "Put in that I am well dressed," he says, but you could put down that Jerry the Booster dresses like a slob and he would never know about it because he does not know how to read or write. But he does happen to dress well. If Jerry the Booster doesn't dress well, then there is something the matter with the top stores of the country. For Jerry will not put a thing over his back that does not come from at least Saks Fifth Avenue.

"I prefer Neiman-Marcus," he says. "Whenever I

need a change of suits, I go to Dallas. Who do you know that goes all the way to Dallas just to get clothes?"

He says that very proudly. Too proudly. Which, as the Supreme Court of the State of New York attests, is the major failure on Jerry the Booster's part. The Pope of Rome told us at the United Nations that pride is behind the troubles of the world. And pride is at the bottom of this whole mess which is going to end a career when Jerry the Booster is sentenced on December 1.

"Look at the trouble you're in," his friend Frankie was saying to Jerry the other night. "Why did you have to go and do that thing?"

"I had to," Jerry the Booster said to Frankie. "I had to go and show everybody that I'm the best booster in the whole world."

"You couldn't leave things well enough alone and bat out a living," Frankie said.

"No," Jerry said.

He couldn't. He grew up in Jersey City of a laborer's family which sent him to school with clean clothes on and the like, but the day Jerry learned to cut out the pockets of his knickers, turning them into two large shopping bags, was the end of his school career. "When the truant officer made me go, they put me in the yap-yap class, the one that got all the dunces in it," Jerry says. "We done basket-making all day. I never learned how to make a letter. What did I care, anyway? You should of seen what I done to the grocery stores."

With this as a background, Jerry was out on the streets stealing for an occupation at age fourteen. Stealing alone, stealing small, and—the most important characteristic of a booster—stealing consistently. So Jerry the Booster, illiterate, able to read only the pictures in the newspapers, always was around with money in his pocket during his formative years. Now unfortunately the money at times was not all that American money should be.

"He was found with twenty-five bills of twenty-dollar denomination, each bearing the same serial number," a Secret Service agent testified in federal court in Newark in 1945.

"What do I know?" Jerry the Booster screamed. "Somebody give me money. What do I know what it is? I can't read."

This inability to read made it very tough on Jerry when he had to sit in Lewisburg Penitentiary for two and a half years.

When he came out, he stayed strictly with the boosting. Teaming up with individuals from the town of Providence, Jerry became the busiest and most imaginative booster in the world.

Now to understand what he did, you must know the details of the department-store boosting trade. To begin with, you never take anything so big that they call out the heavy hitters from the Safe and Loft Squad. A booster takes common things, a suit of clothes, a coat, a good dress, a $150 evening purse. A missing suit, even twenty missing suits, causes a department head to scream. But it does not put heat on a town. And you can make a living selling suits and coats. However, let one Russian sable coat get out of a store and there is hell to pay all over town. No booster living in a hotel wants to bring this kind of sure trouble on himself.

On the road, boosters also must live well. They move from town to town by car, and do it leisurely. They always have the best luggage and clothes. When boosters check into a hotel, they order suites. When boosters check out of a hotel, they do it through a process known as double-dooring the joint.

"It means you come in the front door like a legitimate guy and then when you leave you take another opening," Jerry says. "You find your own door and go. Let the room clerk eat your bill for his dinner."

In his case, it usually meant checking in with two suitcases filled with telephone directories to fool the bellhops carrying the luggage. For the remainder of his stay, Jerry lived off the land, grabbing a fresh shirt every morning from the shop in the hotel.

Getting out of the hotels was easy. He just left the luggage in the room, the luggage with the telephone directories inside, and walked out.

Jerry worked with many people over the years. A team of boosters consists of a man like Jerry, who is the thief, and two or possibly three others. One of the three is what is known as the Blocker. He looks as suspicious as possible. And he places himself directly in line of sight between the sales clerk and the thief. He blocks the sales clerk's view. And he looks so suspicious that the clerk is afraid to take his eyes off the Blocker. The other two, known as Luggers, help the thief grab things and carry them out of the store.

The helpers are a necessity when Jerry operates normally. And normal work for him means being perhaps the worst pest sales help in stores ever have come across. Perhaps Jerry the Booster's major asset is his ability to be a pest. Many people say he never had to work hard to develop this talent. "I know him for years; from the day I know him he gives me a pain in the backside," a friend of his says. In a store, working on a strange salesman, this quality of Jerry's is brutal.

"I'm like two old ladies all at once," he says.

Jerry begins by checking the clothes he says he is going to buy inside out, demanding to look at a suit he just told the salesman to put back on the rack; then in the middle of retrying the suit on he throws it off and asks for another one which is far down the aisle. While doing this, he makes little remarks at the salesman. Not big remarks. Just little things like, "That suit you got on makes you look like a bum; I hope you got better than that around here." In the meantime, with the clerk angry and confused, Jerry the Booster's co-workers take everything but the tailor's sewing machine. Once, in St. Paul, Jerry had a sales clerk tied up for four hours. He ordered $2500 worth of suits. The salesman, shaken from having to put up with Jerry, but elated at the sale, pitched in and helped the floor-boy put the clothes in the boxes. Jerry said he wanted to take the suits with him right away, that he would have them tailored privately. When the suits were all wrapped, and the salesman was just starting to tie the last knot on the last box, Jerry reached for his coat.

"Put them all back; I don't want the clothes," Jerry said. "I don't do business with no rude people like you."

He walked out of the store. The salesman screamed. Although not so loud as the salesman's boss screamed later in the day when he found three racks of overcoats missing.

But Jerry's imagination is so great that many times he didn't need all that help. He murdered Neiman-Marcus in Dallas with the aid of only one other person. This is because he used what he calls his "aplexy" move. His accomplice was the fattest female booster ever to come out of Providence. And on a fine Texas afternoon he walked her boldly into Neiman-Marcus's cocktail-dress department.

A saleslady came up to them. Jerry said he wanted to buy his love a dress. The saleslady smiled sweetly. Jerry the Booster rolled his eyes around in his head. His mouth popped open. A loud gurgle came from his throat. His hands came up to his sides and shook violently. And Jerry the Booster fell backward to the floor in one piece, his right hand held behind him to break the fall. The hand slapped on the floor. He bounced his head after it. The fat booster with him screamed, "My husband!" and as the saleslady went to help, the fat booster from Providence shoved $450 in cocktail dresses down the front of her house dress.

He had his deaf-mute act too. There was the afternoon when he attended a sale at Alexander's department store in the Queens section of New York City. Jerry felt like overcoats that day. He stepped up and put on a size 38. Over that he put a size 42. He topped the ensemble off with a 44 long, which covered the whole works. Out he went, out through the doors and onto Queens Boulevard with his three overcoats protecting him from the cold and the wind but not from the store detective on the sidewalk.

"What are you, a football player?" the store detective said, touching Jerry's shoulders. Jerry's shoulders were higher than the top of his head.

The store detective led Jerry by the arm back into the store. And now Jerry's hands began working. The hands flew back and forth in an approximation of a deaf mute's hand signals. The hands were flying faster when they sat Jerry down in the office with an assistant manager. They were flying even faster when the store detectives removed the three overcoats. They were still flying when the assistant manager said, no, he wouldn't have any part of getting a deaf mute arrested. Only when the store detective had Jerry on the street and the store detective let go of Jerry's arm did the hands stop flying. Then, in conjunction with the right arm, Jerry's hands formed a deliberate and ancient Italian curse.

Jerry's mouth came open. "You rat bastard," he said to the store's detective.

He went along like this year after year, stealing his clothes, ripping the labels out, and selling them that night to wise guys who look for these sales and can be found in every city in the nation. Not really able to read or write, but knowing brands by their looks, knowing the men's department is in the basement at Jordan Marsh in Boston and that it is on the fifth floor of Neiman-Marcus, which he considers the world's greatest store, although weak in security. Remembering whether doors come in or go out, Jerry made his way through life. And then, as the Pope warned the world, and as it happens to so many of us, pride wrecked Jerry the Booster.

"I'm the best," he told everybody one night on the corner of 54th and Seventh.

And on June 20, 1965, Jerry the Booster, a large black suitcase in his hand walked across Fifth Avenue and stepped between the Bentleys at the curb, and he walked, his chin so far out it was not hard to see that he looked like Mussolini, walked right into Tiffany and Company, one of the seven most sought-after stores in a booster's life.

Jerry came into the green-carpeted main floor and walked to the back, to the vaultlike elevator doors.

"Third floor," he told the elevator operator.

Jerry the Booster had been told by a Bickford's waitress, who could read, that a collection of beaut-i-ful porcelain birds, made by Doughty, were on sale at the store.

"Birds?" Jerry the Booster said.

"They cost $1300," the waitress said.

"Beautiful," Jerry the Booster said. "What floor?"

"The third."

Onto the third floor came Jerry the Booster. He came with an eager look and this big, black, empty suitcase which he had boosted out of a luggage store on Third Avenue.

"Where's the Dorothy-Dorothy birds?" he asked a woman.

"Oh, the Doughty birds. They are right over there in the Royal Worcester Room."

Jerry went to the room, a small, carpeted room with a seven-foot-high glass cabinet at one end. The birds, perched on wood mountings, sat on the middle shelf of the cabinet. The cabinet had sliding glass doors which were locked on the bottom. Jerry looked at the lock.

"Beautiful," he said.

"They are, aren't they?" a woman standing next to him said.

"Oh, yes," Jerry said. He loved that lock. "I could move that lock if my fingers were cut off," he said to himself.

He shifted the black suitcase in his hand and waited for the woman to leave. She did. But she did not go too far. Her name is Constance Zebroski, and she is a store detective. She was disturbed by the black suitcase. There is a reason for this. A suitcase in Tiffany's is the same as an open seacock in the *Queen Elizabeth.*

So twenty minutes later, after Jerry the Booster had

pushed the glass sliding doors in and then moved them past the lock and grabbed both the birds and thrown them into the suitcase, Detective Edward Clancy, 17th Precinct, was waiting patiently on the main floor, and when the elevator doors opened, Jerry the Booster stepped out and took the worst pinch of his life.

"I thought you pick up the things upstairs and then come to the checkout counter down here, like you do in the supermarket," Jerry said to Clancy.

"No," Clancy said, "they run this place different than Waldbaum's."

In court, Jerry tried to go all the way. He had a spell, he played deaf mute, he tried to take off his clothes. Finally, seeing it was all over, he said he was guilty.

"Raise your right hand," the court clerk said. Jerry raised his left. Nobody seemed impressed. He was through.

"What can I tell you?" he said over anisette the other night. He is out on bail pending sentencing December 1. "I done my best and it's over. But put down one thing about me. I had heart. I went into Tiffany's. You tell me a booster who ever went into Tiffany's. Jerry the Booster did. Put it down. I was the greatest of them all. I had heart."

"He did have heart," Walter Hoving, chairman of the board at Tiffany's, was saying the other day. "But the thief also had my Doughty birds."

Fat Moisch

According to the various laws and standards of conduct of the place in which he lives, which is the earth, Fat Moisch from Avenue D in Manhattan is a bad boy.

Whenever he comes around, he doesn't *seem* to do anything wrong. Fat Moisch is built like a juke box. In his summer outfit of plaid walk-shorts and white shoes, he sits at the bar and drinks red wine until he falls off the stool. But he has a background of being misunderstood in many places. He has been in trouble with barefooted policemen on St. Andrew's Island, Colombia; in Toronto, Canada, where he issued a group of checks that were classified as "leapers"; and in London, England, where he went on a gambling junket and was discovered checking suitcases in a hotel room which was other than his own.

When Fat Moisch has to come to court in New York City and a judge asks for his past record, the case always has to be postponed for two days while the clerk types it up.

"Your honor," the District Attorney said the other day, "this man is a blight on society."

The judge looked at the file in front of him which gave Fat Moisch's personal history. The file is heavier than a novel on Lewis and Clark. "The defendant does have a long record," the judge said.

"Rumors," Fat Moisch said under his breath.

He was mad that they had him in court. He was appearing in connection with some nonsense about a man who did business with him. After his appointment with Fat Moisch, the man had to go away in an ambulance.

"I'm so bad," Fat Moisch fumed. "I take bets and pay the winners cash money, right on time. But if somebody doesn't pay me, I kick him in the ankles. That's so bad?"

He shook his head and sat back and waited for the judge to come to the one part of his record that they always stop at. And when he saw the judge's head come up, Fat Moisch said a bad word.

"It's the only thing that seems to get them mad," he said. "And I had nothin' to do with it."

He was referring to an incident which grew out of an afternoon of drinking in a bar on Second Avenue near Ninth Street. The bar was crowded and Fat Moisch was broke. A man came into the bar and pushed Fat Moisch to make room. Right away, Fat Moisch got mad at the guy. The guy took out his wallet and ordered a drink. The wallet was a half-foot thick. Right away, Fat Moisch fell in love with the guy. "Get yourself in there, pal," Fat Moisch said. "Plenty of room for you." He put his hand on the guy's shoulder.

The guy threw a ten-dollar bill on the bar. The inside of the wallet looked like a bank. The guy put the wallet back into his jacket pocket. "Ain't you hot with the jacket on?" Fat Moisch said. The guy didn't listen to him. The guy drank up the ten dollars, then pulled out another ten-dollar bill and went into that one. Pretty soon the guy was in an argument with a man in a sports shirt.

"Go to it, I'm right with you, pal," Fat Moisch told the guy in the jacket.

The guy with the jacket got good and fresh and soon he and sports shirt got up and went outside. Fat Moisch was right with them. "I'll hold your jacket," he yelled. The guy gave him the jacket. The fight started and Fat Moisch's first instinct was to run. But he was afraid his man would spot him and come after him. His second instinct seemed better. Fat Moisch maneuvered right behind his man and gave his man a good shove. His man stumbled forward, face first, into a right-hand punch. Fat Moisch's man went down like a piece of wood. Fat Moisch took the wallet out of the jacket. Then he threw the jacket over his man so he wouldn't catch cold on the sidewalk. Fat Moisch strolled off into the afternoon to celebrate.

He went to a bar and began throwing ten-dollar bills from the wallet onto the bar and buying for everybody. He was spending money like it was counterfeit. It was.

Fat Moisch wound up with the Secret Service that night. They said that there was $500 worth of counterfeit money in the wallet. They wanted to know where he got it. Fat Moisch told them the truth. He said he took it from a jacket he was holding while a guy he met in a bar was in a fist fight. Fat Moisch was in the federal detention pen on West Street for two days before he could make bail. He was going to court for six months before he finally got out of the case.

But the arrest for counterfeiting is there forever. And, Fat Moisch was saying in court, he learned something from it.

"Don't steal no money that's bad," he said.

Robert J. Allen

There had been some kind of trouble at lunchtime and the owner of the place came up to Robert J. Allen. He spoke very nicely to Robert J. Allen. He said, "If you don't leave my place, I am gonna take you into the kitchen and hold your hand over the front burner."

Allen left. He went to his friend Adam's house. Adam is a paraplegic, but he's all right, nobody has to worry about Adam. The only reason you have to feel sorry for Adam is that Robert J. Allen stays with him.

"I just bet the Preakness," Adam said. "I closed my eyes and bet $30 across on Tom Rolfe. I got no business making a bet that big. Why dontcha take a piece of it from me?"

"No," Robert J. Allen said. "You'll make me pay if I lose."

He flopped down on the couch and the vodka made his eyes close. Robert J. Allen's mouth dropped open and he began snoring so loud that Adam had to turn the television way up to hear the end of the race. The loud noise made Robert J. Allen wake up. He opened one eye just as the horses were in the stretch. "Tom Rolfe, in the middle of the track," the announcer said. Robert J. Allen opened both his eyes. Tom Rolfe lugged in to the rail. Just a little bit, just seemed to cut off the second horse, Dapper Dan. Robert J. Allen clapped his hands. He loves even the hint of larceny. Tom Rolfe got under the wire first. Robert J. Allen flew off the couch. "We won," he yelled.

"Keep quiet, there's a foul claim," Adam said.

Robert J. Allen was on his feet. "I know we won," he yelled. He ran into the bathroom to shave. When he came out, the result was official. Tom Rolfe had won. Robert J. Allen had Adam's jacket with him and he grabbed the wheelchair and started pushing Adam out of the house.

"Stop it," Adam said. "I want to eat."

"We have to go out and get paid on our bet," Robert J. Allen said. Adam was still yelling that he wanted to eat and Robert J. Allen pushed him out to the car, dumped him in, threw the wheelchair in the back seat, then got in and started driving.

The bookmaker Adam bet with is from the Bronx. His name is Gilly. And as dusk was falling on the Grand Concourse, Robert J. Allen got Adam out of the car and into the wheelchair and he started pushing Adam along the crowded street and at every corner he asked people if they knew where Gilly was.

Robert J. Allen was pushing Adam's wheelchair very fast. Adam told him to go slower. Robert J. Allen started to trot. The wheelchair was going so fast now that Adam had to hold on tight so he wouldn't fall out. Allen stopped at a candy store. The woman inside said that Gilly was in this saloon three blocks down from the Grand Concourse.

"Let's go," Robert J. Allen yelled. He ran out and got behind the wheelchair. He grabbed it with both hands. Robert J. Allen put his head down and started to run.

The door to the saloon was open and they came flying into the place. Adam thought he was going to get killed when Robert J. Allen saw the bookmaker and let go and the wheelchair smashed into the juke box.

"Give us the money," Robert J. Allen yelled at Gilly, the bookmaker.

Gilly walked over to Adam and handed him $180. "My pleasure," Gilly said. Adam had it in his hand and he was counting it when Robert J. Allen's hand reached down and grabbed the loose ends of the money.

"Let go," Adam said.

"Gimme my part of the money," Robert J. Allen said.

"Hey, leave him alone," the bookmaker said. "He made the bet, not you."

"I want money. You mind your own business. This is my friend," Robert J. Allen said. "Tell 'em you're my friend," he said to Adam.

"Will somebody give me some help?" Adam yelled to the whole barroom.

Somebody came over from the bar and pushed Robert J. Allen. Robert J. Allen turned around and pushed the guy back. Adam reached up and hit Robert J. Allen in the back of the head. Robert J. Allen turned around at Adam, and Adam punched up at Robert J. Allen's face. Now there was a mess, and Adam got the wheelchair going and he was running it back and forth over one of Robert J. Allen's feet. Allen was yelling and the whole place was in a turmoil.

And Robert J. Allen's day came to an end with him fighting for money with a guy in a wheelchair. And the worst thing about it all was that it was only 7:15 p.m. and Robert J. Allen still had the whole night in front of him.

Larry Lightfingers

The place was dark. There was a ton of whisky on the table and the headwaiters kept lighting your cigarettes. Up on a stage in the middle of the big room, a blue spotlight was on Barbra Streisand's face while she was singing "Happy Days." It was one of those nights that summer is supposed to be for, but Larry did not like it at all.

"This place has very high security," he kept saying.

He had a valid complaint. There are also so many weekends in a summer and Larry has to get the most out of every one of them. He cannot afford to run into a resort joint that doesn't like property stolen from its guests. Taking things that belong to other people is Larry's business.

In street language, he is known as a heister, and Larry does most of his work in the summer. He checks into resort hotels and kind of stands around until the recreation director gets on the PA system and says, "Everybody on the front lawn in ten minutes for a game of Simon Says."

Larry then swings into action. He proceeds into rooms occupied by people who are out on the lawn with the recreation director. "Before they got time to throw four people out of the game, I'm even for the weekend," Larry says. "Everything I do after that is winter money."

But here, on this night at a beach club out on Long Island, Larry was a loser. He was wearing his best working clothes, a $145 tuxedo, and he was staying in a room that cost $78 a day. And, as he kept complaining, he was not going to be able to steal even the blanket from his bed all weekend.

"Believe me, I know these places," he was saying. "When you check into a hotel, you can tell how tough the place is going to be right off. The first night, you look around the lobby. Everybody is in a tuxedo. But there'll be one guy in a dark blue suit sitting off in the corner. He is trying to be inconspicuous. But at the same time he wants to make sure you know he's there. This is the security man.

"Then, if you don't see another guy like him any place else you go, you know you're in trouble. Very high security means you don't even see the security. Now, I haven't seen a guy who resembles an officer since I saw that one guy in the lobby. And I've been all over this place. You know what that means? This joint is loaded with them. I'm dead here."

He had another drink and said he was going to be glad to go home Sunday night.

As a rule, his summer weekends are not this bleak. His big move is at 4:30 Saturday afternoon, when women guests at the hotel line up to get their jewels out of the vaults so they can dazzle each other at the show Saturday night.

In the midst of a conglomeration of hairnets and spiked heels, Larry stands and smokes a cigar and concentrates so hard he sweats. He memorizes names and room numbers and matches them up with the furs and diamonds coming out of the vault. He will forget the name of his own wife before he loses track of who is taking what to which room.

"After that, I wait for Sunday morning and then bust in," Larry says. "How do you bust in? Huh. There is only one way to get through a double lock. With a bellhop."

Larry originally got into the summer-resort business with two other guys from his neighborhood. They went to a shylock and took enough money to outfit themselves with a good vacation wardrobe. Then they hit the better places and went to work.

He stole his first fur, a mink, in the Poconos.

It was early on a hot Saturday night and the dame at the next table in the cocktail lounge said she wanted to go up and leave the stole in her room.

Larry walked out after her. A bellhop came up to him.

"Do you know something?" the bellhop said. "I know her room number."

"So?" Larry said.

"So I got a key for it." The bellhop smiled.

"That's nice," Larry said.

The whole thing took exactly twenty minutes. Larry was launched on a career.

He says he never does anything in the winter. "I used to read the television listings and when a big name was on a show, we'd take a shot at getting into the apartment. But once we came into this guy's apartment while he is on the television. *The Perry Como Show*. We even checked a set to make sure he was on and wasn't sick or something. So in we came. And here is the guy. Sitting right in his living room. He let out some scream. That's how I learned about television shows being taped in advance."

Since then he has never wavered in his first love—hotels in the summer. "They do Simon Says live," Larry says.

Sam Silverware

When the headwaiter in the night club stood by for a tip before he led the party to a table, Sam reached out and put a folded napkin into his hand.

"What's this?" the headwaiter said.

"A prank," Sam said.

The headwaiter led Sam to a table that was near Egypt. It was next to what waiters call the drugstore. This is the chest where the silverware is kept. Anybody trying to eat at the table alongside the drugstore usually spends the night with waiters bumping into him while they grab silverware and pepper mills and the like for the other tables.

"Enjoy yourself here," the headwaiter told Sam.

"Beautiful," Sam said. The minute the headwaiter started walking away, Sam's hand went out and dipped the drugstore. The hand returned with a half-dozen forks. Sam stuffed them into his inside jacket pocket. "Terrific," Sam said. "They go for $11.20 a dozen. You got to be sick to buy silverware." A waiter pushed past him, grabbed a couple of dishes, and headed away. Sam hit the drugstore again. Hard this time. He came up with eight or nine forks and stuffed them into the pocket again. "The best," Sam said, picking up the menu.

Ever since he bought a restaurant of his own ten years ago, Sam has been around town stealing supplies. He has never bought so much as a butter knife for his own place. He makes sure he always gets the worst table wherever he goes. And he steals everything. When you eat at Sam's, you have shrimp forks from the Plaza, soup spoons from the Drake, knives from the Rainbow Room, and, his big prize, chafing dishes, from the Americana.

One morning during the transit strike, Sam sat in his restaurant and read in the newspaper about the day-and-night negotiations going on at the Americana. "This could be sensational," Sam said. "They must be eating right around the clock. Tremendous." Sam checked into the Americana later that day and began to patrol the halls. On the 39th floor there were three room-service tables out in the hall. Sam began to clap his hands when he saw the chafing dishes.

By the end of his second day in the hotel, Sam's bathtub was full of chafing dishes and he was taking them out two and three at a time and the hotel management was asking the people not to put their room-service tables in the hallways any more. "We are having a problem with missing dishes," a notice said.

Sam steals like this because he is a thief. Not a big thief. He tried to be a big thief once and everybody got mad at him and made him go away to a jail. He is strictly a small thief, and he only steals for his restaurant. He has it figured out that if he cuts down on almost all expenses, his restaurant will show a bigger profit. This is good thinking, but it can be troublesome for the owners of other restaurants. For whenever Sam goes out socially, he steals.

"Look at this," Sam crowed at a hotel one night last week. He had a pepper mill inside his jacket. "You know what these things go for? $12.80."

"Sensational," he kept saying to himself when he hit the buffet table of a private party at an expensive restaurant Saturday night. Sam made a clean sweep of the forks. "Eat with your hands," he muttered. He sat down, and all around him people wound up eating cake with spoons and the waiter was downstairs screaming at the dishwasher, "What do you mean, you don't have forks?"

Through normal restaurant attrition Sam's place ran low on teaspoons a few weeks ago. At 5 a.m. Sam went up to a golf club where he knew the watchman. The dining room was neatly set up for lunch. Folded napkins, cups, saucers, silverware lined up at each place. Sam disturbed nothing. He just took the teaspoon from each place. Then he went into the kitchen and took the reserve supply of teaspoons. At noon, when the club dining room opened for lunch, there were calls for teaspoons from every table. Busboys ran to waiters, waiters ran to the headwaiter, the headwaiter ran in circles.

The people eating lunch had to stir their coffee with butter knives. The headwaiter was in the kitchen, sitting on a chair. "Somebody is crazy," he kept saying. And two psychiatrists who were members of the golf club sat over their lunch and got into an argument over what teaspoons stood for in a man's life. "I don't see how taking teaspoons is a way of hitting back at your mother," one of them insisted. And Sam was down in his restaurant patting the silverware drawer.

"Do you know what you're eating with?" he called to a customer. The customer looked around and shrugged. "You're eating with a knife from the Sign of the Dove," Sam said. "So now you don't have to go there."

One of the problems of being a compulsive telephone talker and preferring to spend your spare time in a bar rather than wash the family auto is that you say and do things you would rather have left unsaid or undone. Despite the fact that he rarely means it when he delivers one of his dire threats (or that he means it only for the next two seconds) or that he has never bitten anyone's nose off although that used to be one of his favorite intimidations, Breslin does sometimes manage to say the perfectly cutting thing and get insulted in return. Like an Irishman of the old country, who would keep a little book in which to record slights, he manages occasionally to put them into his column, at which point all his enemies become his friends again—almost.

People I'm Not Talking to Next Year

All these people today, they run around and put their arms around each other's shoulders and they say how much they like each other and they hope the new year is better than the old year. And all during 1965 they were trying to kill each other and now today, because of a calendar on a wall, they think everything should be nice.

This is not my game. I can remember too well. And I remember everything every person did to me during the year, and herewith, on this day of warmth and understanding, I present the people who did something very bad to me during the last twelve months and because of what they did to me I do not intend to speak to one of them throughout the coming year.

GOLDSTEIN THE PROCESS-SERVER. About a month ago I was walking on Seventh Avenue and this little bum in an overcoat down to his ankles comes up to me. He says, "Parson me, but didn't I see you last night with Johnny Carson?" I wanted to kiss him. Beautiful. "Yes, you did," I said. "Great," he said, "don't tell me your name. I have your name written down right here." Out of the pocket of his overcoat comes a folded piece of legal paper that said the Chemical Bank had put a lien of $1500 on me because I cosigned for another one of Fat Thomas's cars.

"Wear it in health," said Goldstein the Process-Server.

Well, Goldstein the Process-Server could go into the ocean and be drowning this year and I would sit on the beach and say, "I can't hear you, Goldstein."

PEPE. His real name is Norton W. Peppis. Pepe runs a saloon with his partner, John McGuire, and him I intend not even to nod to this year. All year they spend their afternoons at the racetrack. When the horses left, Pepe, who had started out the year with a Cadillac and now has to try to find change for a subway ride, sat down with his partner and tried to figure out how they could get some money. They found a way. On Christmas Eve, the manager of the saloon comes to my house with a bill for $895 they said I had run up in the joint. You should get paid by the hour just to be in the place. And they look to get out on Christmas Eve by sending me a tab. They didn't even have it in them to come around personally. Well, I'm not talking to Pepe and when I see him riding on the subway train I am going to look out the window.

BIG SHOT MAITRE D' AT THE 21 CLUB. All my life I've sat in Mutchie's saloon and read stories about how so-and-so was with this big beauty at 21 last night. Back in October I was out with some guys, and one of them said he'd like to see what this 21 was like and I said I'd like to see the place too. We went to the 21 and I go up to the door and give it a push and we all go inside. You never saw anything like it in your life. All guys with tuxedos on started to run toward us.

"Can I help you?" one of them said. A tall guy. He was in charge. He had both his hands on my chest.

"We are all filled here tonight," he said.

Then he pushed at me hard so that a party of about eleven could come in through the door. He smiled at them and the eleven strolled to the bar.

"You see this carpet on the floor?" I yelled. "I'll come back here with a guy and set it on fire."

One of the other guys in the tuxedos went for a telephone. He was probably going to get the cops.

"You don't want to come in here," the maitre d' said.

Big shot. Damn right I don't want to go into his place. You could take the 21. Take the whole joint and the suckers who go into it. It is a sink compared to Mutchie's saloon, which is directly across from Pier 29, East River, and last night Georgie Brown was seen with Sherry at the bar of Mutchie's, and Nunzi hosted a big party for Jumbo from the fish market.

What follows now is a list of people who I am not

going to talk to. The reasons would take too long to explain. So I just list the people.

Atra Baer, Mike the Brain, Roger Kahn, Mr. Hitz from Bleeck's, B. J. Cutler, Mr. Finelle from the Municipal Building, Miss Stewart from the telephone company, Everett Walker, Harold Anderson, Harry Day, Harrison Salisbury, Jerry the Booster, Seymour the Pirate, Mrs. Pirate, Mrs. Ahearn from Consolidated Edison Company, Hugo the Tailor, Mike Lee, Transit Authority cop who wouldn't let me go up the subway stairs on Thanksgiving Day, Nick Lapole, Max Kase, Boyd Lewis, Jack Powers, Mr. Fiore of Beneficial Finance Corp., Toney Betts, Tom Zumbo, Arthur J. Sylvester, Phil Pepe, Joe Alvarez, Mike Reynolds, Tom Frane, Ed Aurico, Lester Williamson, Louis Kleinsteuber, Al Newman the bail bondsman, Vivienne the housekeeper, and Joey Beglane.

4

In Which Negroes Are Just People

Theoretically, Jimmy Breslin should not like Negroes. The white backlash is supposed to come out of the lower-middle-class areas of Queens, and the ones Breslin calls "my people"—the plainclothesmen and the cops on the beat, the small-time bookmakers and some of the big-time gangsters—are supposed to be part of the great reservoir of hatred and anti-civil-rights sentiment. Maybe so.

Breslin, though, has always been deeply concerned about, well, not so much civil rights as civil inequalities. He laughs at beatniks and eggs the Mayor on to throw the bums out of City Hall when they have a lie-in. He bristles back at the Black Muslim propaganda in a meeting in Chicago. He seems sometimes to be the champion of the scoffers when it comes to the rhetoric of Black Power. But he has consistently drawn a line between poverty and the poor. He hates poverty. He takes the poor as they come.

It is is probably a result of trying to be a curmudgeon too early. He has a poor opinion of so many white people, he can't help feeling that some of the black ones have to be better.

The motor that drives him always forces him out to

where the action is, even on the occasions when he figures the action is not in New York. And one of the action things to him has always been the Negro drive toward equality. In May of 1964 he predicted the troubles that were coming for Harlem and he heard the rumbles of distant trouble in other cities. He didn't try to make a reputation as a crusader; he certainly didn't want one. But civil inequality became something of a running theme in his writing.

The memo that follows, his stories from Harlem, and his coverage of the Selma march indicate just how he saw the picture: it was national in scope, but it was played out through the people in the streets, the men and women who wept and laughed and married and stole, just the way other people have always done.

Dear Jim [Bellows]:

Here, for your information and consideration, is a schedule of ideas and the mechanics of carrying them out which I intend to put into effect starting today. I was out bouncing on the street at 6:30 a.m. today so I might as well do something with all this freaking time. . . .

Tomorrow night (Tues.) I intend to move into somebody's apartment in Harlem. Joe Glaser is in charge of this. I told him I lived bad all my life and I don't have to live with roaches to know what they are like. So he is getting me something he says will be all right.

What I intend to do there is simple. Build five murderous parts, and build them on the hallmark of anything of this sort: small facts, gathered in many places, and gathered in such numbers that the copy can be flat, understated and totally effective because of the facts. Take a woman at the supermarket. Get her order, can by can, and list it and what she paid for it. With almost no comment on it by me, this list will be meaningful to a housewife in Larchmont. Maybe more meaningful than all the big words written of this thing.

You follow this theory with everything. With

the schoolyards, which are crowded at 7:30 a.m. because parents have to leave early and the kids are locked out of the apartments with nothing else to do, they go to school. And with the furniture repossessions and water and gas and electric shut-offs and the gas-station habits—50 cents' worth of gas for a Cadillac. You do this with facts from small people in the street and from merchants and bankers.

But always, you do it with people. You keep the facts alive with people.

Then the violence aspects. Ride with the police for a night. Talk to my man Bumpy Johnson, the first major Negro criminal. Talk to the unimaginative junkies who steal for their habit; "You think I *like* paddin' around in the dark in somebody else's bedroom?" And talk to the X's and their people; the ones everybody expects trouble from. And talk to the colored leaders who have sold out their own people so they can be patted on the heads by the whites.

These are people who have had very few heroes, but they are trying to find heroes right now. Some of the ones they look for are bad. Others are exceptional human beings. Who they will turn to when the heat makes the tar on the roofs soft and sticky and it gets into the masonry and comes through the cracked plaster ceilings and makes the apartments too hot to stay in and everybody spills out onto the streets until 2 and 3 a.m. is the question.

The police walk three abreast on the streets now. Their clubs spin on the leather cords. And all around them, the dark faces look at them. The people believe only demonstrations will get them anything. They never got a thing before they started trouble, they all believe. The credo in Harlem in simple: "Anything that costs Whitey money is good." A demonstration, even the threat of one, forces police overtime. Yet the voting rolls show that in this most important of all areas, the people of Harlem are terribly deficient.

"We are missing two million votes," the Democratic leaders say. "They all should come from Negro areas."

Yet ask the average colored people in Harlem when was the last time they voted, and the answer is a stare. So many of these people do not even know where or how to vote. They have no tradition of voting. In the old neighborhoods, Bay Ridge, say, election day is a ritual. It is a ritual because your father, grandfather, and great-grandfather voted so they could have decent shots at city jobs. Now the city jobs are not needed, because there are insurance men and stockbrokerage workers in the families. But the tradition of voting goes on.

The people in Harlem have no traditions. They have no heritage. But they want one. And in some areas, a very good story Walt Kelly handed me, they are after it. An Episcopal church has started a big voter-registration drive and they came to Kelly for help.

"It's a lot more fun to go on sit-ins," he told the kids.

"We want to do it by voting," they said.

"But if you go on sit-ins you can go to jail and be heroes," Kelly told them. "If you go to all the trouble of getting a big vote out, then nobody will be calling you niggers any more and there'll be no reason for sit-ins and you'll have the same dull life everybody else has."

The entire story is based on one idea: these are people. They are bewildered, uncared-about, and angry. They have a right to anger because white people would prefer to speak of them in great generalities and do nothing about the housing or the type of food they have to eat because of the salaries they make. The question is, as this summer comes up, will their anger show in a legitimate drive or will it erupt as it did in 1936 and 1943?

Now this is a nice, big statement. It is of the type I intend not to use. Not even once. But the small facts, gathered and put together, will say the things themselves.

I would have this thing started and into the office by Friday for the Sunday paper and have another in on Saturday for Monday and the remainder in Sunday. The outline for the entire series will be in by late Thursday.

I feel this is the most important thing I can do for the *Tribune* at this time, and perhaps the most important thing I have done for you at any time. It will work fine, as long as somebody does not throw a garbage can at me from a rooftop. The rooftops, not the sidewalks, are the things to look out for.

respectfully,
j. breslin

Harlem Notebook—I

Inside the church, the heavy air-conditioner in the wall kept the narrow hallway cool. Carroll Tyler and Sandra Hopkins, who had just been married, stood under the machine while the guests squeezed in front of them and kissed the tall, striking bride and shook hands with the groom and then went out through the doors and into the hot Sunday-afternoon sun. Outside the church, the Salem Methodist Church on 129th Street and Seventh Avenue in Harlem, the people's voices were drowned out by the whir of low-pressure tires on taxicabs which kept passing by. On a weekend, taxicabs are a poor man's game and Harlem is filled with them.

Tyler was in a tuxedo. He was nervous, but he spoke in a quiet voice. He is twenty-four and in the

Marines and he has a neat mustache and a strong-looking neck.

"I've got about seven months to go," he was saying. "I'm at Camp Lejeune. That's in North Carolina."

"Where are you going to live when you get out?"

"We have an apartment."

"Is it a neighborhood like this?"

"Well, you know. It's a neighborhood."

"What are you going to do when you get out?"

"I don't know. I'll be a real-estate agent, I suppose. Why are you asking?"

"Oh, I don't know. I was just wondering how you figure out your life or your future or whatever it is on a day like this when you happen to be colored."

"I don't want to know about that now," he said. Then the bride smiled and said thank you and they went out the door and onto the church steps.

There are three small trees, the leaves fresh green, on the sidewalk in front of the church. The well-dressed guests were by the trees and the limousines were parked at the curb behind them. It was pleasant. But the rest of it, the part Tyler didn't want to think about on his wedding day, was there too. Across Seventh Avenue, in the ground floors of the old stone tenements, were the Harlem Swan Fish and Chips, the Dunbar Pawnbrokers, Bea's Hair Styles, and the Vogue Beauty Shop. On the side street, 129th Street, the red sign of the Elks Imperial Bar and Grill showed on a building sitting between two tenements. Across the street from the Elks are the buildings where, the police believe, the young kids who claim they are going to kill white people this summer sit on stoops and stare at the police cars.

And from the windows of the stone tenements, the old people leaned out and looked at the young married couple coming out of the church. Tyler did not look up at them while he helped his wife into the limousine, and he did not look at the hock shop or the Elks Club sign, but it was all right in front of him, standing like the couple of hundred years of history and attitudes that this young guy was walking out of church to face.

In Harlem, words like "history" and "attitudes" come down to plain things. To the paycheck mostly. The paychecks Harlem people earn, and their dissatisfaction with being poor and living in slums, produce the speculation that this will be a summer of racial violence in Harlem. But these same paychecks are why general violence almost certainly won't develop at all. The same Harlem people who have the whites frightened about a race riot are too busy working for a paycheck and too tired from years of being poor to start running in the streets.

In Harlem, from 96th Street to 119th Street, between Fifth Avenue and the East River, the average family income is $3797. From 110th Street to 126th Street, between Eighth and Park Avenues, it is a little higher, $4141. In the lower part of Manhattan, where white people live, income in the area from 14th to 30th Streets between Eighth and Third Avenues is $6892. And, if you want a real contrast, from 63d Street to 96th Street, between Fifth and Third, a family averages $15,305.

Money makes the way of life, and low money shows everywhere you go in Harlem. In a supermarket on 135th Street, in the middle of the Saturday rush, the totals on the cash registers kept showing $7.30 and $10.58 and $5.97 while, at the same time, in a supermarket in Baldwin, Long Island, the figures were $28.60 and $41.12.

In the neighborhood taverns, the bartender puts three thick-bottomed shot glasses on the wood in front of you when you order a drink. All these local bars sell drinks on a two-for-one or three-for-one policy. In Maxie's Café, on 153d Street and Eighth Avenue, rye, gin, vodka, or rum shorties are sold for $.50 per single, two for $.90 and three for $1.20. Cognac and better Scotch sell for $.60 a drink. All chasers except water are $.10 extra. Bar etiquette requires the bartender to place the three shot glasses down and the customer names his game, a single or two for $.90 or three for the $1.20.

The low money shows most in the people. There are 450,000 people living in Harlem, and the talk, and the crime-rate figues, have other people afraid of the Harlem people and afraid to go into the area. The crime figures are high, and the brutality of the crimes of late turns your stomach. But 450,000 people do not run around committing crime. Last week, to see Harlem a little better, and to examine this place some have said is just a big time bomb waiting to go off on a hot summer night, we moved into Harlem. James Putnam, a fifty-four-year-old man who is retired from the Pennsylvania Railroad after thirty-eight years as business-car steward for Davis G. Bevans, the railroad's vice-chairman, was kind enough to put us up in his three-room apartment.

For walk-around company we had James Russell, who calls bartenders "say, my man," and who drinks orange slings as a rule, but V.O. in the Pink Angel, where, he explains, he is "in kind of tight with the barkeep." Mr. Russell is a former Golden Gloves bantamweight boxer and, upon being properly urged, he demonstrates a good, short left hook and gives the impression that he once was a stiff puncher. Also with us was a person who is known, where he comes from, as "the First Division." He is called this because of the firepower he keeps in his pocket. He was along because of many warnings from outsiders that Harlem is a dangerous place for a white these days. In five days and nights we didn't draw much more than a stare because people in Harlem are too busy living like people any place else.

This does not mean that trouble isn't there. Pick up a paper and you see that. James Putnam points out that Wednesday-evening services at his church, St. Mark's Methodist on 137th Street and St. Nicholas Avenue, have poor attendance because so many women have been mugged right in front of the church. Throughout Saturday night, riding in an unmarked Police Department crime combat car out of the 32d Precinct, Sergeant Frank Weidenburner kept advising us, at each stop, to get into the building in a hurry because the bad trouble comes from the rooftops.

On 129th Street between Seventh and Lenox, which is the area where a small group known as the Blood Brothers stored ammunition for a war on the police, and where the few remaining members still hang out, Weidenburner became insistent. His car was answering a radio call which said somebody in the tenement at 155 West 129th had called for police help.

"Any call on that block can be trouble," he said. When his unmarked car pulled up, two radio cars were there, and two more pulled in later.

"Don't hang around out here," he said when we got out. "Come inside the building with us."

Inside, a man of about twenty-five was stretched unconscious on a second-floor landing. Two women were with him. They said the man had been beaten and stomped on by kids from up the block. Then the women began to fight over who was going to nurse the beaten man.

You see things like this. And then, with bright morning sunlight coming in from the patio, you sit and talk to a woman like Jane Booker. Bright, and almost overly sensitive because of her intelligence, she sits and has a glass of orange juice in her new high-middle-income apartment, and she snaps out the things that bother a woman who is colored in New York.

"Why is it," she says, "that every time I get into a taxicab downtown, the driver turns around and asks me, 'What's the number today?' Just because I'm not white, does that mean I have to know the numbers game? Does he do that with any white woman that gets into a cab?"

And over all of this, over the people and their habits and their misery, runs the layer of arguments. The Negro crime rate is high, the whites claim. The police brutality must stop, or it will provoke violence, the Negro leaders say. A Negro comedian gets on television and says some nonsense about a conspiracy in the white press to suppress the Negro. The words in the arguments are big and important-sounding and in the meantime Harlem sits there, with 450,000 people who have no heritage in life except poverty. And with this long, hot summer coming up that everybody talks about, some of them may step out and do things. But only some of them. And then only maybe.

"Riot?" the bartender was saying in Maxie's. "Who's got time for that? People have to go to work every day. Doesn't anybody know that?"

Harlem Notebook—II

In 1936 a Negro boy was arrested while he was trying to steal something in a five-and-ten, and a patrol wagon came for him. But the story got around that the kid was shot to death in the store and taken away in a morgue ambulance, and at 7 p.m. somebody ran up to a jewelry store on 125th Street and put a brick through the window. Now everybody else started to do the same thing, and pretty soon there was a riot.

It was the same in 1943, the year of the last big riot in Harlem. It started when a girl in a bar told off a cop in tough language and when he tried to arrest the girl, the soldier she was drinking with came off the stool and grabbed the cop's club and hit him over the head with it. The cop got up and shot the soldier in the left shoulder. The time was 7:30 p.m. on a hot Sunday night. The soldier, Robert Bandy, was taken to Sydenham Hospital, where he was resting comfortably for the night. But down on the streets everybody was saying that the cop had killed the soldier, and at 10:30 a mob spilled onto 125th Street and smashed every window in sight and did $5,000,000 in damage before the riot ended.

Both times, these riots were aimed solely at the stores on 125th Street, which were owned by white people. In the middle of the 1943 trouble, the Chinese proprietor of a chop-suey joint stuck a cautious hand into the window part of his store and put up his famous sign: "Me Colored Too."

Now, twenty-one years later, all except two businesses on 125th Street are still owned by whites. From Lenox to Eighth on 125th, the jumble of ground-floor credit jewelers and three- and four-story-high department stores is solid white except for a barbecue stand and the Carver Savings and Loan Association. And the grumbling about it from Black Nationalist and other groups has been loud. One CORE group has called for every white business to take on a Negro partner.

Like everything else about the racial question in New York, there is more than one side to all this. The Negro groups say that the white man is making a living off black backs and then running away to his suburban home to live with other whites and leaving his customers sitting in a tenement with a new television set and a thick payment book.

But yesterday afternoon Frank Schiffman, the owner of the Apollo Theatre, sat in his office and talked about it a little differently.

"I have a vacant store I own right down here on 125th Street," he was saying, "and I'd prefer a colored tenant. So far, we can't get one. To tell you the truth, we've been rejecting white applicants in hopes of getting a colored tenant. But I'm not going to do it too much longer.

"Now, look," Schiffman said, "it's a very simple thing. These people don't have the money to buy into businesses, and when they do, a lot of times they do not run them too well. It isn't their fault. It all goes back to the beginning. When my son and grandsons come home from school I can sit down and do homework with them. I've had an education. But some of these people come up from the South and the mother and father can barely read and write and the kid is put into school up here. How does this child compete with the others, who get help at home? It's not an easy thing. In the South, there used to be laws against educating Negroes. So who is to blame? The one down on the street who can't run a business because he never had any training, or the people who sat around for a century and made sure he never got a chance to have the training?"

This is a view held by many people of both colors in Harlem, and walking through the streets supports it. If there is one thing, aside from the number of people, which catches the eye during foot tours of Harlem, it is the number of vacant stores. They are all over, and they stand vacant because the old owners busted out trying to make them go and now nobody has the cash or flair to move in and shoot for themselves.

Yet this situation doesn't seem to be producing the kind of deep resentment which can spill over into a riot. The people you see walking the streets of Harlem don't act inflamed about their lot in life. They act like people with a jailhouse outlook on life. They are locked into a square section of New York which has physical boundaries almost like prison walls. And if they riot, they riot, like prisoners, right in their own confined areas, and they know that sooner or later the guards chop them up and the whole thing turns out to be a waste of time.

So these people sit in bars or in candy stores or on their stoops or they hang from their windows or drive their cars and, instead of acting like mean people ready to attack whites, they act as if they are serving out a life sentence.

There are a lot of evidences of this. Big, obvious evidences, such as the painfully low attendance at the last civil rights demonstration. And there are small evidences, too. CORE has a campaign to stop people from buying a certain band of beer. "Of 3500 employees, only 57 are Negro or Puerto Rican," the CORE leaflet reads. There are stocks of these leaflets in bars, right alongside the ballot box the offending beer company places in bars to handle voting for its promotional contest to pick the prettiest Negro girl. All the people in the bars ignore the pamphlets and spend their time talking about the contest, which seems to be one of the most popular things in town.

This apathy shows in the voting, too. Less than 40 per cent of the eligible people in Harlem bother to vote. In low-income areas that are white, the figures run between 60 and 65 per cent.

"People are becoming more aware of civil rights," Joe Tittle, a district captain for Assemblyman Lloyd Dickens, was saying one night. "We have 680 registered now. That's up about 125. How many people in the district? Roughly, 5000."

"Do you have 50 per cent of your people registered?" he was asked.

"No," he said quietly. "Not near 50 per cent."

Which is the crime the people in Harlem commit against themselves. And while they don't vote, automation is slowly knocking them out of jobs and the relief rolls creep up. The Department of Welfare center on West 124th Street has a case load of 7400 now, as against 6900 three years ago.

During all this, the major commerce in Harlem goes on. It is numbers, and on Lenox Avenue little shops sell such as *Aunt Sally's Policy Players' Dream Book,* which tells you such highly valuable things as: "ABSENCE—To see absent persons in your dreams. 411." This means if you have a nightmare about a guy you owe money to and have not seen around for some time, go out and play 411.

Aunt Sally's book runs 122 pages and the last entry in it is for a wood sorrel. That's 203.

The Harlem Riot

The shirtless children ran through the gutters and played with the broken glass and the dull brass cartridge shells from the riot of the night before. The flat sky was an open oven door and its heat made people spill out of the tenements and onto the stoops, or onto milk boxes set up on the sidewalk, and they sat and watched the children pick up the brass shells and pocket them as if they were prizes.

They watched the cops too. The cops were everywhere, four and five of them on a street corner, wearing white steel helmets, and the people of Harlem watched them and hated them yesterday afternoon.

"When I see a white cop, I can't help myself, I just can't stand looking at one of them," Livingston Wingate was saying. "I'm supposed to be a responsible person and I try to rub it from my mind. But right now, when I look across the street here and see those white cops, I get disturbed. I just can't stand looking at them."

Wingate is an official. He is a lawyer who has worked for the government in Washington. He now is one of the major figures in running HARYOU-ACT, which has been formed to help young people in Harlem. When people of position talk the way he did, the trouble is bad. And yesterday afternoon, while everybody in Harlem waited for the sun to go down and night to cloak the streets and make moving around easier, you wondered just how bad it would become.

Some of them wanted to get at it in the daylight. The fire trucks had 129th Street, between Madison and Fifth, tied up during an alarm at 2:15 in the afternoon, and to make room for a hook and ladder coming through, the guy driving us pulled in to the curb in the middle of the block.

Right away, somebody moved off the stoop: a kid with a shaved head and a gold polo shirt. He was about nineteen and he went to another stoop, where three other kids were sitting. He said something to them and they looked at the car. Then they got up and came onto the sidewalk and the one with the shaved head walked across the street and spoke to a crowd on another stoop.

Then he came walking back, looking at the car; and when you stared back at him, his eyelids came down and made his eyes narrow.

"What are you lookin' at, you big fat white bastard?" he said.

"Oh, come on, it's too hot for this nonsense," we told him.

"We're goin' to show you what's nonsense," he said. "We're goin' to stick some nonsense right into your fat white belly."

A fireman, rubber boots flopping on the melting tar street, walked over from an engine. He had an ax in his hand. A new ax. Big, with a light yellow wooden handle. The kid with the shaved head didn't even notice him. He just kept walking past the car and went back to the stoop where three waited for him.

"What the hell are you doing here?" the fireman said. "Don't you listen to the newspapers?"

"We're trying to get through."

"They were stoning us last night," the fireman said. "You don't know what it was like here. They were trying to kill us. Get out of here if you got any brains."

Then he went back to the truck. The other firemen came out of the tenement and climbed onto the trucks. There had been no fire and now the three trucks were starting to pull away.

"Hey, fat white bastard," the shaved head called out. "Why don't you stay around here till these trucks leave?"

"Oh, come on," he was told.

Two trucks left, and then the hook and ladder moved by, and the minute it did, the guy driving us in the car pulled away from the curb and started up the block. The kids came out from both sides. They were walking at first, but then one of them ran and tried to get in the back door on the right-hand side, but now the car was moving too fast and he couldn't make it and then, with the car heading up the block, you saw his bare black arm pulled back and then come up and something came through the air at the car.

Whatever it was, it exploded when it hit the street behind the car. Who knows what it was? Molotov cocktails were all over the place Saturday night.

Maybe it was nothing more than a firecracker. You couldn't tell. If somebody snapped his fingers on 129th Street in Harlem yesterday afternoon, the noise made you jump.

It all came down to this in Harlem. All the talk and all the speeches and all the ignorance and all the history of this deep, vicious thing of black against white which they classify under the nice name of civil rights came crashing down from the rooftops inside garbage cans. The symbol of a couple of hundred years of sinful history became a black arm pulling back and then coming around to throw something at a white cop.

And there seemed to be no way to talk to anybody. For a while the big main avenues of Harlem seemed quiet and police-state orderly yesterday afternoon, the people sitting on the side streets with a bitterness which went right through you when you saw it in their faces.

There seemed to be nobody who could stop what everybody thought the night would bring.

At 4:15 p.m. we drove to the Mount Morris Presbyterian Church with Judge James Watson to hear Jesse Gray address a rally. Gray is an irrational man who is a force in Harlem only because of the white press, which failed in its obligation to check out people it writes of. Publicity made Jesse Gray, and yesterday afternoon was to be his great chance for rabble-rousing.

Then Jesse Gray got up and this church turned into something you've never seen before.

"Before today is over, we'll be able to separate the men from the boys," Gray said when he got up.

"Only one thing can solve the problem in Mississippi, and that's guerrilla warfare," Gray said. "I'm beginning to wonder what's going to solve the problem here in New York."

He threw the line out into the hot airless church and he waited for the answer he knew would come. He got it.

"Guerrilla warfare," they shouted.

"Oh, my God," Judge Watson said in the back of the church. "Oh, my God."

It was a little before five o'clock on a Sunday afternoon. A long hot night was in front of everybody.

The Rochester Riot

Rochester

They had the personnel carriers on the other side of the field. They were parked side by side, baking in the hot afternoon sun, heat shimmering from the machine guns on top of them, and the caterpillars under them were ugly and out of place on the park grass. Machines that men used for killing never look nice when you put them in places where children play.

The General was proud of them. He wanted to make sure Governor Rockefeller saw the personnel carriers.

"Now over here," the General said. He pointed to the machines. Rockefeller stopped and looked over at them. "We have machine guns mounted on the top," the General said. "A fifty and a thirty. And we put the troops down in there. A squad in each. When we move one of them in, believe me, it breaks things up in a hurry. Would you care to go over and see them?" Rockefeller said nothing. He turned his head away from these ugly things with the machine guns on top of them. And now, with sadness on his face, he walked in the other direction.

"Bad," somebody said.

"A shame," Rockefeller said.

There was nothing else to say. He was the Governor of the state and he was walking through this big grass field which was filled with vehicles and pup tents and National Guardsmen, and across the street, in the red brick armory, the state troopers slept in T-shirts on cots with their .45s on the floor. And all of it was to keep people who live in New York State from destroying each other in racial violence. This was something we always felt belonged to Little Rock or some place like that.

Rockefeller walked over to a cluster of Guardsmen who were in fatigues and he reached his hand out to them.

"I just want to thank you very much for what you're doing for all of us," he said. "I don't know how to thank you." He did not say it like a politician looking for votes. And he did not smile. Nobody ever smiles during a race riot.

This was, it appeared yesterday, exactly what started in Rochester last Friday night. In Harlem and Bedford-Stuyvesant, the junkies and the shiftless ran in the streets and looting was more important than civil rights. Rochester is different. Rochester is the real thing. It was kids who tried to kill the Chief of Police and then went into the streets and split his force into pieces. But it was kids without police records who seemed to be in the majority. And colored adults did not wring their hands and say how wrong their kids were. They liked it. So late yesterday afternoon, when Rockefeller left Rochester, the state troopers in the armory got off their cots and strapped the .45s onto their black garrison belts and the Guardsmen started to line up in the park and everybody said it was going to be a quiet night, but nobody was sure.

"Oh, I saw troublemakers out there," Lloyd Stevens, a detective, was saying, "but it wasn't all troublemakers. I mean the troublemakers were there. But I'd say that most of these kids out there have never been in trouble before. They were no juvenile delinquents or anything."

Connie Mitchell sat at her kitchen table and smoked a cigarette and said the same thing. She is a member of the Monroe County Board of Supervisors, the first Negro ever elected to the board, and she lives in the neighborhood where they rioted on Saturday night.

"These kids, I've known them since they were four and five years old and now they're in high school and I had hopes for them as leaders," she said. "But they went out. They told me, 'We love you and we don't want to hurt you, Mrs. Mitchell, so you stay right there on your porch." I saw mothers right on this block out on the porch crying. They were pleading with their kids not to go out. And do you know what the kids told them? They told them, 'Mother, you just don't understand.'"

Laploys Ashford of the NAACP sat with her. "It's not narcotics," he said. "There's not much narcotics up here."

"I came up under Joe Louis," Mrs. Mitchell said. "You know, the picture of the good Negro. But these kids were brought up with Little Rock and Birmingham on television. We didn't realize it, and now they're gone. They won't listen to me. We've lost them."

She looked down at the table. "It's no good," she said. "It's no good. The fever still is there."

Up on the corner two kids were killing time and watching the helmeted state troopers at the other end of the block.

They said their names were John Johnson and Robert Faber and that they were sixteen and in Benjamin Franklin High School and that they had nothing to do for the summer.

"I get up about 11:30 and I walk around," Johnson said.

"All day?"

"No, I go over to my friend's house and play cards."

"We play basketball at night," Faber said.

"Why don't you get a job?"

"Job?" Johnson said. "When school closed I went to the Board and got papers so I could work and then I went around. They would tell me to come back and I never heard from them, so I figured they didn't want me."

"Isn't there anything you can do?"

"Go to the fields," Johnson said. "At four in the morning this bus leaves and you go out to some field and pick cherries. You work, then something happens and you got no work after six hours and you come home with four dollars. The man owns the place, he takes the cherries into town and sells them to the merchants for money and they think they're smart, makin' money off a black man's back. Huh. That stuff's over."

Late yesterday afternoon a plain car pulled up in front of Connie Mitchell's house and a young guy got out.

"Touhey," he said. "I'm with the FBI."

"She's inside," somebody told him. Then the agent walked into the house to try and find out what had started the race riot in Rochester. Everybody in Rochester was doing that yesterday. These are puzzling times for white people in New York. Only the colored people seem to understand what's happening. They sit on their stoops up here and look at the kids who walk around with bandaged hands from the riot, and they say they know what it is and they do not mind it at all.

The curfew began at eight last night. The white man had his state troopers in helmets on the streets. It is, for now, the white man's solution.

Nowhere Else

Selma, Alabama

In a room off the ancient, imposing lobby of the Albert Hotel, right under a framed sign which says, "Chancery Sale of Eight Likely Negroes," Joe Lapchick's kids are playing basketball on the television. They are playing too slowly, trying to kill too much time between shots and they have everybody in the room worried. And then they are only two points ahead and the game is down to seconds and Villanova plays for the last shot. But this Schaffer tries to come across the middle and he walks and now one of Joe Lapchick's kids grabs the ball and Madison Square Garden in New York comes into this little room off the lobby of a hotel in Selma, Alabama.

Now Joe Lapchick, looking dazed, is on the screen.

The lines are deep in his old face. Then his fist goes up into the air and everything in the day here changes. The misery of the civil rights struggle is two blocks away, where the beatniks kiss each other in the street and the white cops spit curses at them under their breath. The Half Moon Café is only around the corner. The Reverend James Reeb was murdered in front of it. But for this little minute yesterday afternoon, Joe Lapchick and his kids put Eighth Avenue into this room in a hotel in Selma. Lapchick won't forget yesterday for the rest of his life. And nobody who was stuck here will forget what this last victory of his did to a miserable day. Here was the good which human beings are supposed to have. It was right on the television screen in front of you. It was nowhere else in Selma.

Selma March

Selma, Alabama

United States Highway 80, between Montgomery and Selma, is fifty miles of asphalt with a yellow dividing line and a roadside of deep green grass which runs for long stretches without being cluttered with advertising signs. United States Highway 80 does not run through buying country. It runs through farmland that has been picked clean and through swamps with squirrel-colored moss trees standing dead in the muddy water.

And it runs past black pigs rooting in the grass and white-faced cattle sleeping against wire fences. Past tin-roofed gas stations sitting on red dirt side roads, and a Negro in a leather cap holding a brown mule while it grazes.

It is a lightly traveled, deserted road with cars cutting down it at 70 miles an hour, their blue-and-orange license plates saying, "Heart of Dixie." United States Highway 80 is a road in the middle of the State of Alabama, and today everybody in the world looks at it.

Today, a march is to start down the highway. It is a march of fat young white girls in sneakers and raincoats, wearing glasses, and Negro boys in windbreakers. Of sloppy white men in beards and needing haircuts, who peer through thick glasses. And also of white ministers, Roman collars loose on their thin necks, and white nuns in flowing black robes, and college students and bleak-faced old Negroes. And there also will be people like Ralph Bunche and the Reverend Martin Luther King, and Army troops will be all around them while they walk out and put the civil rights movement in the South onto Highway 80.

The world will be watching it all. But there may be very little to see outside of people walking. For the march is through down country, where a screen door shutting is the only noise of a day, and where excitement runs slowly through people.

"Where you from?"

"New York."

"Uh-huh," he grunted. He was about forty and wearing a brown rain jacket. He was looking out the window of Byrd's Lucky Dollar truck stop. His hands were stuck into his pockets and his mouth was busy chewing gum. He chewed and looked out of the window for a long time without saying anything.

"New Yawk," he finally said. He chewed the gum some more.

"Hope somebody kills me 'fore I go to New Yawk again."

"What's this thing tomorrow look like to you?" he was asked.

"Circus."

He walked over to the door, chewing his gum. He looked out the window.

"I give up goin' to the circus when I was a keed."

His friend sat on a stool with his back to the counter. This one had on a plaid shirt and dungaree pants and work boots. His scalp showed white through the close crew cut. He had high, tanned cheekbones and narrow eyes and he took cupped-hand drags on his cigarette.

"What I resent is all these taxes bein' used to pay for this thing tomorrow," he said. He scraped his boots on the rough cement floor.

Byrd's Lucky Dollar has a low ceiling of wooden beams, tables and chairs at one end, and this small lunch counter at the other end. On top of the counter were two napkin-holders, three bottles of catsup, a jar of chili peppers, and two bottles of McIlhenny's Hot Sauce, New Iberia, La.

Then the man by the window began to talk without turning his head. "Last night over in Lowndesboro, this nigger woman came over to a white lady and she says, 'Who's the boss of the country, Johnson or Governor Wallace?' That's just what this nigger woman said. Now they gonna give her a vote." He chewed his gum again.

"All they got to be is twenty-one, black, and breathing, and they vote same's any man."

"Do you figure there'll be any trouble on this march?"

"Don't expect so. Ev'time you hit one them people, you help 'em."

"Well, I hope to hell there won't be—"

"Mind your tongue," the crew cut sitting on the stool said. "We civilized people here. We don't allow anybody talkin' like that in front of our women." He looked around. The one waitress was at the stove in the kitchen behind the counter. "You damnyankees come down here and think you can talk the way you please front of our women. Well, jes' remember we civilized here."

He took another cupped-hand drag on his cigarette. The one at the window kept chewing his gum and looking out at the empty road.

"Well, I'll see you."

The one on the stool said nothing.

"Be no trouble tomorrow," the one at the window said. "We got other things to do besides watchin' niggers with their white girl friends walk 'long the side of the road."

Lowndesboro sits a mile off Highway 80. It is a cluster of new red brick ranch houses and old plantation homes with twelve pillars at the front and busted cars and broken yellow school buses in the overgrown back yards. There is also the Lowndesboro Baptist Church and J. C. Green General Merchandise, tin-roofed and whitewashed wood with high wooden steps leading up to it.

Leroy Greene, who is Negro, stood in the doorway of his long wooden shack, which sits in the mud by the side of the road. In the windowless room behind him, five small kids, boys and girls dressed alike in filthy smocks, ran around.

"I tell you," Greene said, "I don't know much about this march. See, I work in Montgomery. This here is in Selma and I don't get over there too much."

"Well, do you think it will help?"

He stared out at the road—that blank stare Southern Negroes carry like a lunch basket.

"I don't know," he said. "That thing is over in Selma, and I work in Montgomery."

"Well, don't you think Martin Luther King is right?"

"Martin Luther King, oh, he right."

"Do you know that he's leading the march and that it's a big thing?"

He stared.

"You mean you don't know all about the march? It's only just down the road from you."

"It in Selma," he said. "I don't work in Selma."

A dull-faced woman came and stood beside him. She had on a flowered blouse, wrinkled black Bermuda shorts, and red bowling shoes that had no laces in them.

"All these kids yours?" she was asked.

"Uh-huh."

"What's your wife's name, Leroy?"

"She's not my wife," he said. "I just stays with her."

The kids came and crowded behind their legs. On the porch an old black and white spotted dog lifted his head, then dropped it back on his paws and went to sleep again. And Leroy Greene and the woman with the five dirty kids stood in the doorway and looked at the mud in front of the wooden shack, and the march on United States Highway 80, the march for the right of Americans to vote, was a million miles away from them. And what the South, and the North, does to a person who has black skin was set forever in their dull faces.

Selma Leaders

Selma, Alabama

The Reverend Martin Luther King stood at the top of the steps to the red brick church and talked to the crowd that was standing in the sun in the street. Now, he kept telling them. Now it is going to be done. Now we are going to be like other people. Now we are uneducated and poor. And now we are going to change. Each time he said "now," a murmur went through the people in the back of the crowd.

When he finished talking, the people in the street reached for each other's hands and they pulled themselves into long rows and began to sing. They sang "We Shall Overcome" and the people holding hands in one of the rows began to sway from side to side. Then the row behind them started swaying, and then all the other rows began to sway too. Everywhere on the street there were people in this back-and-forth motion, and they were singing, and bright sunlight was all over it, and now everything was happening.

It was funny to see it. The people really were doing nothing. They were just standing in front of this church and singing and swaying. But each time they sang ". . . we are not afraid . . ." each time one of these rows of people slid back and forth, some more of the town of Selma, Alabama, came apart. And some more of the South, and North, and the rest of the country came apart too, because nothing ever again can be the same after yesterday in Selma, Alabama.

Here on Sylvan Street, a rotting piece of the Negro section of a Southern town, simple little people stood up in the sun and asked for a thing which was theirs and never had been given to them because they are black. They are people who have been beaten because they are black. They have had friends and relatives killed because they were black. They have been laughed at and spat at because they are black, and they have been held down on the dust of the streets and made to be dirty and uneducated for all their lives because they are black.

Yesterday they stood up from the dust and they asked for the right to vote which is the start of the right to live. And they asked for it gently, and in prayer, and with the dignity of human beings. And then they left Sylvan Street, and they marched out onto United States Highway 80, and they put all the beauty of the march on Washington back into the civil rights movement, and now it never can be stopped. There was greatness in yesterday.

It was in the old women, black faces and gold teeth, Sunday straw hats on, singing in high-pitched voices that cracked when they began to cry. And in high school girls, pin-neat, white socks against their black legs, their eyes closed while they made a prayer of their song. And it was in the old black men, and the young black boys who never want to find themselves old and living on streets like the ones around them. And it was in a student from Yale and a minister from Chicago and a Catholic nun from Los Angeles with her chin out and her mouth shouting ". . . we are not afraid. . . ." And these people came off the street and out onto Highway 80 and they overcame everything.

Nellie Moore, twenty-two, stood in the street, wearing a white sweatshirt. A rolled-up pink blanket hung from her shoulder. A big silver medal flopped from her neck. Her hair was frizzy and her face expressionless. She didn't look like anything at all.

"Who got whupped last time?" one of the march leaders called out.

"Me," Nellie Moore said.

"Then you can't stay out all night," he said. "We can't have anybody who got whupped."

"Ah'm staying out," Nellie Moore yelled at him. He shrugged his shoulders and walked away.

"What happened to you last time?" she was asked.

"Tear gas," she said. "Then some man tried to beat on me with a club. But he didn't hurt me none."

"And you're going to stay out there this time?"

"Yup."

"What do you think you can get out of this march?"

"School for mah kids. Ah has four children. Ah wants them to get schoolin'. Ah didn't have no right schoolin'. Ah went to the grade school and then to the Ira B. Hudson High School. That's the school for us. But Ah want them to go to regular school. He say if we vote, we get the right schoolin'. Ah wants that. My husband, he workin' in Georgia. He go there to get work. Ah wants my kids to have schoolin' so they can get work where they live."

Up at the head of the street, Sheriff James G. Clark, Jr., stood like the Confederacy. An olive snap-brim detective's hat sat above his moon face. Pale blue eyes, flashing anger, looked out from under thick eyebrows. A button saying "Never" was stuck in the lapel of his blue suit. The jacket was unbuttoned and his big stomach showed under the blue shirt. His hands were jammed into his pants pockets.

"Niggers," he said. "This is a new low. If I had my way there wouldn't be a one of 'em take a step off of this street. What do they want? They get everything they want. All this is, this is a bunch of niggers standing around with homosexuals and listenin' to Martin Luther King. A No-belprize winner. Pffft. Just another nigger to me."

He stood there with his hatred. And then when the

march started, Nellie Moore walked right past Sheriff James G. Clark, Jr. She walked by him holding hands with a colored girl and a white minister, tossing her head in laughter. The last time she tried to walk past Jim Clark she was beaten, but yesterday she was laughing and she didn't even bother to look at him because he didn't count any more.

They overcame Sheriff Jim yesterday. They overcame him with a brigadier general of the paratroopers, who stood on the street in field uniform, gun belt on, arms crossed, his eyes crinkling in the sun while he watched what was going on. Alongside him four MPs sat in a jeep. The two in the back held rifles that had fixed bayonets. The general was flown into Selma on orders of the President of the United States because the dignity of Sylvan Street has gotten to Lyndon Johnson too, and now he uses the words "We Shall Overcome."

Everybody walked past Clark yesterday. Past him and past his men, who sat on motorcycles with cigars in their mouths, and past the side-street bums and all the other Tobacco Road people who wanted Selma to stay as it has been since 1865.

At 12:47 p.m., Martin Luther King came down off the church steps. He walked up to the corner and out into the street. The Army general turned around and called to an officer, "Move on out." Jim McShane, the Chief United States Marshal, swung into a light blue car, and the car started moving slowly. Newsreel station wagons came in behind him.

Then with one line of kids in front of him, King reached out and took Dr. Ralph Bunche's hand and started walking. Behind him, a narrow line of people stretched down Sylvan Street. The march to Montgomery had begun.

They went past the deputy sheriff, who stood alongside the station wagons and cursed. They walked up Alabama Avenue, under trees that were starting to bud, and past a Coca-Cola sign that proclaimed: "Selma Progressive and Friendly."

They came past the Purity Ice Company, the Central City Laundry, and the yellow brick City Hall with the third-floor jail in which this town's police put a Nobel Prize winner. Then they swung out onto Broad Street, with its Pilcher-McBryde Drugs and the American Acceptance Corporation, loans.

A fat-faced guy sat in a car in front of the loan company and he squirmed around and looked out the back window to sce King go by. The guy's finger came out and pointed to King and it shook up and down. "Crimson Tide, National Champs," the metal sign on his car said.

"Look at him," said Paul Screvane, walking behind King. "He's just like a guy who got knocked out and now he's up demanding a rematch in front of his friends. He's dead and he won't admit it. The whole town's dead. This place got taken apart today."

King, walking in high-topped work boots, led them up to Pettus Bridge, which goes over the Alabama River and comes down onto Highway 80. It comes down to a tangle of fifteen-cent-hamburger stands, car-washes, fried-chicken counters, and used-car lots.

Two weeks ago the state troopers and loafers came out of this jumble and charged into the crowd of marchers and beat them. Yesterday only a few loafers gathered in knots. They were mostly silent because this march of little people, dressed in the clothes of little people, and carrying blankets and knapsacks, crushed anything in its way.

Farther along the road the whites stood in twos and threes and called out obscene things, mostly about the nuns who were marching together. Once a fat woman in slacks and a pink blouse ran out onto the roadway and spat at the nuns.

"Walking with nigger trash," she yelled.

Nobody else bothered to look. Here was a woman named Meletta, sixty-one, her face carved out of coal, marching because her boss told her on Friday night that he would fire her from her floor-cleaning job if she marched with all these niggers. Yesterday he and the other better-off people in Selma sat home and saw nothing of the march, but they worried about the change in all these Melettas, these good niggers who never wanted anything.

And with her was Charles Evers, Medgar's brother, and Phil Carey of the Electrical Workers and an entire unit from the National Maritime Union and Constance Baker Motley from New York City and a minister from Nebraska and college students from any place. And the beatniks who had hung around Sylvan Street all week, disturbing everybody, suddenly became lost in a crowd of orderly people who walked with great dignity and sought things they now were going to get.

And the fat woman screamed something out again and then she ran into the street again and spat.

"Nuns walking with nigger trash," she yelled.

But her words, and what the words represented, were so small in the face of the immenseness of the people marching that even she seemed to know that she was standing there with this life of hers, a life where there is somebody lower than she is, always somebody to call nigger, running out of her hands and becoming part of the past.

On Highway 80

Selma, Alabama

Patricia Anne Doss, ten, stood in the red dirt and twitched her black toes to brush away the ants crawling over her feet. She put her head between the strands of cattle wire and looked at the people walking on the road.

"I know why you marchin'," she said.

"Why?"

She smiled and looked down at her toes. "I know why you marchin'. I know it good."

Jesse Daniels, thirteen, wearing cut-down Army fatigues, was sitting up on the rotted wooden gate. "I knows why," he said. " 'Stead of one goes to school this place, t'other go to the other place, everybody go to the same school. We get smarter. That's why they marchin'."

Back at the head of the long dirt path, their families stood on the porch of the tin-roofed shack and the women held babies on one arm and shaded their eyes with the other so they could look through the heat shimmers and see the people marching down the highway.

Farther along the road, at a rutted turn-off leading up to a construction site, workers in tin hats sat on the hoods of cars and displayed the best of local overalls culture.

"Hey, boy. You, boy. That's right. Coon-lover. Turn around here so's I can take your picture."

A bearded white marcher turned around and one construction worker stood up on the car bumper and took his picture with a small camera.

"Greenwich Village You-niversity," the worker said.

"New Yawk coon-lover," the one next to him yelled.

The pictures the worker took will be used to give visual aid when the children at home are taught that this civil rights march had nothing to do with these nice local niggers at all. It was a thing strictly for beatniks from New York.

"Coon-lovers," they yelled boldly.

Then they go back to their jobs and this line goes past them slowly, pushing up the road, silently eating away a method of life that has existed for a hundred years.

All day yesterday the civil rights march from Selma to Montgomery trailed along U.S. Highway 80, with the great Hookworm Belt, Lowndes County, stretching out from both sides of the road. At the head of the line was Dr. Martin Luther King, the Nobel Peace Prize winner who walked like a sharecropper. Behind him, two abreast, were the marchers. And there was a line of cars, sanitary vans, water trucks, and jeeps. The road was clear, the walking easy, and it was a sparkling Alabama day. And all around were people who work for the United States government and carry guns.

Off to the side, Army helicopters sat with the cattle in the sweeping fields, then took off and flew low over the woods to watch for anybody who might be out to get himself a good nigger at three hundred yards or so. Jeeps blocked the red dirt side roads. MPs with slung rifles stood alongside. Truckloads of troops were parked under trees in spots where somebody thought there could be trouble.

On the highway, business-suited FBI agents and United States marshals walked near the marchers, or rode slowly behind them in rented cars. Generals stood on the road or came past in cars. They were looking, giving orders, looking down at clipboards, then looking up and giving orders.

This march doesn't look like much, really. It's just a rumpled line of people, many of them exhibitionists. But the generals have tight faces. One of them, the name Graham sewn on his fatigues, runs from spot to spot. He reports to Lyndon Baines Johnson personally if something goes wrong here.

There are a lot of people to protect. The marchers are limited to exactly three hundred. But this is a changing group, with new ones coming in from Selma and others shuttling back, and crews of workers up the road busy setting up a camp for the night. And there was Albert Turner, who was marching along at the end of the line yesterday.

He had on tan unfinished cowhide work boots, black pants, and a white sweatshirt. He is twenty-nine, but he has a little weight on him and he grunted while he walked along. Sweat showed on the two creases on the back of his neck. He is just a bricklayer from Marion, in nearby Perry County, and he marches with no ceremony, and with his head down, and he was the last one in line yesterday. But if Albert Turner wanted to make this march by himself he would rate every gun-hand that the government had on the road. Albert Turner comes with a fairly legitimate beef.

On a Friday night in 1960, Turner came home from his job as a bricklayer and sat down with his wife at the kitchen table and began to match money with his bills. Oh, he had enough money. Turner was a brick-layer, and they get $3.00 an hour, $3.50 in some spots in Alabama.

Bricklaying always was considered niggers' work in the South, and it paid accordingly. But there was a building boom in 1947 and then a strong union came in, and the South found that it had figured wrong again. Here was a nigger job that all of a sudden was paying people like Albert Turner $150 a week.

What bothered Albert Turner on this night was the figures on his pay stub. It said that $27.52 had been taken out for income taxes. He looked at the stub and a strange thought ran across his mind: If the govern-ment can take $27.52 a week, then it can give back something to Albert Turner. Like a vote in an election.

"I'm goin' to go down to the courthouse Monday and register to vote," he told his wife.

"Albert, they'll throw you in the river," his wife said.

"I work almost a whole day for that $27.52," Tur-ner said. "How'm I gonna stand there and lay brick all day when I know I'm not gettin' anything for it? Some-body stealin' a day's work off me. That's it. They take the tax, then I vote."

On Monday he appeared at the courthouse, and a registrar, anxious to get back to his cows, growled when Albert stated his business.

"All right, boy," he said "Sit yourself down and answer this here test."

He handed Albert a sheet which had twenty-five questions. They asked for name, address, place of em-ployment, names of friends and relatives and their ad-dresses and places of employment, and other pertinent information that would aid the White Citizens Council in times of anger. Turner filled it out anyway.

He has a degree in mechanical art from Alabama A & M, and his penmanship was quite clear on the exam. He handed it to the registrar. The registrar took it from him and didn't look at it.

"You done failed, boy," he said. "You done failed on two of these here questions."

The somebody came up and asked the registrar to sign something. The registrar reached for a pencil, curling his fingers around it as if it were a pneumatic drill, and went to work.

"I though he'd hurt himself with that pencil," Albert was saying while he walked along yesterday.

From the time he failed that test, Albert Turner decided he was going to vote. He began to agitate, and he blew jobs and had to travel to be a bricklayer. But then people from the Justice Department began to come around and Albert got hope and he kept talking it up with people and going back again and again to register.

He was threatened. A few weeks ago he led a night march in Marion. The state troopers jumped them with clubs and gave Albert a going over. Then they went through the town and grabbed his friend, Jimmy Lee Jackson, in a place called Mack's Café. They beat hell out of Jimmy Lee. Shortly thereafter he was shot to death.

But Albert Turner kept agitating and showing up at rallies and yesterday he marched along Highway 80, grunting and sweating, and Tobacco Road doesn't know what it got itself into when that registrar told Albert that he had done failed his examination.

Here he came, walking along past the sign that says: "Welcomc to Benton. Churches: Baptist, Presbyterian, Methodist." And then, up at the crossroads, was the Benton Service Station and Byrd's Lucky Dollar truck stop, and in front, parked at the roadside, were cars with white painting on their hoods and doors. "Welcome coons," the lettering said. "Go home, scum."

And the whites stood there, these real outdoor whites, with their sunglasses and tanned faces and thin lips, and MPs sat alongside the cars, and a helicopter flew very low overhead and back down the road where the truckloads of troops were parked. Albert had a lot of backing yesterday for this thing he wants.

John Doar, the Justice Department's man in charge of civil rights, stood in the road and pointed out Albert yesterday.

"We've known him a long time," Doar said. "He's a man. He's worth the whole thing."

Marching Aisle

Selma, Alabama

Out on the highway, most of the people connected with the march already had left the field across the street from Steel's Service Station, and now the black faces sat on the steps leading into Steel's and looked out onto the road.

The front of Steel's roof comes out into a shed, and two gas pumps sit in the dirt under it. The front of the store has tin advertising posters nailed all over it. Most of them are signs for Goody's Headache Powders and Tops Mild Scotch Snuff. Thc tin signs serve a purpose. They cover the holes in the front of the store.

Inside, an old man sat on a campstool, holding his hands out to a rusted, pot-bellied stove. The tin floor around him was crowded with hundred-pound sacks of Jazz Scratch Feed. The shelves in the store were a jumble of empty cardboard boxes, a few yellow boxes of Jim Dandy Grits, and ginger snaps. A jar of pigs' knuckles was on the counter. The meat freezer was empty, except for small containers of milk, and its glass window was smeared. A woman stood behind it, holding a baby.

"They gone," she said.

"How long ago did they leave?"

"They gone," she said.

"They jes' leave and go away," the old man at the stove said.

The march was farther up the road. They were wet and they walked with plastic coverings over their shoulders. It was the middle day of this march, and Dr. Martin Luther King was in Cleveland for a speech. But his people got closer to Montgomery and Governor George Wallace, and Army trucks came out of a side road yesterday and pulled out onto the highway with red and white signs reading "Explosives" on their tailgates. The wooden cases on the floors of the trucks had stencils on them which said there was .30-caliber ammunition inside.

Alabama Schoolhouse

Selma, Alabama

The Rolen School sits in the dirt off United States Highway 80 in Lowndes County, Alabama. It is a public school of the State of Alabama for grades one to six. It has eighty Negro students and three Negro teachers. It is open from 8 a.m. to 3 p.m., but from the road it looks like a deserted shack.

The Rolen School is a wooden building that was a church when people in Lowndes County wore Confederate uniforms. It once was painted yellow. The building sits off the ground on small piles of loose red bricks. It has ten frame windows. Nearly all the panes are broken. Beaverboard, put up on the inside, covers the broken windows. The school has a tin roof. Yesterday part of the roof was flapping in the breeze coming through the fields. In the winter the wind comes strong and keeps blowing parts of the roof away and the students sit in class under the cold sky.

A shack in the dirt field behind the school serves as a bathroom. There is a small coal bin on the side of the school. A tin basin, used by students for carrying coal inside to the pot-bellied stoves, is on the ground next to the bin. A long-handled ax stands against the building. The students gather wood at lunchtime and chop it for the fires inside. The school has a church entrance, with five wooden steps leading up from the dirt. The steps are rotted and an adult cannot stand on them.

The principal, John Bowen, who also teaches the fifth and sixth grades, stood outside the school yesterday. He is forty and has gray-topped hair. He wore a long-sleeved dark blue sports shirt. His arms were folded in front of him and he spoke quietly.

"Nobody is allowed inside the school without a permit, we were told," he said.

"When did they tell you this?"

"Well, when all the people started coming around here they told me that."

"I see. They don't want us to get a look at the place."

"Well," he said, "I work for the county school system. You shouldn't work for a person, then give him bad publicity. But I have to say you can't learn in this school. There's no way to learn here. It's just impossible."

"If you'll excuse me, I'm going to go into your school without this permit."

The inside of the school was divided into three rooms. The first and second grades were in the room on the left. There were eleven small black faces with big eyes sitting on benches around a wooden picnic table. A girl was on her stomach on another bench, looking up at the visitor. The teacher, Josephine Jackson, wearing a pink dress, sat at a bridge table in the corner, next to a big rusted stove.

Beaverboard covers the classroom window, but light comes in through large holes in the side of the building. The holes give the kids a view of the fields. The kids also can look through a huge hole in the floor and see coal ashes and empty pork-and-bean cans on the ground under the classroom.

"We use coal when we can get it, and wood in the winter," Miss Jackson was saying. "It run to, oh, 'bout twenty-five degrees here in the winter. We hardly ever get near zero. The children wear hair rags and overcoats. They don't have gloves. When it gets too cold they sit with their hands in the coat pockets."

"Can you get anything done here at all?"

"Well, I try as hard as I can."

"Do the parents know what's going on?"

"Oh, I don't think they understand either," she said. "They went to the same kind of school as this and these children here will have to send their children to a school like this and, oh, I guess it never will come to an end."

The kids sat at the table and watched with big eyes. One girl put her head on the table and looked up, a finger stuck in her mouth.

Arthur Lee Williams, in overalls, red shirt, and sneakers, looked up, turned around, and looked at the visitor. Then he mumbled something and broke into a giggle and buried his face in the shoulder of the kid next to him.

"What'd you say?"

The kid next to him answered. "He say, 'Stop there, little preacher.' "

This should have been a big laugh, but there is nothing funny in the idea that any white man who would visit that school would have to be a minister.

Arthur had a torn, thumbed workbook in front of him. There was scrawling all through it. There was not one legible letter on page after page of scrawling.

"Do you have a bright one?" Miss Jackson was asked.

"That one," she said, pointing to a little girl in pigtails and white sweater.

The top of the girl's workbook said her name was Janice Cosby. On the first page she had printed, "See the kitten. The kitten says mew mew." It was neatly done.

"Do you like the school?" she was asked.

Her eyes brightened and her head shook up and down. "Yop," she said.

"Do you do any writing at home?"

"Yop. In the back yard when I get home."

"Would you want to write something for me now?"

She grinned and picked up a pencil and, carefully, and neatly, and proudly, she printed, "Sunday is the day before Monday."

"That's very good," she was told. She beamed and began printing something else.

"What does her father do?" the teacher was asked.

"Farmer. Sharecropper."

"And what happens to the girl here?"

"When she gets old enough, she goes into the field and picks cotton and doesn't come to school any more."

A door with cardboard panels led to the next classroom, which was for the third and fourth grades. A Coca-Cola machine was in one corner of the room. A big blue metal gas-station sign, "Firestone Tires, the mark of quality," was nailed over a hole in the floor in the middle of the room. Old Alabama license plates were nailed here and there around the room to cover other holes in the floor.

A heavy woman in a striped dress stood against the wall and watched the seventeen students, who sat on benches and did nothing. She said her name was Lillian Pierce and that she was sixty.

"I been teachin' around between twenty-eight and thirty-nine years in this county," she said.

"Where did you go to school?"

"I went to schools right in this county," she said.

"This is awful," she was told.

"Awful?" she said. She looked surprised. She didn't understand.

The fifth and sixth grades were in the back room, a big bare place with cement blocks and pieces of charred firewood lying on the floor. A kid in a raincoat was hammering a nail into a bench that was falling apart. A small cluttered table, with an old blue globe on it, was in the front of the room. There were no blackboards or charts hanging on the wooden walls.

Seven or eight boys sat on the other benches, doing nothing. Two girls were standing at a door leading out to the back of the school. One boy, in a blue shirt with ripped shoulders, leaned against the wall in the other corner of the room.

"What grade are you in?" he was asked.

"Sixth."

"How old are you?"

"Twayelve."

"What do you want to be when you grow up?"

"What I want to do? I want to wait. Wait on tables."

"Is that a good job?"

He smiled. "Oh, my father he say that a very good job."

The books were on a shelf behind him. The flyleaves all carried the stamp: "This book is the property of the State of Alabama, County of Lowndes."

The books consisted of a Bobbs-Merrill reader put out in 1939, a book called *Conrad's Magic Flight*, also put out in 1939, and an arithmetic book whose title page was so ripped that its publication year could not be determined. But its approach to arithmetic was in the same small print, with no visuals, which the visitor remembered seeing in about 1939.

A hand bell tinkled in the next room and kids walked out the door into the yard. It was lunchtime. Most of them stood in the dirt or went in front of the building and sat on the top step. None of them had anything with them to eat.

"Hey," one of them was asked, "don't you have anything for lunch?"

He shook his head yes. "Light bread and hot sauce. I eat it on the way to school."

"Don't they get any lunch to bring?" Bowen was asked. He shrugged. He could see the visitor did not understand Lowndes County, Alabama.

A little one sitting alone on the step watched the visitor carefully. The kid had on a sweatshirt with red lettering: "Four Seasons C.C." The shirt had not been washed in a long time. His dungaree pants had holes at the knees. There were no tongues in his little brown boots. His bare feet showed through the laces.

"What's your name?" he was asked.

His eyes narrowed and he moved his mouth. "Uh," he said.

"What did you say?"

His lips shook and he gurgled something again.

"He Akin Grant," one of the other kids yelled over.

"Let him say it himself. Come on, now, what's your name?"

The little kid's eyes narrowed and his lips moved and he tried to talk. And then his eyes filled and he sat there afraid, and crying, and then you could see that he had something the matter with his mouth and that he could not form words.

The visitor started to put his hands on the kid's shoulders, but the kid got up and ran, crying, over to the side of the porch and jumped off and went back behind the school.

"How much of this do you have?" Bowen, the principal, was asked. "This kid needs help. What is this, letting him come here like this?"

"I don't know much of anything we have," Bowen said. "What do we call normal? How do we measure what is normal and what isn't when he have a situation like this? They're all so far down here. They don't have any hope particularly. The school building is here and a couple of teachers is provided. Then nobody cares whether these kids come or not. It don't matter. School for these kids is just a period between childhood and growin' up and workin' in the fields."

The lunch period ended and Bowen said good-by and went back into school with these little children who are being brought up as semi-human beings.

The visitor to the Rolen School got into the car and drove out onto the highway and back to Montgomery. The marchers were by the airport now, and the line was long, numbering in the thousands, and the people walked along and clapped hands and sang. They marched in the sun because of things like the Rolen School, which stands for every step of every foot which has touched United States Highway 80 this week.

But farther up the road, the sunglasses-wearing state police stood by their cars and they sang, "The niggers are coming," and the white people standing on the sidewalk laughed. And in downtown Montgomery the great Tony Bennett, here to entertain the marchers, was told not to go out on the streets because everybody is mad about his being here and he is liable to get hurt. And in the State Capitol, which sits under a flagpole that has the Confederate flag flying over the American flag, the legislature yesterday passed a special resolution condemning the ministers who are in the civil rights march and calling attention to all "the fornicating" going on among the marchers. And the Governor of the State of Alabama, which, in the year 1965, in the United States of America, has the Rolen School as part of its great educational system, sits in his office and says he is not going to give in to this mob rule of Communists.

Montgomery Greeting

Montgomery, Alabama

The sidewalks were nearly empty, with only small groups of Negroes watching, but the white faces were everywhere. They were at the lobby doors of the Jefferson Davis Hotel. And they were looking out from the street-level windows of the Dixie Office Supply Company and McGehee's Drug Store and Weiss Opticians. And they looked down from open windows in the Whitley Hotel and the Exchange Hotel, and the big First National Bank building was twelve stories of white faces pressed against windows and looking at the street below.

At first the faces were set and the lips formed curses. Dr. Martin Luther King, the enemy, was coming by. And behind King were some rows of straggly-dressed people in shoes that were caked with mud. The faces at the windows smiled, and one face would come up to another and both faces would break into a laugh.

Then the people kept coming. They came in soggy clothes, with mud on their feet, and they walked in silence and with their heads up in the air, high up in the air, with the chins stuck out and the eyes straight ahead, and they came for an hour and a half and the faces at the windows changed.

The cursing was gone and the smiles were gone and the owner of the Ready Shoe Repair Shop stood with his lips apart and he watched the life he knew disappear on the street in front of him. And a man in a white shirt and dark tie was leaning out of the sixth-floor window of the bank building, leaning far out so he could see how long the line of marchers was, and he shook his head and pulled it back in and all the faces at the window around him stared blankly.

And Mrs. R. C. Howard sat in a green easy chair at the second-floor window of Jay's Dress Shop, sat with one shapely Southern leg over the other, a cigarette held out between manicured fingers, and the salesgirls stood around her with their arms folded, and they all tried to see what this thing was on the street in front of them.

"They are *so* sloppy," one of the salesgirls said.

"But there are so many of them," Mrs. Howard said.

"Look at that white girl holdin' hands with that big ugly black thing," a salesgirl said.

"I don't know," Mrs. Howard said. "I tell you, I've never seen this many people together in all my life." She sat motionless and the cigarette burned down while she stared at the street.

Up Montgomery Street the marchers came. They trailed out of the Negro section, with its mud roads, and they came onto the flat asphalt and went by the hotels and office buildings and they came around the fountain where Montgomery Street twists into Dexter Avenue and now they came straight up Dexter Avenue, up the six-lane street, with their heads high and their eyes at the white Capitol building at the top of the hill and they walked through Montgomery and changed the face of the South yesterday.

John Doar walked first. He was a half-block ahead of the march and he strolled along, a tousled-haired white guy in a quiet green plaid sports jacket and striped tie. He chewed on an apple. He is the Assistant Attorney General of the United States in charge of civil rights. He is forty-two and he has put in the last five years, the big years of a man's life, worrying about these colored people who were behind him. Four years ago he came into Montgomery to handle the Freedom Riders, and when he walked out of the bus station for a minute, his assistant, John Seigenthaler, was jumped and had his head split with a lead pipe. But yesterday, John Doar walked up Dexter Avenue as if he were out for the air, and a guy alongside him kept talking about what was happening.

"It's all gone," the guy said. "The South is all gone. A whole way of life is going right into memory."

"That's right," Doar said. "That's just what it is."

A few yards behind him, Jim McShane, the Chief United States Marshal, stopped and took off his sunglasses and looked up at something that was sticking out of a building window.

"That's an ABC camera," a man called out from an unmarked car behind McShane.

"Oh, that's right," McShane said. "For a second there . . ."

Then the marchers came. There were the known people. King, the old Phil Randolph, the stiffness of the years in his legs, and Roy Wilkins, and Whitney Young. But there were few that could be recognized. Civil Rights, when it comes out of the lecture halls and goes into the backroads of places like Selma, Alabama, does not attract many personalities. It attracts only people whose names are nothing, and who have nothing that shows, and they take chances with their lives, and yesterday they walked through Montgomery, these nameless little people who changed the ways of the nation, and with them were people from everywhere, white people and black people, and they walked together in a parade the South never has seen. And they showed, forever, on this humid day in Montgomery, Alabama, that what they stand for cannot be stopped.

"I want to get whupped," Alexander McLaughlin said. "I told my wife yesterday that I feels left out of this thing. I want to go out some place and get myself whupped so's I can feel I been in it."

He was an old man with a white card saying "Washington" sticking from the breast pocket of his gray suit.

"Come down with me and you get yourself a good whupping," the old woman in a plaid kerchief called to him. "Oh, Ah guarantees you a good whupping."

"Where you from?" McLaughlin said.

"Madison County, Mississippi," the old woman said.

"They whup you for all times in Madison County," somebody in the back yelled out. The old woman shrieked and clapped her hands and everybody laughed and kept walking toward the white Capitol building on the top of the hill.

"I'll be in Madison County," McLaughlin said.

Roland Cooper, State Senator from Wilcox County, stood on the white marble steps of the Capitol building and watched the line of marchers coming up the hill. Roland Cooper is a solid man. He had on a gray business suit and his hair was cut and combed and his shoes were shined, and he owns an auto agency and a small cattle farm in Camden, Alabama.

He is no street-corner redneck. He is a businessman and a politician and he shakes hands and says hello affably. He was out on the steps yesterday, watching this long line of sloppy people come up the hill toward him, and when the first rows reached the speakers' stand set up in the plaza, they stopped and Roland Cooper, standing for everything that the South used to mean, made fun of them.

"Never saw so many coons all together in mah life," State Senator Roland Cooper said.

"Damn," he said. "Don't that look like Nigger Penn over yonder there."

"Who?"

"Nigger Penn. Jes' some nigger from mah home town. If Ah catches him here . . ."

He looked to see if the face in the crowd was the one he knew.

"You know something?" Cooper said. "Ah'm good to niggers. Why, Ah've got two of 'em working for me now at the auto agency. One's been with me seventeen years, the other eighteen. Ah got one on the farm. They like me. Ah'm good to niggers."

"How much do you pay them?"

"Pay them accordin' to the work they do."

Up on the stage at the foot of the steps, Harry Belafonte stepped to a microphone and began to sing.

You waited for Cooper to say it. "Tell you one thing," Cooper said after a while. " 'Tain't anybody can equal niggers for keepin' time to music."

"What do you think all this means?" he was asked.

"Don't mean nothin', don't mean nothin' at all. Jes' take a look of them. They jes' a pack of coons."

He kept looking at them. And they kept coming. Far down the street, around the fountain, the line coiled and the people kept coming up the hill and the sun was breaking through the clouds now and lines of Army troops stood with their rifles at parade rest, and FBI agents walked through the crowd with hand radios, and helicopters flew overhead, and Roland Cooper stood and watched his world change and he didn't even know it, and he will not know it until he sees, someday, the registration figures in Wilcox County, Alabama, where niggers never have voted.

But the Roland Coopers were buried yesterday. They were buried on Dexter Avenue, which was decorated with flags of the State of Alabama, a final touch of small-boy toy-breaking which this state loves. And they were buried by people who came winding from a huge field of deep mud behind a Catholic hospital and school in the Negro section, four miles away.

The marchers gathered in a section of town which has places like Council Street. On Council Street, yesterday morning, a little boy sat and banged his feet on the tin porch chair they had put him on while he sucked on a smeared plastic bottle. Next door a man dozed on a bench on the porch with a red hat stuck over his face. The house was a tangle of boards nailed together under a tin roof and sat up on cement blocks.

A little girl in a red dress and bare feet stood in the garbage in the weeds at the curb and bent over a pipe that was sticking up. She turned something on the pipe and water came out of its rusted end. She bent over and started to drink the water.

"Don't you have water inside?" she was asked.

"No," she said, "this the water."

On the porch a fat woman in a cotton dress and white butcher's apron held a baby in her arms. The baby woke up when a helicopter flew low over the house, and the fat woman began to jiggle the baby back to sleep.

The march started here, and it was going on for people who live on the Council Streets everywhere in this nation. And it wound through the Negro section, past toothless old women who kept calling out, "Ah never thought Ah'd see this," and then it came down into the white section, down onto the wide streets, and at a little after four o'clock yesterday afternoon the speeches were over and the people started singing "We Shall Overcome."

And when they sang it, they held hands and swayed. Thirty thousand people stood on the main street of Montgomery, Alabama, and held hands and swayed and sang "We Shall Overcome" and the voices went out from the street and echoed off the buildings behind them. And the faces in the windows of the buildings were blank, all of them blank now, and these black people singing in the street, these ignorant niggers who would have been shot to death for causing this kind of trouble six months ago, seemed to glow with each word of the song.

You have not lived, in this time when everything is changing, until you see an old black woman with mud on her shoes stand on the street of a Southern city and sing ". . . we are not afraid . . ." and then turn and look at the face of a cop near her and see the puzzlement and the terrible fear in his eyes. Because he knows, and everybody who has ever seen it knows, that it is over. The South as it has stood since 1865 is gone. Shattered by these people in muddy shoes standing in the street and swaying and singing "We Shall Overcome."

A businessman came running down the steps of the Capitol building and reached out and grabbed you in the middle of the song.

"Look," he was saying, "I saw you talking to Roland Cooper before. Now Roland Cooper is a sincere man, don't get me wrong. But he just doesn't know. Life has passed him by. This here thing is a revolution. And some of us know it. We really do.

"Now can you please do me a favor. Go over and talk to Red Blount. He's the biggest contractor in town. You see Red Blount, he thinks different. He knows what's going on. Red Blount knows that this is a revolution and he's going to live with it.

"Do me a favor. You saw Roland Cooper. Now please go and see Red Blount. He knows what's going on. The world's just passed Roland Cooper by. It's passed all of us by, unless we start to live with it."

The Retreat

Montgomery, Alabama

Fat Thomas, who in his retirement decided to see Alabama two weeks ago, rolled into the Jefferson Davis Hotel, Montgomery, Alabama, and registered as "Martin Luther Fats." The room clerk took this with a smile. The same kind of smile the sheriff of Dallas County gave when he saw Fat Thomas. And the same way Mr. L. B. Sullivan, Police Commissioner of Montgomery, smiled at Fat Thomas. In fact every place Fat Thomas went in Alabama, he made people feel good. They loved the idea of speculating on how many people it would take to carry Fat Thomas out of town on a railroad tie.

"You people don't have enough tar to handle me," Fat Thomas kept telling them.

As his daytime headquarters, Fat Thomas chose a back booth of the Selma Del, which is in Selma, Alabama. He spent much of the time ordering small snacks for himself. By the middle of the week, waitresses in the Selma Del were walking around with no shoes on. At dusk each day, Fat Thomas would come across the street and set himself up on the third floor of the Albert Hotel, where Bob Gay, proprietor, had a private saloon set up. Fat Thomas would drink gin at a white leather bar and Bob Gay would call up all his friends and they would come up to the saloon room and sit on a couch and watch Fat Thomas drink.

"Man down here, if he's big as you, can't get enough work to feed hisself," one of the locals observed one night.

"I've got a hard-working girl friend," Fat Thomas said.

Between meals, Fat Thomas toured the town a little bit, and what he saw on his tours disturbed him.

"All they do is sell guns down here," he said. "A guy goes into the store and orders a pound of baloney, a hundred rounds of ammunition, and a loaf of Wonder bread."

Fat Thomas, of course, was called on to take quite a bit of abuse from the loungers and state troopers around Selma, and from people in such places as Byrd's Lucky Dollar truck stop in Denton, Lowndes County. Fat Thomas said nothing in return, but he kept making notes in a little book.

Over in Montgomery, everybody in sight insulted Fat Thomas.

"You fat beatnik," they yelled.

Even the owner of the shoeshine stand tried to

abuse Fat Thomas. "Don't you give that damnyankee no shine," the owner said to the Negro who was doing the shining.

"In Harlem they put two men on me and they sing for me when they give me a shine," Fat Thomas told the Negro kid.

"Don't you listen to him," the owner said. He came over to the shoeshine kid. "Don't I get you out of jail?" he asked the kid. The kid nodded yes. "Then don't you give this fat white trash no shine," the owner said.

"I'm gonna do something," Fat Thomas said.

"Sit in? We have a way to handle all you sit-ins round here," the owner said.

"I said sit down, not sit in," Fat Thomas said. He got up on the shoeshine stand, took a deep breath, and then sat down hard. The shoeshine stand was made of pretty old wood. When it splintered, one of the arms flew right out the door and onto the sidewalk.

However, because of Fat Thomas's size—he weighed approximately 485 during his stay in Alabama —the locals began to recognize him and regard him as a prime target. Evil rumors about what would happen to Fat Thomas if he showed again in Lowndes County began to make the rounds. Fat Thomas got riled at this and late one night, loaded with gin, he was mumbling something about going out to buy some Wonder bread and bringing his friend Bad Eddie down from New York for target practice.

Then there was a bit of trouble in the bar of the Jefferson Davis, caused when somebody called Fat Thomas the fattest nigger-lover ever to live, and the bar was closed to him thereafter. And everybody in town began to scream insults and finally Fat Thomas got on the plane and left for New York. He was relieved to be out of Alabama, but agitated by his treatment there. He couldn't wait to get to the Atlanta airport, where, over cold tap beer, he took out the little book he had been marking up all during his stay in Alabama and he jammed himself into a phone booth.

He started calling up every place that had abused him. He told them all the same thing. "Go out and buy yourself a Dalmatian dog so he can bark when he smells the smoke," Fat Thomas yelled into the phone. "Get a good Dalmatian dog. And make sure he got no laryngitis. Because your joint is going to have an accidental fire in the middle of the night very soon."

Then Fat Thomas hung up, drank his beer, and got on the plane for New York, which is where he and everybody else belongs.

5

In Which He Has Some Difficult Times

I OWE THE NEW YORK HERALD TRIBUNE NEWSPAPER SAFE THE SUM OF $50 WHICH I WILL PAY BACK WHEN THE SNOW GOES AWAY.

SIGNED
JAMES E. BRESLIN JR.

The New York *Herald Tribune* witnessed many examples of odd behavior on the part of its employees in the course of 141 years of publishing. One of its distinguished veterans of the North African campaign evened up his expense accounting at the end of the war with the simple entry. "Purchase of camel, $1000." Another alumnus, later known for the foppishness of his clothing, once smashed all the bottles behind the bar of a local speakeasy by raking his gold-headed cane across the shelf when he suspected the proprietors of mulcting one of the paper's copy boys. There were people who didn't meet deadlines; there was one reporter who couldn't be taught to use a period (he used commas so that he could print page-long sentences and say he'd only written two or three sentences) and there was an editor once who sat at his desk talking to himself in a very loud voice.

But there couldn't have been anyone to match Breslin for the energy he brought to bear in complicating his own life. He could work thirty hours straight covering a fire and remember exactly the accent of the survivor who supplied two lines of copy but he couldn't ever find five minutes to do an expense account or remember for more than an hour where he spent the money he had been advanced.

Allied to this problem was the one in which he found it impossible to complete a story. It wasn't that he couldn't write it. It was more that he never felt it was finished. For his columns in the daily paper this meant that most of the time his was the last copy to be moved down to the composing room at night because Breslin was fixing it up until the moment the managing editor tore the last of it from his typewriter. But it usually made the paper. He was also supposed to write articles for the paper's Sunday magazine, *New York,* and there was no managing editor to come rip the stuff away from him, so he managed to miss a fair number of deadlines. His usual tactic in response to this was to claim he was being sabotaged ("They're tunneling under me again!" he would shout) or else to turn furiously to the attack and suggest reams of story ideas that should be appearing in the magazine and weren't—presumably through the indolence of the editors.

The following memos also refer to a subject Breslin would alternately refuse to recognize and finally accept: his health. He would work around the clock for two weeks, spending his nights in a variety of bars, seeing the New York hidden from tourists, and his days interviewing politicians and other notables. He would pour out columns on deadline and magazine pieces after deadline and memos in between and suddenly come up barren of thoughts and have to go away for a while. He would be furious with the syndication people, who had their headquarters in Chicago; he would be cuttingly funny to any editor within reach; and then he'd suddenly shut off his motors and let his wife feed him steak and take him away to the beach somewhere.

Buddy [Weiss]:

This magazine is getting so freaking arty (see "East Village") that I want to do a piece on my own "in" places and people.

Such as, places:

Mutchie's (In).

Pike Slip Bar and Grill (Out). This is where people who owe Mutchie's a lot of money sneak when they have to cash a check and don't want to do it in Mutchie's, where he will take out what they owe.

Irelands Thirty (In). This is where the greenhorns from Ireland hang out and they have good, fresh ideas and good, fresh mouths, too.

PEOPLE:

Marvin The Torch. (In).

Joe Meschery, the dishwater at 21 (Out). He has been working at 21 for so long that he now thinks he is one of the customers and acts snooty.

And so on . . .

And in doing so, I want to point out that, as always, the major work is done not by these bearded bums in Bohemia settings, but by Walt Kelly in the Orient Room, etc.

J. BRESLIN

Buddy [Weiss]:

Thank you very much for your patient and find handling of today's atrocity. It is a pleasure to do business with you and I would buy a drink, but I got to go home.

By the way, this is written on Kerr's [1] typewriter because I broke my own in two places and this Collier [2] gave me the loan of his and I broke that too, but I didn't mind that so much because he is turning this office into a pigpen.

[1] Walter Kerr, *Herald Tribune* drama critic.

[2] Barnard Collier, Latin American correspondent.

I'm pretty sure Collier is against me. So is the typewriter repair man. He fixed the C key three times on my typewriter and what he does, he just fixes it so that it falls apart when I am in the middle of a column. This machine of Kerr's is all right, but I know he doesn't like me. Although he is not trying to hurt me as much as Bob Bird [1] is. Crosby,[2] of course, talks to Buchwald [3] on the phone and they agree to each write three more lines of copy a day and pretty soon I will be writing a little 2-column box. "Overheard in New York" and it will consist of one leftover Leonard Lyons anecdote. If Lyons will give it to me. He doesn't think too much of me.

I'm going home to sleep. That Sheldon Zalaznick [4] upstairs is doing things to me and I want to be wide awake and able to see what kind of a tunnel he is digging.

take care,
J. BRESLIN

TO MR. BELLOWS:

Me and my medical problems are fine. I have cut butts in half, coffee by 75 per cent, and had nothing to drink Thursday, Saturday, and Sunday and nothing today, nor is anything planned for today and tomorrow, except tomorrow night a little bit.

I'll lose 30 or 40 pounds over the next couple of months and that should do it. My man Jackie even had me out on the golf course for a few minutes Saturday but I can't get my arms past my gut so the clubhead moves at rather reduced speed and I said to hell with it. But I'll be all right.

[1] Robert S. Bird, national correspondent.
[2] John Crosby, columnist.
[3] Art Buchwald, columnist.
[4] Sheldon Zalaznick, Sunday editor.

I am returning the clips and the expense account tomorrow morning and I should be in a complete state of grace around here with various departments by then. Besides that, you could ask anybody, Breslin walks this earth with only the finest of intentions and the purest of thoughts. I've always felt that my trouble was that I was too good, too easy, too pliable, too charitable.

Take care.

J. BRESLIN

TO SHELDON ZALAZNICK:

One day next week I am going to have a time-and-motion-study man assigned to me by the firm in an effort to rearrange my working methods and get better production. I intend, of course, to bust out the time-and-motion man and send him to a job at Chase Manhattan, where the ———belongs. In the process of bending the poor bum in half, I am going to have so many bookmakers coming into the office and so many phones going that it just could be a light piece that would work. The time-and-motion guy does not know I am looking to bust him out in order to get a story, so any pictures will have to be done on pretense they are simply little things for promotion. For a finale, I'm bringing a five-piece band from Pepe's into the office to help me work.

I am absolutely, on pain of losing $50, going to write the story of Italian feasts and how the Franciscans took the crap games out of the hands of the people.

Later today I will deliver it to your desk by some late hour. But I am going to do it and I feel it is light and nostalgic and amusing and I would appreciate your putting it in as soon as possible because I have conscience pangs when the magazine comes up without me in it.

J. BRESLIN

His biggest hang-up, though, has always been on money. He doesn't really want very much. He just wants enough to live on. Only it takes a great deal for him to live, and one way or another he is always a few steps behind. When he writes memos about money, Breslin is almost unfailingly humorous. He makes it sound like a big joke. But he knows that it isn't such a funny subject at all when the going gets rough, and the columns show his fascination with the dark as well as the light side of spending more than you earn.

JANE:[1]

Here is some expenses from many sources and I got to catch up here and there. Could you make me out an account for them? Tab the plane tickets (which were for the Liston fight and were bought by myself) as special research for Harlem series if you have to, but get me the scratchsky back.

Now I spent from Thursday night, May 21, until Saturday, May 30, in Harlem. I spent from the 21st until the 25th right there, just like I was on the road. The other days I took a cab up there and a cab back to the office to write and then another cab up there at night and then a cab back across the Triborough to Pepe's to get a lift home at dawn. The cab uptown runs about $2.25 and to Pepe's runs about $3.25.

I also spent the following sums while going around with, and here are names to use. Names are names. Whether I saw them or not doesn't matter. Jimmy Booker, Livingston Wingate, Roll On Davis, Jesse Walker, James Putnam, Sandra the Hooker, Fat Thomas, Pepe, Sgt. Hackett of the 32nd, Leroy Groom, Jean Booker, Mrs. Stewart, Joe Yancey, Billy Rowe, Paul Zuber, Clark Terry, Count Basie, Soldier the Photographer, Hardy the Bartender, James Russell.

I spent money that I can remember like this: I

[1] Jane Noakes, secretary to the editor.

give Jimmy Russell a $20, of which he blew in most of it waiting for me and taking cabs in various joints, etc. I blow $32.50 in Pauline's Interlude on Friday night, May 29. I blow $12.25 in Count Basie's the same night and $6.25 in Arthur's and $11.00 in the Golden Door and I was with, as the story showed, Fat Thomas and a lot of other people.

Then I blew in $15 early one Sunday morning to go home for a couple of hours.

I was not spending much in restaurants at all. A $2.00 piece of liver over the first four days was a big food bill. Figure it out, would you?

I was in Maxie's Bar and Hardy's Bar mostly and spent only a little there, $5 here, $3 there.

Now as for the other items attached:

The Riviera billhead is expenses from the Liston-Patterson fight in Vegas last July. See if you can hide it onto this one as something special. It is a legitimate bill and I paid it, so don't get worried about me trying to rob this joint. I don't do it; I just want to start trying to break even and I got a long way to go because I am behind thousands around here.

The Loew's Midtown Inn bill is from staying over in the snowstorm for some reason.

Now as for the telephone company: It comes to $722.18 paid in. Of this, I got to charge this joint 70 per cent.

With all of this, I am only trying to start to recoup. I am not hustling the joint. If I am hustling this joint, I am going to go and kidnap Whitney and take down a real score. So if some accountant starts questioning, don't you even get involved. I will speak to him and verify everything personally.

jbreslin

Breslin's world is peopled with those in trouble over money. Someone who is not in trouble over money is either too rich or too stupid to be traveling on the same circuit. To him, money is a very personal thing so that, whether it's Eddie Gilbert or a member of the United Nations or a "honeymooner," the joys and sufferings are individual. He talks whole books about shylocks and their customers but he can't listen for two minutes to the balance-of-trade problems. There aren't any people involved.

Money Men

You could see the cards right away. There were fourteen of them, taped to the door like Christmas decorations, and everybody on the way to work stopped to see what they were about. Each card was the same. "Urgent you call this office immediately," the handwriting said. Underneath it, in print, was the name, address, and telephone number of a loan company. It was eight o'clock in the morning. Within an hour the whole block knew that Leon Berger was in trouble with the finance company.

"They did more than that," Leon says. "Another time they called my sister up at midnight and told her I was going to be in a lot of trouble if I didn't pay. She called my wife up right away. My wife jumped out of bed and started screaming that I was keeping another girl. How am I going to keep another girl? I can't even keep myself. But my wife kept arguing with me and I didn't get to sleep until four o'clock. I went to work half dead. I'm not in the office twenty minutes when the boss calls me in. He wanted to know about this money the loan company called him up about. For $311, they were trying to wreck my life."

Things like this happen every day, and in every part of New York City, because finance companies, with no specific laws to slow them down, go after people in debt sometimes as if they were chasing dogs off the sidewalk.

People borrow money from finance companies because they happen to need it. They are supposed to pay it back in monthly installments. The installments are not cheap. For a loan of $800, spread over two years, the payments are $40.27. At the end, the finance company gets back $966.48, or a profit of $166.48 on the loan. Shakespeare wrote a big thing about this kind of action.

Now some of the people who borrow run into trouble and can't make the payments. Most of the time they have to keep the matter secret because very few men want their wives to know they borrow money. The minute they fall behind in payments, they are in the hands of the finance-company agents. The agents are generally young, but they act like they went to school in Leningrad.

Out in Freeport, Long Island, there is a guy named Stewart working for one of the loan companies and everybody calls him "the Hero." He chases people as if they had his own money. If you are a late payer, he goes to the house next door and tells them that you owe money. That's one of his better moves. His best one is to show up at the train station in the morning and catch his man in front of a crowd of commuters, then start yelling, "What's the matter? Why don't you pay what you owe?"

This isn't just one case. Nor is the whole subject restricted to just a few people. New York is a city of credit. When there is credit, there are people in trouble. And there is always some sick degenerate sitting at a desk in an office who can't wait to get personal pleasure out of somebody else's trouble. There is no way to stop him, short of a sawed-off shotgun, which is warmly endorsed here, but rarely heard of. The situation calls for a strong law.

Yesterday State Assemblyman Michael Capanegro, Democrat from Queens, began drafting a bill that he is going to introduce to the next session of the legislature. Capanegro's bill calls for the establishment of a commission to control the orderly collection of debts while protecting the dignity and privacy of small borrowers.

"I want to stop the repetitious, consistent, and constant molesting, phone-calling, house-visiting, calling of employers, and general intimidation and harassment of individuals by loan companies," Capanegro said. "Loan companies have the legal remedy of the courts if people do not pay them back. I want them to use that remedy. Only a minute percentage of non-payers are of the type known as 'dead beats.' Most non-payers are simply up against it in life. Their problems should be ruled on by a judge, not by some vicious, power-crazed individual working in a loan-company office."

Capanegro's proposed law is not quite so far-reaching as two that once existed. One was sort of natural law. Under it, you invited the finance-company guy into the apartment and had friends present. All grabbed the finance-company guy, threw him under the shower, then turned him out into the street. This worked best in the middle of winter. By the time the finance-company guy hit the corner, you could ice skate on his overcoat.

The other law was the one put on the books in Boston by James Michael Curley. He ruled that no Civil Service employee could pay back money to a loan company unless his wife said in writing that she would let him. This was one of the great pieces of American legislation. Right now, the best available is Capanegro's, and it appears to be good enough.

Poor Penmanship

There was, in the twelve-month period which ended September 30, a total of $2,100,692,783.33—you begin this figure by saying "two billion"—in transit items returned unpaid by the New York Clearing House. A transit item returned unpaid is a banking term which describes a check that is headed back to the man who cashed it for a person who told him the check was the same as money. It turned out to be not quite.

In places less formal than banks, a transit item returned unpaid is known as a "bum map" or a "frog."

The one who issues the transit item returned unpaid is known as a "paper hanger." In some less fashionable neighborhoods he is called "the next patient."

The New York Clearing House handles all checks for banks and yesterday a Mr. Fitcher, on duty here, said he did not have an actual count of the number of checks his place returns.

"We would have to weigh the bad checks on a scale to come up with that figure," he said.

Later a banker sat down in midtown and after considerable figuring said that, for this calendar year, transit items returned unpaid appear to be off to a smashing start.

"There are about 350,000 bad checks on hand in New York City today," he said. "This would indicate that there was a bit of a rough period for some people toward the end of last week. The average tends to be closer to 300,000 bad checks each day."

The weekly bad-check average for New York, then, comes to something over 1.5 million pieces of paper plastered on merchants, saloons, grocery stores, candy stores, and other places of that sort.

In addition, a man from the returned-item section, Second Federal Reserve District, said his place handles 14,000 returns a day. These are checks drawn on banks outside the city.

"Now this does not necessarily mean that they are returned because of insufficient funds," he said.

"You mean there is another reason?" he was asked.

"Yes. A great number of checks are returned because they are postdated."

A postdated check is a piece of paper which was given the name "head check" by Al Weill, a fight manager.

"A head check," Weill said, "is a thing where the money is in your head and not in the bank. When you get the money you're thinking of, you get it to the bank ahead of the check."

These figures do not reflect the number of forged checks going around the city. Forgery is a criminal matter and has no place here. We are dealing only with calculated risks which do not work out too well. There seems to be an imposing number of them each day, but mention of this to people connected with banking produces a strong reaction.

"Less than 1 per cent of all checks written are returned for insufficient funds," Merle Miller, of the American Banking Association, says. But Mr. Miller is including all payroll checks issued by companies, and they never bounce. If they did, nobody in the country would go to work.

Bankers generally are unconcerned about bad checks. The fact that the banks charge anywhere from $2.00 to $3.00 for each bad check written could possibly have something to do with this.

The rather surprising thing about these 1.5 million bad checks which move through town each week is that traces of them are found in the better places.

A spokesman for Sherman Billingsley of the Stork Club said, "Why, of course we receive bad checks here. Doesn't everybody?"

A breakdown of figures tends to back this up. There are 78 million bad checks issued every year, and this comes to 9.75 bad checks per year per New Yorker. In dollar volume, the figure comes to $250 per person.

"You say less than ten bad checks a year for every person?" My friend Mr. Mutchie mused in his business establishment yesterday. "That seems awfully low. I don't want to get personal but I know of people who bounce that many in a week."

He pondered this for a moment, then came up with a sensible reason. "Of course, I may be different," he said. "Most of the people in here work for newspapers."

The Honeymooners

"I got to go to work and I need some money," Henry called upstairs to his wife, June, yesterday morning.

"I'm in the middle of changing the beds up here," she called down. "You always do this to me."

He does. Henry sits at the kitchen table for so long on some mornings that June finally gives up and goes upstairs to start her work. This is Henry's game. He knows that once June goes upstairs she won't come down again, and then she won't be able to see what he is doing when he takes the household money. This is why Henry gets to work so late once in a while. Sometimes June just doesn't get up from the breakfast table right away. Henry does everything he can think of to kill time while he is waiting her out. Once, he played tic-tac-toe for forty-five minutes while June sat at the table and listened to some show music she liked on the radio. Henry got in trouble with his office that day because he was so late. But he couldn't help it. He needed the money.

"Well, how much do you need?" June finally called down the stairs.

"Just ten dollars until I get to the office," Henry said.

"Oh, it's in my gray purse. On the top of the refrigerator."

"Thanks," Henry said.

He flew at the gray purse. He opened it up and saw that June had three $20s and a $10. Now Henry worked quickly. He took out the $10. Then took a $5 out of his pocket and put it into the purse and took out a $20. Later in the day, in the supermarket, June would say, "Damn, I thought I had another $20 here and all the time it was a $5."

"Got it?" June called down.

"Thanks," Henry said. "I got to run now. I'm late. I'll see you tonight."

Then he went out the front door and into the morning sunlight. Here it was only the start of the day, and he was a success already. He had stolen $15 from his wife.

This is only one of the ways in which Henry steals from his wife. He uses a lot of different methods and some of them are very good because, at this hardest and most common of all games, Henry is a champ.

Now, nearly every working guy in New York steals from his wife. He needs to pay off loans the wife doesn't know about and also to go to lunch and eat like a United States Senator. And, at the end of the day, he stands at the bar and waves a hand at the bartender and says, "Give us another here," and the little secretaries from the office say, "Oh, we shouldn't have another," and then the guy winks at them and says come on, and they have another drink with him and the guy pays the bar tab with the money he got out of his wife's purse in the morning. She was going to give it to Consolidated Edison. He gave it to Seagram's.

All of this, of course, means marital trouble. With working people, there is almost no other kind of marital trouble except money trouble. Those big professors sit down and write books and say that sex is the major problem in marriage. Every time I read that, I break in half. Sex is a joke compared to a late notice from Household Finance. Send Theodore Reik around, and the married people will pull his beard.

Any trouble Henry has ever had in his marriage, for example, is because he lives over his head and has to make up for it by being a sneak.

A little while ago June was two months pregnant. Henry also had started on something: a new twenty-four-month loan from the finance company. He came home one night with the money and the loan papers all together in a little bundle. He hid the package, like it was hashish, under his pajamas in the bureau.

In the morning, June, because of some great maternal drive, was up at 6 a.m. and she attacked the bureau, muttering about how she wanted everything in her house in order. By 6:20 Henry was awake with his wife hitting him in the face with the papers from the loan company. The cash was in her other hand.

"I took it out so we'd have it to pay for the baby," he said.

"We have over six months to save," she yelled.

"No," he said. "I wanted the money right away. In case you have a miscarriage."

June waited until Henry was going out the door to work. Then she threw her cup of coffee on him and slammed the door.

The Art of Saving

One of the great arts of modern living is to go through a whole week without spending more money than you earn. It is practically a lost art. Nearly everybody we know has a shylock next to his bed each morning, testing his breath with a hand mirror to make sure he is alive.

But there is one fellow who does thing differently. He works nine to five in an office in Manhattan, and everybody calls him "the Chief" because he saves so much money that someday he is going to have enough to run for President.

Nobody who ever lived saved money at a faster rate than the Chief. He is a Langley Collier with youth. Take what happened last week, when he had to move because he found an apartment in Bensonhurst that was $5 cheaper than the one he had. He took the apartment, then came home and called the moving men. They told him the price was $25 an hour. The Chief nearly fainted. Then he sat down and thought it out.

The next morning at 7:15 he made the shape at the 86th Street stop of the BMT's Sea Beach line. The Chief had two kitchen chairs with him. He pushed through the rush-hour crowd into a car, then put down one of the chairs and sat on it.

He rode five stops on the Sea Beach line to 18th Avenue. Then he got off with his two kitchen chairs and took them to the new apartment. He asked the landlord if he could leave the kitchen chairs in the basement of the house.

"I'm going to move little by little," he told the landlord.

He sure was. Because the Chief found this test run great. He could do a little bit of moving every morning, and still be at work on time.

The next morning at 7:30 the Chief showed up at the 86th Street station with his wife and her cousin. They came along because they had to help the Chief carry the living-room couch onto the Sea Beach train.

This time there was trouble. A lot of people standing in the station started to complain.

The Chief's wife was embarrassed. "I wish I could go right through this platform," she said.

The Chief shrugged. Then he sat down on the couch and opened his newspaper and waited until the train was coming. When it pulled into the station, the Chief got up and he and his wife and her cousin picked up the couch and, with the wife's cousin walking backward and the Chief and his wife walking frontward with the living-room couch, they came into the crowded subway car like Indians knocking down a fort wall, and people fell all over themselves to get out of the way.

Then the Chief and his wife and her cousin sat down on the couch and rode the five stops. It worked fine. And it was the last time the Chief's wife had to help carry the furniture on the subway. The Chief took a living-room chair the next morning and found he could handle it by himself easy.

"The only other time she had to take anything was on the last day," the Chief said. "I asked her to help me with the pots and pans. It worked terrific, and I saved a lot of money."

Yes, he did. But, as noted before, there is great art to this type of maneuver. The average guy can't pull it off at all. The other night proves this. After looking at the Chief's bankbook, we decided to save a dollar cab fare by walking home.

On the way home we passed this joint we know.

Just as we got settled, somebody played the juke box. The juke box in this joint is a loud one, and right next door is a Chinese laundry. The laundryman and his wife sleep in the back of the store. The two don't get along. When the juke box goes on loud at night, the Chinese laundryman gets up and starts to hit his wife because he figures the noise from the juke box will drown out her yells.

He is half right. You can't hear her yelling in the saloon. But the lady who lives in the back of the antique store next to the Chinese laundry can hear it fine. She is old and nasty, and when she hears the yelling she gets up, puts on some clothes, goes to the saloon, and sometimes starts a fight.

She stole a man's change from the bar the other night. He got mad and said the bartender did it. We put in with the bartender. The guy told me to mind my own business. The bartender got mad at the guy, the old woman screamed, and then everybody got busy. We just did make it out and into a cab. Let the Chief do his saving. We'd rather stay alive.

What Blackout?

Just around 5:30 p.m., when the television set faded, the lights dimmed, and winter darkness came into the room, Fat Thomas, sitting on the couch in his house, knew what it was right away.

"I should have paid the bill," he said.

His friend, the Count, was sitting with him. "How much do you owe them?" he asked.

"I guess I owe them enough for them to turn the lights off," Fat Thomas said.

He got up from the couch and stepped easily past the coffee table and walked through the blackness to the kitchen to get a candle. He had no trouble finding his way. Since becoming legitimate, Fat Thomas has had his lights turned off so many times that he can see in the dark better than anybody in the world. "They should make me a fighter pilot," he said.

He spent the rest of the evening reading magazines by candlelight. When he went to bed he was certain that the lights in his house were off because the little Irishman who covers the neighborhood as a collector for Consolidated Edison had tiptoed to the side of the house and turned off the power. The week before, the little Irishman had come with a judgment and asked Fat Thomas if he could step in and turn the lights off from inside the house. "You can if you got a shotgun with you," Fat Thomas told him. The little Irishman got mad. He said he would be back, and that if there wasn't any money waiting for him he would take the electricity out of Fat Thomas's hair. So to Fat Thomas, Tuesday night, the greatest power blackout in the history of the Western world, was just another evening with candles because he hadn't paid his bill.

He was not alone. If you look around the newspapers today, you will be hit in the face with a ton of statistics about subway passengers aided, kilowatts lost, hotels overloaded, and stairs climbed. But nowhere will you see the only statistic of the whole night which means anything. It is the number of people from Toronto to New York who sat and watched the lights go out in their houses and yelped, "I forgot to make the payment." And then spent the rest of the night pretending that nothing was wrong and worrying that the neighbors would find out.

At 7:10 p.m. on Tuesday night the phone rang in the darkness of Mr. Norton W. Peppis's apartment in the Queens section of New York City. He groped for it and picked it up.

A friend was calling. "What are you doing?" the friend asked.

"I'm watching Huntley and Brinkley on television," Mr. Peppis said.

"You're what?"

"I'm watching the news on television. I want to

know current affairs. What do you think I am, some dope?" Mr. Peppis said.

He hung up the phone and sat alone in the darkness for the rest of the night. He cursed himself because he had forgotten to pay his light bill. "I win a pound of money at the track today and I bet you they shut me off for something like $11.75," he muttered. He sat there for the rest of the night and when he got a call later on, he told the guy to hang up, that he was in the middle of watching a good movie on television.

There was no reason for people not to think this way. Everybody knows that an electric company consists of only two things: a little Irishman who collects past-due bills, and a crew of strong Italians who make big holes in the street. Otherwise, an electric company is a mirage. Anybody can have one. You get a big color picture of Niagara Falls and put it on the wall and you're in business. The financial page is right about utility stocks being up or down. It's ridiculous. Go out and ask the little Irishman if his feet hurt him today before you buy stock in an electric company. The other joke is the way they consider the president of a power company an important man. As Tuesday night showed the world, he's the president of a toy.

So the only one to really blame for Tuesday night is the little Irishman who sneaks around and shuts off the lights.

"When I get service restored," Fat Thomas grumbled at midnight, "I'm going to hold his hand in the toaster."

A Broke Weekend

The former Rosemary Dattolico, prominent Queens housewife, is mad this week. She is mad because she is broke. She is broke because on Saturday, on her way to the supermarket for the week's food for her husband and five kids, she pulled in front of a saloon owned by a person named Pepe, honked the horn for him to come outside, then asked him to please cash her check so she could shop.

The check, a good one too, represented the former Rosemary Dattolico's money for everything in the house for the week of October 16 to October 23. Pepe asked her what she needed the money for. She said she had to shop for food. He said, "How would you like to give me the check for a couple of hours and then, later in the day, go out and do some real shopping?"

"Who gave you the horse?" the former Rosemary Dattolico said.

"He was in last night late," Pepe said. He mentioned the name of a prominent private handicapper who is very big around town. The private handicapper was enthusiastic about a horse called Count Banish, 10–1 in the morning line. Pepe also said that he was unable to do anything about the race because the band had to be paid off. The band, a four-piece outfit, was inside the saloon, looking out the window in the door to make sure Pepe did not try to run away.

"I have to go back in there and tap out on the trumpet player," Pepe said. "The only way I can get anything down on the horse is to borrow your check for a while and give you the cash tonight."

"I don't know," the former Rosemary Dattolico said. "I got five kids home."

"Yeah, and do you have a mink stole home?" Pepe asked.

"What race is it?" the former Rosemary Dattolico answered.

The race was the fourth. It was held at Aqueduct Race Track. It went off at 3:11 1/2. The field of nine ran six furlongs. The fractions were 0:22 3/5; 0:46 3/5; 1:12 2/3. The horse called Count Banish went off at odds of $11.90 to a dollar. Count Banish ran without mishap and finished seventh.

On Saturday night the former Rosemary Dattolico served scrambled eggs for dinner.

"I'm too tired to make a big dinner," she explained

to her family. She was holding back three cans of corned-beef hash for Sunday dinner.

The former Rosemary Dattolico spent Saturday night at home with her family. Halfway through a movie on television, she turned the sound up so loud nobody could hear a word, which was good because she had to call Pepe at the saloon. Since half the bet on Count Banish was his, he owed her money which would enable her to fake through the week.

"He took the cash register and went to a card game," the bartender said. "He must have felt lucky or something. He said he'd call you in the morning." When Pepe called in the morning, he said he did not feel lucky. He said he was going up on the roof of his apartment building and jump off.

On Monday morning the former Rosemary Dattolico's children, sensing her problem, gathered to comfort her, as children always do.

"Am I going to get my new shoes today?" her son Kevin asked at breakfast.

"No."

Kevin's foot came out from under the table. "I have to get new shoes today," he said. "Look at the ones I got on. I can't wear them after today. You said you'd get me new shoes today."

"Shut up," she said.

"How can I go to school with shoes like this?" he said.

"I'll break your toes and then you won't need shoes," she said.

The rest of the day consisted of an unhappy man named Hugo, from the tailor's, who wanted more than a smile for his dry-cleaning delivery, a milkman who went away with empty bottles, a paperboy who was informed that she had a headache and would he come back Saturday; and on Monday night the former Rosemary Dattolico announced, after dinner, that she wanted to go out and get some air by herself.

She went to Pepe's saloon and took a seat by the cash register. It was a slow night, but she sat there grinding it out, grabbing every dollar that came in, from eight until midnight. And yesterday, out shopping for the bare necessities, she spent fifteen minutes arguing with the butcher over a piece of pot roast.

"I had to wait out a martini-drinker for two hours to get this," she said. "I want value."

6

How He Saw the War in Viet Nam

In 1965 Breslin and the *Herald Tribune* decided it was time he went out to see what the Viet Nam fighting was all about. Carol Glaser, the secretary on the City Desk who used to handle his mail and some of his less outrageous errands, left this memo of what happened.

The first thing Jimmy did on Wednesday, July 21, when he was told he was going to Viet Nam was to run up to Gallagher's to make plans.

Today, Friday, Mr. Bellows told him to get his cholera and typhus shots. He wouldn't let me make an appointment with the doctor. But an hour or two later I heard him conning Walt Kelly into going with him and Kelly made an appointment for the two of them at Kelly's doctor for tomorrow to get their shots. Jimmy thinks Walt is going, but Walt thinks his wife won't let him. Jimmy needs to take his Health Passport with him to the doctor to have him sign it as certification that he has his shots, but Jimmy won't let me give him the passport. He says he'll lose it. I'll have to call the doctor and see if I can get it to him by messenger for certification.

Yesterday Jimmy wrote Senator Kennedy requesting information talk and has appointment today with him. Kennedy called back about 1 p.m., said he was in New York for the day, at the Hotel Carlyle until about six and would like to talk to him today. He also said, "I hear you cried when the doctor gave you your shots." Jimmy has appointment at 3:30 to see him.

Before he went to meet Kennedy he went downstairs to the bar with Walt to make more plans.

I gave him his transit visa to fill out and he wrote his name, admitted he had five children, but wouldn't tell me how old he was, where he was born, or his draft status. Also he didn't know his passport number, but said his wife had it. After the ordeal of the visa, he left and said he'd see me Monday.

Monday: I came in this morning to fill out papers only to discover Jimmy had gone to Montauk for the week. Finally got his number from Jim Bellows, who called him for me. I spoke to him, got some of the information I needed, and told him I needed his signature. He told me to sign. I told him I wasn't going to spend the rest of my life in Riker's Island for him, so put in another call later and decided to mail them in case he calls me back with an address where I can mail them. He insists I get hold of Walt Kelly and fill out all the necessary papers for Walt, who, he insists is going with him. But Walt tells me his wife won't let him. Walt got his shots with him on Saturday.

What Breslin set out to do was tell the story of the war in terms of men who were fighting it. He wasn't going to deal with strategy or campaigns. He was just going to try to tell an ordinary reader back home what it might be like for some of the men involved.

Little of Breslin's anguish at what he saw actually got into the columns. He wrote very personal copy but he knew that few readers were interested in what was happening to him. They wanted to know what was happening to the soldiers and the civilians that he saw and spoke to.

Visit to a Little War

Travis Air Force Base, California

The ground-crew man kept waving his black-gloved hands for them to keep coming, and they moved slowly over the white concrete runway toward him. The blue truck came first. The big jet transport, which had no windows on its sides, was behind it. Then there were two red firetrucks which always come out when they land a plane that carries people who are wounded. Otherwise, there was no change in the routine of the air base. Transport planes taxied onto runways and took off. Straight across the field, in front of low sand-colored hills, B-52 bombers waited in the dusk with their nuclear bombs inside them. The ground-crew man's black gloves still waved and the truck led the plane right up to a knot of people who stood with their hands over their ears. The jet's engines roared and the kerosene fumes were thick in the air. Then its engines ran out in a whine.

A wide cargo door in the side of the plane came open. A nurse stood in the doorway with a clipboard in her hands. She was dark-haired and tanned, and wearing blue slacks and shirt and a heavy flying jacket with captain's bars on it.

"How many do you have?" one of the officers on the runway said.

She looked down at the mimeographed sheets. "Twenty-six from Viet Nam." She shook her head. "No, I missed one. Twenty-seven from Viet Nam."

"All litters?" the officer said.

"No, we have twelve ambulatory," she said. "And one psychiatric."

The ground crew pushed a covered chute up to the plane. The officers who had been standing on the runway started walking up the chute. A hospital bus backed up to the chute; white-uniformed medics ran out of the bus and up the ramp and into the plane.

The litters were stacked in tiers. The inside of the plane was warm. Only sheets covered their broken bodies. The medics carried them up to the hatch and into the cold Northern California breeze. Each time, the nurse told the medics to put the litter down.

"You have to cover up," she said, and she bent down and pulled olive-drab blankets over them and tucked the blankets in. Then she looked at them. "Now lie on your back, please," she said. The young, smooth faces went back and the white pillows came up around their cheeks. They were silent. Their eyes, opened very wide, looked straight up.

They came, one after another, in casts and with bloodstains on their sheets, and the nurse's tanned hands pulled olive-drab blankets over their broken bodies and she talked quietly and looked into the face of each of them. Then he would be gone and the medics would put another piece of the war in Viet Nam at her feet. And she would bend over and reach for blankets.

She did not bend over when they brought Sergeant Philip Vogel out. He was the last. Both of his legs were in casts that were dark from the blood seeping through them. The bandages on his body began at his chest. A sheet covered part of him. Plastic bags and tubes from a colostomy showed from under the sheet.

"Don't put anything on my legs, please," Philip Vogel said.

She shook her head. "No, I won't put anything over you," she said. She stood and looked at him. "Get him out of the cold right away," she said. The medics took Philip Vogel down the ramp and into the bus. The doors shut and the bus rolled away and went off the runway and up a hill to the light green hospital building.

They bring them in like this almost every night at Travis Air Force Base. Broken bodies from a small war in a place in Asia. They come in on jet planes that land unnoticed while the nation watches programs on television. They used to come home as heroes. Now they are a way of life.

They put Philip Vogel in a room on the first floor of the hospital. They gave him a cigarette and lit it up for him and then the medic went to get a doctor for him. Vogel's brown eyes looked up at the ceiling. There was no animation in his long, straight face. He took the cigarette out of his mouth and, without being asked a question, he started talking.

"On the second night," he said. "They attacked us on the second night. According to the S-2 there were four hundred guerrillas. It was only my second day there and I got hit. A hand grenade. The VC hit me with a hand grenade. No, what's the use of saying that? I was in a foxhole one night at 10:30 on guard duty and the guy with me was asleep in the higher portion of it. I heard a noise. I didn't want to fire and give away my position. I tried to get out a hand grenade and it didn't clear the bunker and it came back and got me. It bounced right back. Right back at my feet and got me everywhere. I have a colostomy. I'm twenty-five and I have a colostomy. I was going to marry a girl. She's in Pennsylvania. If I ever heal up I can marry her. We got the most modern weapons in the world. I never saw one of them. Never saw one. They move in the grass like snakes. Hey, aren't you gonna do anything about my feet, man?"

The medic heard him and came into the room. He started to take the pillow out from under Vogel's feet. Somebody across the hall began to scream that he couldn't breathe. Then there was a gagging sound. The medic let go of the pillow and ran out of the room.

Vogel looked around the room. "May I have an ashtray, please?" he said.

"Where are you from?" he was asked.

"Baltimore."

"What are you going to do with yourself when you're finished with this?"

"Do? I don't know what I'm going to do. I like the

Army. The Army's good. I didn't want to go to Viet Nam. The second lieutenant, he was running to different men's positions. He got shot right in the head. I saw it."

He closed his eyes. "It hurts," he said. His teeth came down and dug into his lip. He started to moan. His teeth came up from his lip and a yell came out of his mouth. A doctor and a nurse came into the room and they bent over Philip Vogel, who had a hand grenade bounce back at him on his second night in Viet Nam.

In an office at the end of the corridor, Ben Griffin, an officer from the base, sat at a desk and went through some forms.

"We got a plane coming in from Viet Nam tomorrow," he said quietly. "This one is carrying coffins."

Colonel Sam

Saigon

The first time Sam Wilson came to Asia, he walked into the jungles of Burma with a carbine in his hands. He was a captain of the lead detachment of a group which the records say was the 5307th Composite Unit (Provisional). The newspaper and movie people called it Merrill's Marauders. The enemy in Asia then was the Japanese, and Sam Wilson spent three years fighting them behind their lines.

Sam Wilson is back in Asia again, this time as a colonel. He is back in a gabardine suit with a red tie and he stands at the candlelit bar of his huge apartment, a half-gallon of Chivas Regal in front of him, a houseboy padding in with a bucket of ice, and Nat Cole's voice coming over the stereo set. There are no guns lying around the place. There is very little talk of them, either.

At forty-one, and after twenty-four years in the Army, Sam Wilson says that killing people doesn't accomplish a damn thing.

"The Big Red One," he was saying, talking about the United States 1st Infantry Division here in South Viet Nam. "Let's roll them in here, they say. Roll in the Big Red One. We'll flatten these bastards and then go home.

"Oh, Christ, what a waste of time. You roll in the Bed Red One here and, do you know what you're doing? Just taking the tarpaulin off the field so you can start to play a ball game. This is a political fight we're in here. It has violent military overtones. But it's going to be won or lost politically. Not with any big fire-fights."

Wilson tipped the Scotch bottle and poured another round. The room next to the bar had tile walks going around a garden that was lit with Japanese lamps. The center of the ceiling was made of a wire screen. Rain made a waterfall sound as it came through the screen and into a pond in the middle of the garden. Sam Wilson wants to live good. He is going to be here a long time. He is in the Special Forces, but he is attached to the United States Operations Mission. He is in charge of political action in the thatched-roof hamlets and villages which make up this country. Canned milk for babies is Sam Wilson's top weapon.

He is six foot two, 195 pounds, with blue eyes and light wavy hair and outdoors on his face and big hands. He is practically inaccessible around Saigon because he works an eighteen-hour day between his office and the hamlets out around the country where he has men stationed.

He is in the school of Edward Lansdale, the retired major general who has come here to direct counterinsurgency operations. And those who know something of Viet Nam tell you to see Sam Wilson if you want to find something hopeful.

"Once the Viet Cong get into a hamlet and establish this VC infrastructure, as the book calls it, once they digest the hamlet, you can roll in the Marines and bring all the firepower in the world with you," he was saying. "And for that month that you're in there, you own the hamlet. But when the tail end of that column leaves the hamlet, the VC owns it again. And don't you try and go back and spend the night there. So how can you win here with a gun?

"I'm proud I'm a soldier. Hell, I should be out fighting to be a brigade commander in the 101st Airborne. Only we're doing it differently now. We're developing a new kind of soldier. A politico-military breed. Take me. I spent most of the last five years in Russia and the satellite countries. I'm 95 per cent fluent in English and 100 per cent fluent in Russian. And the job here is to fight them for the people. Get the people. They do it with a tight, cohesive organization. They make every man a chairman of something in the hamlet. They give the man dignity. Even if he's the chairman of the firewood-organizing committee, he gets a chance to conduct a meeting once a month and be on top.

"The other government, the one that runs Viet Nam, that stops at the district level. Saigon? That's a word to most of these farmers. Some place distant. Once in his life the farmer might meet his district chief. The farmer lives and works in hamlets and villages. That's where there is no government influence. Our job is to bridge the gap and put something in there. We don't do that, then we win nothing around here. Shoot 'em up. Christ, shoot hell out of them. But you win around here by doing things that aren't exciting."

Wilson's job sounds like another of these advance-social-worker affairs which, after a few successes with much fanfare, amount to a few drops of rain into the sand. But it is the only way out in this intricate country. Every aluminum casket shoved onto a freight plane at Ton San Nhut for delivery to a house in America is a life lost for nothing unless these social and political things take hold.

"I'd like to go and get a look at those caves they were hiding in," the Marine colonel at Chu Lai was told recently.

"Oh, you can't see them now," he said.

"Why?"

"Because our people are out of the area now and the VC has moved back in. You'll get shot if you go near them."

These were the caves the Marine operation swept through in the big American battle they fought here. The operation was a smashing success. Except you can't go back, or the VC will shoot you in the back.

"Rice," Sam Wilson was saying, "they need rice and old tires to make more sandals out of, and cloth so they can make some clothes, and salt. And nuoc mam, the fish sauce they put over everything. And canned milk for babies. Past this they don't know about anything, and they don't need anything. Get in there with supplies. Then work with them. Make them understand the only way they can have a free life is by a decent government. I got men all over the country living in these hamlets with them. They're the ones who are going to be the success around here. If there's ever any success.

"Force? Here, look at this picture. I'll show you what force does."

He took out a copy of the English-language newspaper published in Saigon. The front page had a picture of a big Negro Marine holding a rifle on six Viet Cong prisoners. The Viet Cong sat on the ground, with that on-purpose scrawny look they can affect so quickly.

"If those six prisoners had their chance, they would take that Marine and mutilate him while he was still breathing. We know that," Wilson said. "But the people looking at the paper only see this big round-eye standing over the six poor Viet Cong prisoners. Even the Vietnamese people on our side, they don't say anything about it, but they resent that round-eye towering over the poor prisoners."

"The Marine is a Negro. Doesn't that make any difference?"

"As long as he has round eyes, the black guy is a white guy to them. They don't like him. Let me tell you, the more roundeyes we bring over here in our Big

Red Ones, the more people we're getting into an area where all the people are going to resent us."

He finished his drink and looked at his watch. "When a kid gets killed over here, he's just as dead as they were in those great big wonderful battles in the forties. You got to work for these kids. Work to try and straighten this out for them. Come on, I have to go out with my troops."

Sam Wilson's troops were in a villa twenty minutes away by car through the rain. The troops were sitting with Vietnamese girls on a tile floor, drinking orange soda. A Vietnamese man with tinted glasses sat on a stool in the middle of the floor, playing a guitar and singing little songs the troops seemed to know. Sam Wilson stood by the door and watched.

"The man playing the guitar is Pham Duy. He's the leading composer in Viet Nam," Wilson said. "The troops are college students who came over here for the summer. I worked their asses off. They got put in hamlets and they stayed there all summer. Some of them got shot at, some had bombs thrown at them, all of them were threatened. But they worked and got things done. You're looking at one of the only success stories in this war."

Roger Montgomery, a student at Wesleyan in Connecticut, came out on the floor and sat down with the guitar and started to sing, "Michael, row the boat ashore." The students and Vietnamese girls sang with him.

"You're a colonel of the coffee house," Wilson was told.

He called one of them over. The student had glasses and a mustache. His name was Allan Samson. He was twenty-six and a graduate student at the University of California at Berkeley.

"This is a much more useful thing to do than student demonstrations," he said. "It's difficult to learn anything in the United States about the problem here. I feel the information put out by the government about Viet Nam is not worthy of an intelligent person. I feel my being here is a channel of protest against the government's information policies. Let them tell the truth. Then one can see more readily that we should be here. McNamara said there is only a nine-thousand difference in the weapons captured by both sides. The figures he used were true. But he slanted them badly. The VC capture mortars and we capture homemade weapons."

"Where did you spend the summer?"

"In Vinh Long, in the delta. A couple of potshots at me. But that was nothing. Everybody who comes here gets shot at. It's the initiation."

"Did you get anything done?"

"We accomplished quite a bit," he said. "The picture changed in our area. Not forever. You've got to remain working. But it did change."

Another one came up. He introduced himself as Dan Grady, twenty-five, who attends the Fletcher Law and Diplomacy School at Tufts.

"I worked with VC defectors in Phan Thiet," he said. "Returnees in that area were averaging 2.5 a month until July an August. Then it went up to 19 per cent. I think we had something to do with it. They are drafting thirteen-year-olds. They're hurting themselves. And we worked on our program. We're beating them in that region now.

"But the American military are hurting us. They should get their ass kicked," Grady said.

"Here you go," Sam Wilson said.

"Well, they should get their ass kicked," Grady said. "The indiscriminate use of air power here is hurting our effort. A lot of civilians have been killed by air strikes that don't accomplish a thing except to make some general feel good."

"Someday I'm going to get used to my men talking like this," Sam Wilson said. "Someday."

"Look what we're working with," Grady said. "They have a sect here, the Cao Dai. They worship Victor Hugo and Winston Churchill as their saints. It takes great patience and understanding to get to them. Then some ass orders an air strike and an American bomb kills one of their sect. How can we talk to them then?"

Sam Wilson was outside the room, standing under a portico and looking at the rain.

"I know there's no sex appeal in it," he said. "We can't give out big stories about operations we went on and how many people we killed. But I'm going to tell you something. I've tried it both ways. I killed more sonsofbitches than you've seen. Killed all the time. Christ, shot them right in the goddamned head. And I'm telling you what we're doing here is the only way."

All around Saigon, planes were dropping immense flares to light up the ground for night strikes at the Viet Cong, who creep up from the ground when it becomes dark. American soldiers were on duty everywhere, their weapons aimed through coils of barbed wire. Sam Wilson's troops sat on the floor and drank orange soda. He said they were more important than regular soldiers.

"You can win a war with these kids," he said, "not with any soldiers."

A Little War of Rats

Saigon

George Sunderland rolled over on his cot in the hut and his foot caught the mosquito netting and pulled part of it onto the bed. Mosquito netting should hang straight, from the rod on the ceiling over the cot down to the floor, so that the rat crawling up it follows the netting to the ceiling and does not get a grip on the cot with its feet. Sunderland's foot made a fold in the netting and the rat crawling up it came into the fold and onto the bed. The rat's small mouth moved and its teeth came through the netting and into Sunderland's foot. Sunderland kicked the rat and the rat fell under the cot. The rat crept away with its tail dragging across the dirt floor.

George Sunderland, who is a sergeant in the Special

Forces, had to be taken out of his camp at a place called Plateau GI the next morning. The doctors started treating him for rabies by sticking aluminum needles into his stomach.

Viet Nam, which is a little war of rats, is like this always. It is a place of sneaking and gnawing and of people who see nothing and hear nothing and spend days finding nothing, and who are hit in the back by a shot that comes from nowhere. Nothing seems to happen, and then a Marine battalion is sent home after seven months and it has not been in one action and it has 10 per cent casualties.

It is a place where people are hurt and die in little situations, and very little is heard of it because it is all so scattered. But it is here.

The big-bladed fan in the ceiling spun slowly over Richard Nixon's head while he sat on a couch Saturday night and said he thought the military part of the war could go on for two or three more years. He was sitting in the tile-floored living room of a house that is three blocks away from a street called Pasteur. On Pasteur one night this week, the four Air Force men were standing and waiting for a bus to take them to the airport, and one of them saw the hand come over the wall and he let out a yell when he saw the grenade fall onto the pavement. The four started to run but the grenade went off and caught them all in the back.

Everywhere in Viet Nam the days gnaw at people who live them. In a place called Can Tho, which is in the delta area, the Vietnamese have a hospital building, a sickly-yellow place with blue shutters, and behind the building is a sluice and hands and arms and legs are always in the sluice, because Vietnamese army doctors do not repair things the way Americans do. They amputate.

And at a place called Duc Co the two Vietnamese questioned the Viet Cong prisoner who had just been caught out in the thick forests which surround the camp. The Vietnamese were in fatigues. The Viet Cong prisoner wore black. The three squatted down, which is the way Vietnamese talk best. The two soldiers spoke in the bird language of the country and the Viet Cong answered them. The two soldiers showed no anger. One of them reached out with his hands and took the prisoner's right hand and held it. He seemed to be talking to the prisoner with feeling. Then the soldier gripped the prisoner's middle finger and began to bend it back. The soldier's voice did not change. He kept talking in one tone while his hands brought the finger straight up, a brown muddy finger rising from the prisoner's hand. Then the soldier tipped the finger straight back and there was a little sound when the bone of the finger and the knuckle of the hand broke.

The prisoner let out a little cry. Tears came out of his eyes. The soldier let go of the finger. He clasped his hands and put them between his knees. He squatted there and kept talking. The prisoner squatted in front of him, the brown muddy finger back on the top of his hand. Everybody walked past them and did not notice it at all. These things are a way of life in this little war.

"This is Nutcracker 91 to Navy Jet Flight 42," the pilot of the forward air controller's plane said. "Do you have me in sight yet?"

"Ah, this is Navy Jet Flight 42. I have a sighting of a large town with canal flowing east to west."

"Roger, 42, follow canal east to coordinates WQ 960-963, until you see canal empty into river. I'm at 1800 feet. Ah, there are choppers at 1500. Come in at 3000."

"Roger, following canal," the Navy jet pilot said over the radio. "Should see you in two minutes."

The forward air controller's plane, an observation plane called an L-19 circled the area, which was green, watery land. His job was to spot targets and direct the jet planes to them over the radio.

After a long pause, the Navy pilot's voice came into the forward air controller's headpiece.

"Nutcracker 91, have you in sight," the Navy pilot's voice said.

"Roger, there is target at left of canal. Hit tree line on west side of canal, repeat canal, for about 100 yards. Church out about 1000 yards to left of tree line." The forward air controller was speaking easily as he directed the jet, which was over him in the sky some place. "Do not hit church," the air controller said. "Repeat, do not hit church at 1000 yards to left of tree line. Church is out of bounds. Repeat, church is out of bounds." The pilot of the jet plane did not hear anything after the words "tree line." A crackle on the radio, confusion in the words he heard through the crackle. But he thought he had heard it all.

"Roger, Nutcracker 91," the jet pilot's voice said into the forward air controller's earphones.

The jet came out of the sky, came low over the ground, and a long white cylinder dropped from under it and disappeared into the trees and the trees exploded in smoke that had fire in its middle. The plane kept going. It went right at the church and something came out from under the plane's wings and went up against the church and part of the wall of the church became smoke. The little girl and her mother who were on their knees praying in the church were killed.

The Rusting Rails

Phan Thiet

The railroad which runs beside the sea from Phan Thiet to Nha Trang is a long, rusting strip of 1-meter-gauge track. Green and yellow painted 900-horsepower Diesel engines pull trains along these tracks whenever the people in charge of the railroad can find an engineer with guts to take a train out. The Vietnamese, who do not like to show any emotion at all, weep openly whenever a train is scheduled to leave. Just outside of Phan Thiet, the Viet Cong like to sit on the railroad tracks and have their lunch and they become very angry if a train comes along and disturbs them. This situation bothers Lieutenant Colonel Dinh Van De, province chief of Phan Thiet. He takes it as a personal insult whenever anybody tries to blow up one of his railroad trains.

"We catch some of these people trying to do this and all we give to them is a month, two month, three month in prison," Dinh Van De was saying yesterday. "This is not enough. I have asked the commanding officer of the Second Corps Area if, with all my conscience, with all my responsibility, I can do something else to them."

What Dinh Van De wants to do is exciting. As stated in writing, he wants to capture a couple of Viet Cong trying to put a mine under his railroad tracks. Then he wants to order a whole town out to the railroad tracks to be witnesses. Dinh Van De then would make one of the Viet Cong sit down on top of a mine. The other Viet Cong would stand off to the side and push down hard on the plunger that makes the mine go off.

"That's a beautiful idea," Dinh Van De was told recently.

"Thank you," he said. "It very necessary."

"It's too bad your railroad isn't electrified," he was told.

"Why is this?" he said.

"Because then you could make them kneel down on the tracks and stick their tongues onto the third rail."

"Oh, I see," Dinh Van De said. His eyes gleamed.

After this exchange of ideas, Dinh Van De picked up an attaché case and said he had to go to Nha Trang. A railroad train was scheduled to depart in the afternoon. Dinh Van De went out to the landing strip and waited for a plane.

The railroad station was at the end of a row of alleys of sand which run between long rows of yellow cement huts where women sit and sell black-market Cokes while they nurse their babies.

The engineer of the train was standing alongside the Diesel. His name was Lai Chong Duong. He wore black pajamas. His assistant, Chu Van Chich, wore gray pajamas. Another man, probably the conductor, stood with them. All three were so afraid they were holding onto each other's hands.

The train consisted of an engine, two flat cars loaded with lumber poles and crates of nuoc mam. Nuoc mam is a sauce made of rotted fish and it is the most popular thing in all of Viet Nam, which is why you never should invite a Vietnamese into the house. After the flat cars there were one passenger car and then three cabooses loaded with Vietnamese soldiers who already had their guns sticking out the windows. The train had not moved an inch yet, but they were ready to fight for their lives. The war is going very well in this district.

The passengers clustered about the one car. They were women in brown shirts and black pants who carried long poles with live ducks and chickens hanging by their feet from the poles. And old men carrying packing cases which were so heavy the men staggered as they walked. They immediately put their cases down and started shoving the women. They wanted to get a choice location, which is a spot down on the floor so the head doesn't show in the window.

Finally Lai Chon Duong went up the metal steps to the engineer's seat. He went up the steps as if he were going to jail. Chu Van Chich, his assistant, followed him. Chu Van Chich followed because two policemen stood behind him and made him go. The conductor said he was sick and wanted to go home. The policemen took him and stuffed him onto the train. With a loud sob, Lai Chon Duong started the train and inched out of the station.

Through the town of Phan Thiet, all five blocks of it, Lai Chong Duong and Chu Van Chich stood erect in the cab of the Diesel engine. The train passed through a wall of rolled barbed wire and sandbag bunkers. Past this, the train was out in the countryside.

Lai Chon Duong bent over a little bit. Chu Van Chich took something out of his pocket and dropped it onto the floor. He bent down to pick it up. The train moved through rice fields, with the breeze from the ocean making the rice seem to be waving good-by to the train. The rice fields slipped away and now the real countryside began.

Mr. Lai Chon Duong did a knee-bend. He ran his train by reaching up. His assistant, Mr. Chu Van Chich, squatted down and put his hands on top of his head. Every few second or so, Chu Van Chich would jump up to look out the window to see if the tracks were still there. Then he would come back down into his crouch. The countryside became wild and hills overlooked the train tracks and the train moved along with Lai Chon Duong flat on his stomach now and Chu Van Chich jumping up and down to look out the window.

When the shooting started, it was tremendous. Nobody knows who shot first, the Vietnamese soldiers in the cabooses or the Viet Cong up in the hills. But everybody certainly fired a gun. Now it could be seen that Lai Chon Duong was not afraid after all. He was smart. He was streched out on his stomach. Chu Van Chich was beside him, bouncing up and down so quickly the sweat poured off him. The train went through heavy shooting. It ended. Only snipers would be aiming at the train for a while. The next concentration of Viet Cong undoubtedly would have a big cannon set up on the side of the tracks, and they would blow the train into the next province.

Finally, on one leap, Chu Van Chich let out a howl of glee. He began running in place. Up ahead, where the train had to cross a wooden bridge, he could see that the bridge had been tampered with. During the night the Viet Cong's great 400 HQ section, sapper platoon, had come with two water buffalo and sixteen old ladies and moved the railroad tracks and the bridge three feet to the right. It would take the government a week and a million dollars' worth of equipment to fix it.

A great smile came onto Lai Chon Duong's face when he got off the floor and saw the trouble on the tracks. He quickly placed his railroad train in reverse and, with a minimum of gunfire, backed it through the hills and into Phan Thiet again. In a week or so, when the bridge was fixed, the train would be ready to run again. Two weeks after that, when the search party finally caught up with Lai Chon Duong and Chu Van Chich, they could schedule a trip.

So there was no train ride to Nha Trang this time. And there is no train ride to any place in Viet Nam. The fighting has gone so well that a railroad train, even an armored train, can't go more than six miles out of Saigon. The last time a train tried it, the Viet Cong stole the engine, turned it around, and ran it at the Saigon station at top speed.

The Day I Company Got Killed

Chu Lai

Eighteen rifles, stuck in the hot sand by their bayonets, stood in a semicircle in front of a tent. A camouflaged helmet rested on each rifle butt.

The rifles were symbols of the men of the 3rd Battalion of the 3rd United States Marine Regiment killed at Van Tuong last week in the biggest American battle of the Viet Nam war.

Inside the tent, the battalion commander, Lieutenant Colonel Joseph Muir, knelt with his men at memorial services. Colonel Muir appeared to be holding back tears. Some of the Marines sobbed.

"They did not come back," said the chaplain. "O god, for those who fell in battle, we know you are with them. And for those who are here, we give you thanks."

The black mountains of Chu Lai come down to the sea with rice paddies in front of them and then a wide area of orange sand that is covered by lifeless bushes that are shoulder-high. The South China Sea, flat and lukewarm, begins where the land ends.

It was here, on the sand and in the bushes, and under a terrible sun, that the United States Marines fought a battle for the first time in this place in Asia called Viet Nam.

They fought all day Wednesday and into the night, and they fought again on Thursday. Their big American tanks and armored vehicles were useless to them. The enemy, these little Asians in black shirts, knocked the armor out right away.

The Marines were hit with shots coming out of the bushes in the sand. They fought with rifles and machine guns. When the Viet Cong were not on the sand any more, the Marines went into the mud of the paddies after them. The fighting was continuous and the dead were everywhere and now everybody knows that America is in a war.

The Marines say they killed 564 Viet Cong. The Marines do not give their own casualties because this is a war. But their dead were in the sand Wednesday and Thursday, waiting to be put in boxes and sent home to America. The broken bodies of the wounded were being taken to field hospitals. And the rest of them, the kids of eighteen, nineteen, and their early twenties, have had their lives changed forever by this day on the sands and in the mud in front of the black mountains of Chu Lai.

"A lot of boys came off that ship," Daniel Kendall, nineteen, a lance corporal, was saying, "and a lot of men are going back."

Kendell is from Boston and he is in I Company. He thinks I Company is the best company in the Marines and when it was put together in October, back at Camp Pendleton, San Diego, they got to know each other right away because they all knew they had thirty months to live together. And on Tuesday afternoon, when they were taken out of their tents at Da Nang and put on a cramped troop ship without being told where they were going, nobody in I Company was worried.

"We all know what we're doing," Terry Hunter, twenty-two, a corporal, said.

"We got the smartest officers and the best noncoms and the best men," George Kendlers, who is twenty, called out.

"India Company is the best in the Marines," another one of them called out.

"Yeah, we're the best," the kids started to yell, and the gray ship pulled out of Da Nang and went into the sea. They were given chili and rice and cold milk. They liked the cold milk. It was the first they had had since coming to Viet Nam.

"They give us this, they must have some wild operation planned for us," Kendlers said.

None of them had been in action before, outside of having a few stray shots thrown at their camp. After dinner, they were told where they were going. They were going to land on the beach twelve miles to the south of the town of Chu Lai.

"Intelligence says a lot of Viet Cong are dug in in the area," one of the officers said. "But this is one of those things. You may not fire a round. Or you might get your behinds shot off."

"Just remember what you've been taught," Bruce Webb, the company captain, told them. "When you're fired on, go down, then come up and shoot. Don't just lay there. After you shoot, move. Move even if bullets are all around you. You run up less casualties when you move."

They went to bed at 9 p.m. and were up at 4 a.m. and had eggs and pancakes for breakfast. At 6:50 a.m., with the sun breaking over the black mountains in the distance, I Company came through the water and onto the sand and bushes, and it was the first time they ever had been in action.

Walking quietly, with no talk, they went into a small cluster of filthy huts with dirt paths between them.

They call these places villages here. The village was empty. On the paths leading from the village to the sand and bushes, they found women and children hiding. The women held their children and looked at the Marines and said nothing. The women knew where the Viet Cong were. But they would not tell the Marines. The Marines were the enemy.

A second village was approached. To get to it, they had to go over a small bridge. The front of the village was lined with bushes and shrubbery. I Company moved up to the bridge. They started to go across it when one of the bushes in front of the village moved and a machine gun began firing from a trench under the leaves.

The Marines and mortars dropped into the village. They called for an air strike. Armed helicopters lumbered in. Swept-wing jets dove at the village after the helicopters moved away. When the air strike stopped, all the bushes began to move and there was firing both ways and then black shirts were climbing out of the trenches under the bushes and running back through the village. I Company came after them. They came across the bridge and into the village and Captain Webb was talking with two corporals, a radio man and a runner, and they were going along one of the trenches with the bushes over it when the booby trap exploded. It killed the three of them. I Company now knew what war is.

"He's not dead," another officer kept telling them. "They're taking him out by helicopter. He's all right." The officer didn't want the men to know that their commander had been killed in the first half-hour of the first action of their lives.

Now they were out into this sand with the bushes and the fire was coming at them. Not concentrated fire. But a shot here, a shot here, a machine gun from somewhere else, and all of it coming from holes and bunkers as they came through this sand, with the bushes tearing at their hands. Every few minutes, Michaels, was was carrying the radio, would hear something on it and he'd call over to those around him.

"Smith got hit. He's dead."

"Smith," the one near him would say. He'd turn to somebody else. "Smith got killed." It would go down the line.

They moved over three Viet Cong bodies killed by their machine guns. A helicopter was downed in one of the rice paddies in front of them. A line of tanks and armored carriers was going in to get out the helicopter pilots. I Company was to go with them. There was a line of eight armored vehicles. The tanks went first. The first tank pitched through the sand and into the mud of the paddy and nothing happened to it.

The Viet Cong fired at the second vehicle. It was an armored carrier, and they tried to get it with a .57-millimeter recoilless rifle. The shot missed. The I Company Marines in the carrier were climbing out to fight. The second shot from the .57 hit and covered the carrier with black smoke and the bodies fell out of the black smoke and into the mud.

The water ran out at noon. Fire was too heavy for helicopters to land with supplies. The Marines of I Company went through the sand with the sun glaring at them and the shots trying to kill them and they were licking their lips and trying to forget about water while they fought. These should be stories from a book about 1944. They are about 1965.

In the afternoon, a young boy popped up in front of them. He had crawled out of a hole which had an opening so small you could walk by it and not notice it. He pointed down into the hole. The boy started running. A small hand came out of the hole. Then a black shirtsleeve. Then a rifle. The Viet Cong pulled himself out and started running. The I Company machine-gunners caught him in the middle and his body fell in two parts.

I Company dug in for the night. There was firing all night and all morning and Michaels, the radioman, kept calling out to the ones near him the name of buddies who were killed.

Friday, their faces orange from the sand, their lips encrusted with it, their eyes bloodshot, Terry Hunter, Daniel Kendall, and George Kendlers sat in a foxhole with their rifles and a 3.5 rocket-launcher and they were in with another oufit because I Company was not in the battle any more. I Company had been blown apart. The others who were left had been taken back to the beach.

"It's still the best company in the Marines," Kendlers said in the foxhole. "We just had bad luck. Up on the hill, when the captain got killed, I wanted to go right in. When they started shooting at me later, I felt good. I didn't want to be the only one who didn't get shot at."

"We're all real good buddies," Kendall said.

"We always went to the Pike together. Back in Long Beach. I Company always was together."

"The Pike? Is that a gin mill?"

"Gin mill? No. It's an amusement park. It's got rides," Hunter said.

"Dancing," Kendall said. "You know, an amusement park."

Somewhere close, artillery was going off. Jets screamed in the sun overhead. They sat with their chins down so the sand wouldn't blow into their eyes. They talked about an amusement park in Long Beach where young kids go. Then Kendall's eyes came up and he saw a guy walking toward them from another hole.

"What are you, soft?" he yelled. "You'll get shot right through the ass doing that."

The other two looked up. They all looked the same. Three kids in a foxhole with faces that are very old.

Number Wan

Saigon

Cruz had a sling made out of radio wire hanging from the top of the open doorway on his side of the helicopter. He stuck the black grillwork barrel of an

M-60 machine gun through the sling and out into the air. He pushed sunglasses over his eyes and looked down the barrel of the gun at the colorless land under him. The land, the Mekong Delta, went for miles.

Flat, with lines cutting it into domino-shaped fields; nothing seemed to be growing in it. Then a cloud moved across the sky and it reflected on each piece of land as it went over and now you could see that the whole place was olive-drab water. Canals ran through the watery land at intervals.

Cruz, his hands on the gun, kept looking for motion. There was none. Then his head moved. "There you go," he said. "Look at that."

Straight down, a string of sticks hugged the bank of a canal.

"Sampans. Sitting all by themselves," he said. "Nobody's around here any place and all of a sudden we got sampans. The VC travels by sampan around here. Damn. Look at them."

He kept looking down his gun at them, and the helicopter went straight down and the sampans went out of view.

"What can you do?" Cruz said. "We don't know who they are, so we can't shoot at them."

He let go of the machine gun and fumbled under his flak jacket to get at a cigar. He unwrapped it, lit it, and sat back in his seat.

The helicopter landed at Ca Tho, where a company of Vietnamese troops filed up the tail ramp and into the belly of a four-engine C-124 transport. They sat on red canvas bucket seats along the sides. Two lines of them sat back to back down the middle of the plane. When they took off their helmets, black straggly hair fell onto their foreheads. They began to lean on each other, their feet sprawled into the aisle. Most of them were asleep before the ramp was pulled up.

A thin-faced American master sergeant carrying two carbines came in and sat by the door. "Look at this," he said. "They just walked off and left them out there standing against a wall."

The back of his neck was red and criss-crossed with wrinkles. The fatigue cap was pulled down over his eyes. Little veins broken by whisky bottles stood out on his cheeks. This one was an old soldier.

"I'll say one thing for them," he said. "They sure as hell can sleep a lot."

"Are they yours for good?"

"Hell, no. Trainees. We've had them for fourteen weeks. We've got some more work to do, then they get sent into companies. They don't go as a unit."

"How are they?"

"I don't know. Half of them must have disappeared. Already AWOL, like nothing. So many of them have gone off I'm worried about it gettin' to me. I'll wake up some night and run away myself."

"How do they run away?"

"Like nothing. Every time they get dismissed and they start walkin' around and goin' places I get worried. You see them walkin'. They may never come back."

"Are they all like this?"

"You can never say that. I've been with them around here for almost a year. I've seen plenty of them stand right up there and aim and squeeze one off in spots where a lot of guys I know would keep their head in the mud.

"You know," he said, "this is the third one of these things I've played in—Europe, Korea. To get things done in this one just drives you crazy."

"How did you get stuck for this with all that service?"

"I didn't get stuck, I volunteered."

"Why?"

"Because I'm a soldier."

"That's a good answer."

"You say that now. It takes a war to make a people say that. Otherwise a soldier's a bum. I was on East Baltimore Street one night and a guy says to me, 'You're living off the country. You're just a bum.'

That's what a soldier is, just an ignorant bum when there's no war. But now! Oh! We love you."

One of the Vietnamese soldiers was up from his seat. His thick lips parted into a smile when he saw the sergeant take out cigarettes.

"Ah." The kid smiled.

"Here," the sergeant said.

The kid came over, took a cigarette, and leaned over for a light. He straightened up. "Number wan."

He said this is an army saying meaning "very good."

"You got a girl?" the kid was asked.

"Ah." He smiled. "Number wan Saigon."

He smiled and went back to his seat.

"What can you say about them?" the sergeant said. "Half the time they don't even get paid. Then they give their money to some guy who gets sent to the post office to mail it home for them. And the guy comes back and says he lost it or something. And the government says it isn't responsible. What can you do if they don't even get paid?"

"Is their food any good?"

He made a face. "Our captain was in talking to their officers about it the other day. These kids were getting pork every day for weeks. Lumps of fat pork. You can't feed troops like that, but what can you do? Somebody's stealing the money for the food."

He leaned over and spat on the floor.

"They steal the money and feed them crap and then one of us has to go out with them and risk his life."

The plane landed at Tan Son Nhut field outside of Saigon. It came to a halt. The engines shut down and the ramp in the back of the plane came down. Outside, the afternoon rain was a wall of white water.

"We'll sit here for an hour waiting for transportation," the sergeant said. "They're taking this company to a barracks some place."

The kid who had taken the cigarette from the sergeant got up and walked to the head of the ramp. He looked out at the rain; then he took off his helmet and put it on the floor. He pulled a fatigue cap out of his hip pocket and put it on. He did not turn around to see if the Vietnamese captain was looking at him. The kid walked straight down the ramp and he was running when he was at the bottom. He disappeared in the rain.

While he ran away from the plane and went to his girl, the sergeant stared at the two carbines the kid had left against the wall.

"Why did they have to pick this place for a war?" he said.

A Day at the Races

Saigon

The sergeant was with his fat girl friend. He said that her name was Lind and that he liked her the first time he saw her, which was the night before. She was the only girl in the bar who didn't have gold teeth. After introducing his girl, the sergeant did not introduce himself by name because he said his wife in Georgia would get very mad if she ever knew about him going to the racetrack in Viet Nam with a fat girl friend.

The sergeant and his girl were sitting at the small bar in the clubhouse of the Course de Saigon, which the Vietnamese think is a racetrack. It is a place that is overgrown with weeds and has a gloomy wine-colored cement grandstand. The sergeant and his fat girl friend were drinking Scotch out of dusty glasses. The barmaid was an old toothless woman who had her hair pulled straight back in a knot. She was short, and only her face showed over the top of the bar.

"A couple of old buddies of mine are downstairs," the sergeant said. "They know this chink from Hong Kong and the chink knows his way around here. Stick around, we'll get our hands on some money here."

He ordered another drink and the toothless old lady bartender reached between two seltzer bottles to get the sergeant's glass. The old lady picked up the glass, pushed a cockroach the size of a dollar bill off the bar, and then splashed Scotch into the dusty glass.

The sergeant was thirty-four and in the Special Forces. He is a professional soldier. His fat girl friend also was a professional. The sergeant had on a blue polo shirt and dark slacks. He said it was the first time he had been out of fatigues in weeks. His girl friend wore Vietnamese national dress, a white high-collared thing which splits at the waist and goes down to the ground, flowing white trousers, dirty feet sticking out from under them, and the right hand held out for money.

"Maw-ney," she said.

"That's all you know," the sergeant said.

"The chevaux," she said, meaning the horses.

"No, you don't bet now," the sergeant said. "You bet when this chink from Hong Kong tells us what to bet. He knows his way around here.

"I got about 7000 piastres left," the sergeant said. This was about $70.00. "I've been down around Mito four straight weeks now. I'm looking to have some fun. But I'm not looking to give my money away to my girl friend here. It's bad enough she robs me all night, she doesn't have to do it in the daylight."

This made great sense. Around Mito, where the sergeant stays, the Viet Cong have a nagging habit of shooting guns off at all hours of the day and night. It is particularly hard on eardrums. If a person's job conditions are of this sort, the least he should be able to do is get a little help at the racetrack from a chink from Hong Kong.

The man was downstairs. He was talking to the sergeant's buddies, three regular Army men. The man from Hong Kong was a heavy-set Chinese in sunglasses. He wore a white long-sleeved shirt and tan slacks that were sharply pressed. Field glasses were around his neck and a racing form, printed in Vietnamese, was in his hands. One of the Army men, an old sergeant named Fred Bruder, who comes out of racetrack country, Laurel, Maryland, was going over the form with the man from Hong Kong.

"These two bastards here never run before," he said. "They must be gonna do somethin' here."

"Aho." The Chinese smiled.

"You see?" Bruder said to the ones with him. "I told you this place was a joke. This place isn't for horse racing. It's for embezzling."

The horses were numbered 10 and 3. To win a bet in Saigon, a man must pick the finish one-two.

Bruder and the other two went up the stairs to the bar, where the sergeant was holding hands with his fat girl friend. Bruder informed the sergeant they were betting 10 and 3 in the race.

"Did the chink tell you?" the sergeant said.

"He give it to us," Bruder said. "Hell, you know I don't listen to touts. But they fix so many races around here that a legitimate handicapper like me is wasting his time unless he gets in on the larceny."

"Maw-ney," the fat girl said. She held out her hand.

"All right," the sergeant said. He pulled out a thick wad of Vietnamese money and handed her 1000 piastres, which is a huge bet in the Course de Saigon. It amounts to $10 American. In Viet Nam, they will re-channel a river for that kind of money.

The sergeant watched his girl walk to bet the money. "This one, at least she's got teeth," he said.

He was right. Much probably has been said about the beautiful almond-eyed Vietnamese girl. She does not exist. It takes a major talent search to find a girl here with good teeth in her head. Clean feet is too much to ask.

The horses for the day's racing were in a long line of stalls in back of the grandstand. A wooden fence separated the racing fans from the horses. This was to keep any honest people away from the horses. Two Chinese men in sunglasses were directing the grooms. A bucket of water before a race is the finest way there is to make sure a horse will not run so fast.

The jockeys' room, a cement building with a scale

out on the porch, was crowded with young kids in pajamas who jammed around the jockeys. The jockey who was to ride No. 10 was found. He was a miniature boy in red silks who was fifteen and weighed 30 kilograms, 66.6 pounds, and gave his name as Phuoc.

"How much does he get if he wins the race?" an official was asked.

"Two thousand piastres," the man said.

"How much does he make if his horse doesn't win the race?"

The official said he didn't understand the question. The jockey, who of course knew no English, smirked. His friends giggled. The jockey got off the scale and walked away. Jockey Phuoc would steal from a candy store.

Back in the stands, the sergeant watched through field glasses when the horses came on the track. "I just bet another thousand piastres on the 10 and 3," he said. "I need some money."

Across the track, the horses lined up for the start. They lined up in a pack, with little men in pajamas standing in front of them and running at a horse when it would try to start. Then with no noise from the stands the race began. It began with the men in pajamas letting one horse run out by himself. The horse got a six-length lead. Then another horse followed. When this one had a real good jump, they let the others come on. The first horse out was No. 8. The second horse out was No. 5. It was suspected that these were the horses they wanted to win.

The sergeant dropped his girl friend's hand. "I'm a sonofabitch," he said. "You can't do this when the sun is still out."

The No. 8 horse led all the way through the weeds. The No. 5 horse received a serious challenge from No. 2. The jockey on No. 2 immediately corrected this by standing up on his horse and yanking the reins so far back he nearly dislocated the horse's neck. Jockey Phuoc, on No. 10, was, as ascertained early, the world's smallest thief. His horse tried to run a little on the turn and Jockey Phuoc immediately stood up in the stirrups. This is a common thing in Saigon. A week ago there was a riot at the track when the jockey on the horse leading in the stretch pulled the horse to a complete stop. Another jockey rode his horse through a hole in the fence. The people ran onto the track and tried to kill both of them. All money was refunded. Of all the characteristics which make up the Vietnamese, the only worth admiring, and the one never mentioned by Henry Cabot Lodge, is their magnificent regard for stealing. It should be protected at all costs. The government should use night raids by B-52s to save larceny in Viet Nam.

Downstairs, in front of the cages where they pay off, a line of kids and grooms and jockeys pushed against each other. They had formed up during the race with their tickets on the two horses they knew would win. There wasn't an American in on the thing. The payoff was 160 for each two piastres put up, and the Chinese from Hong Kong stood at the back with two others. They were waiting until the line cleared so they could cash in their tickets. Then go upstairs and tout the Americans into betting on wrong horses so the price could be built up.

It was evening when the sergeant and his fat girl friend were seen again. They were drunk in a bar on Tu Do Street that had brown rats running across the floor, and the sergeant said he had been robbed all day at the racetrack and now he was going to finish what was left and leave.

"I got to get a helicopter back to Mito," he said.

He left at 5:30 a.m. and flew back for another month of being shot at.

War and Riots

Saigon

The radios sit on bunks and on boxes in the mess halls, and out in the field they are on top of the sandbags and every hour the music stops and the news announcer begins: "Rioting in a section of Los Angeles . . ."

And the Negro soldiers stand and listen. And they talk. But they talk with uniforms over their black skins. Yesterday morning two of them, wearing fatigues, were standing in the sun and dirt of Bien Hoa, where the 1st Division troops stay, and they talked about this news which had just gone off the radio in the tent behind them.

"They ask you why you're here, you can't be straight at home," a tall one, smoking a cigar, said. He comes out of St. Louis.

"Why shouldn't they?" the other one said. "How can you come over here and say to the people, we going to liberate you, when you got to go out in the streets and riot to liberate yourself at home?" This one talking was from Paterson, New Jersey.

"It's none of our business," the one with the cigar said. "They got us here as soldiers, not a race. We got to be soldiers and just walk right by anything else."

"Lemuel Penn," the one from Paterson said. "What about him? He was a lieutenant colonel and he's coming home from camp in Georgia and the Ku Klux Klan shot him. Nobody do anything about it. They got us over here defendin' Georgia. Next thing you know they'll have us fightin' for South Africa."

"That's just you talking," the one with the cigar said. "When you in the Army, anything you say is just talk. It got nothin' to do with what's going on."

"That's all it is," the other one said. "When you finished talking you go right back to what you got to do."

"And you do it or you got trouble, black, white, or any other color," the one with the cigar said. They laughed.

In the USO club in Saigon, which is in a building on a wide, filthy street which has a flower market in the middle, two Negroes from a communications outfit sat down with green mugs of coffee and right away one of them began talking about it.

"Sixteen dead," he said. "What a scene that thing must be."

"This is the custom," the other one, who had a mustache, said.

Whenever there are one or more colored soldiers any place they start talking about the riot in Los Angeles. "If you're alone, do you talk to yourself about it?" they were asked.

"I think it's fine," the one with the mustache said. "Makes me feel good."

"Them easy credit places," the one with him said. "Boy, they must be catching hell right about now."

"What does it mean to you, right here, as soldiers?" they were asked.

"Nothing," the one with the mustache said. "You can be a rooter. But you just a rooter in the stands and that's all. And you don't get into any conversations with any Vietnamese about it. All that does is get you all raveled up."

"Sure," the one with him said. "How can you sit in a bar some place and explain to somebody why you're here and they got these riots going on? So what you do is just concentrate on being a soldier. There gonna be no civil rights marches in Saigon, I can guarantee you that."

In another room, a Negro in the Air Force sat at a piano. "I don't bother getting into it," he said. "You know, you go into a bar and the girl sits down next to you and she points at her skin and then she points at mine. That's supposed to mean we're all the same. Hell, I know she's trying to con me out of my money. I'm colored to her, same as I'm colored to anybody else."

Outside, the street was jammed and little children wearing only dirty pajama shirts went to the bathroom in the gutter. Saigon is a low-class Harlem and the skin of the people runs from yellow to cocoa, but the minute a Negro serviceman comes into Saigon he heads for bars that are crowded with other Negroes. They are down by the docks.

For years Negro merchant seamen coming into Saigon found themselves comfortable only in these places. No whites go in them. Neither do many Vietnamese, outside of girls looking for payday. The Vietnamese, even the Viet Cong who scream of the race riots in Los Angeles, do not want very much to do with Negroes.

Reuben Simmons was talking about this later in the day. Simmons, a Negro, is an agricultural expert for the United States Mission to Viet Nam. He was sitting in the screened-in-front row of the house he is renting here.

"The Vietnamese?" he said. "They are more color-conscious than we are in the United States. You don't find any of them out taking sunbaths if they can help it. He's death on sunburns, a Vietnamese.

"Then at the same time one of them will say to me, 'Your riots in Los Angeles? How do you feel being here helping us, with all this racial trouble you have at home?' How can I talk to them? There is no way that I can explain Los Angeles to them. They wouldn't believe me. I would tell them what it was like in 1941. I was working for the government and I had to stand in the street in Sixtin, Missouri, and watch them pour gasoline from a truck over a Negro's body and then burn it up. I could tell them how far we have come since then. And how far we are going to go."

"In the Bombay paper," a friend of his said, "they run marriage ads which say: 'Single civil servant wants to meet girl with wheatish complexion.' The whole Orient has its color problems."

What about the effect of the riots on the Negro soldiers here? Simmons was asked.

"None," he said. "This is a controlled situation. They're in the Army. They happen to be Negroes. They can listen to the news on the radio and have their feelings about it. And that's all."

Paid to Be Here

Pleiku

We have had so much of it that now it has become a business. In 1917 and then in 1942 people went away to fight for their country with tears and glamour, and everybody cheered at the movies and mooned over love songs about war and slogans for children became the property of adults. The next time, in 1951, it all came up flat. Korea depressed everybody, and soldiers fought because they were drafted. And now, in this place in Asia called Viet Nam, we have reached back into ancient history. Now we have men who fight a war because they get paid for it.

"The government's been paying me for seven years getting ready for a thing like this," Don Fenton, a captain in the Army, was saying. "It's my job. This is the busy season. I've been taking the money for doing nothing. Now I'm earning it. What do I get? I get $850 a month while I'm here. That's not bad? Hell, it should be better. It's about time people learned that they have to pay a soldier."

Fenton is thirty. He came into the Army five days after he graduated from the University of Connecticut in 1957. He had no military background in his family. His father worked for the gas company in Hartford, Connecticut. Fenton took a job in the Army because he thought it was a better one than the others he could get. After eight months in Viet Nam, Fenton still thinks he has a good job. There are a lot of people in Viet Nam who think as he does. To them, making war is an occupation.

Fenton was standing in the compound at Pleiku. It is a cluster of old red tile-roofed French buildings and newer white cement ones put up by Americans. And then tents heavy with the smell of waterproofing oil and huts made of sandbags and rolls of barbed wire and sentries who are not put out for show. Fenton was back in Pleiku from his station in a place called Tan Canh, which is out in the jungle-covered hills.

While he talked, Fenton kept fumbling for a cigarette. His fingers kept jabbing onto the side of the package instead of going inside it. Nobody walks away from Tan Canh with the same nerves he brought with him.

"I found it interesting," Fenton was saying, "interesting, worthwhile, and necessary. The only bad thing with it is that I'm married. I had to write my wife about some of it. She knows where I was stationed and she's read the names of villages in the newspapers. Finally she wrote me and said she'd rather know all about it than keep getting these 'everything fine' notes. So I just started to write her and say that there was an operation in such and such a place and that I was there. I'd leave it at that.

"Oh, I don't like being away from her. That kills you. But she understands. My career depends on how well I do over here. How could you be in the Army and want a future in it and not come to Viet Nam?"

The Army used a careful process to put Fenton in Viet Nam. There were no middle-of-the-night orders and a hurried telephone call to home or a last kiss in a crowded waiting room some place. Fenton went to Viet Nam the way Wall Street banks send representatives to the Far East. He received his orders last April. In September he was in a school at Fort Bragg. After that he attended a language school in Oakland, California. On January 18, trained for the jungles, able to speak Vietnamese, his wife and new daughter home with her mother in Hartford, he flew to Viet Nam as a professional soldier. Fighting was a clinical thing, his living.

Once they wrote mystically of soldiers thinking about how they would react the first time they came under fire. This is of the forties. The professionals of 1965 step out and go to work with a gun. "Scared," Fenton was saying, "scared as hell. But that doesn't get in the way. You're paid for being here."

In July, a place caled Dak To was overrun. Fenton led a group of Vietnamese in to relieve it. They were caught on a road in an ambush and fifteen were killed. When Fenton talks about it, he draws diagrams of the L-shaped ambushes the Viet Cong set, and he describes it flatly.

"I have 125 days to go here," he was saying. "When I go home I'd like to be assigned some place near a college so I could go for a master's degree. What do I want it for? Why shouldn't I want to get one? Education never hurts you in any business. And that's all the Army is. A business."

An hour away, on the edge of the landing runways at Da Nang, Pappy Hilbert sat on a packing case and smoked a cigarette in the Marine helicopter he flies in. Pappy is not a captain. He is a sergent in the Marine Corps. He looks at it from a working man's viewpoint, not an executive's. But he has been in the service for eighteen years and he intends to stay until he's too old.

"I'd have to get me a job payin' me four dollars an hour to make the equivalent of what I'm makin' now," he was saying. "I understand in the States it can get pretty hard to get a job you like. Here, I know anything happens to my wife or family, they just go to the hospital on the base in the States. And I know the kids are gettin' a good schoolin'. Like today. It's raining, it's miserable. I can just set over here and know everything's taken care of.

"Hell, I tried it the other way. I went out and I was a truckdriver, then I hired myself out as a fry cook. I went into a union and got me a job as a second chef. At this place in Santa Ana. I got no satisfaction out of it. What the hell, cookin' for people. At least here I'm gettin' satisfactions."

"Out of what?"

"Out of keepin' them alive. A man gets a lot of satisfaction pickin' up these kids in hills gettin' hit and gettin' them back here."

Pappy is out of Jacksonville, North Carolina. He has a wife and three kids living there, near Camp Le-

Jeune. It is his second tour in Viet Nam. He spent thirteen months the first time. Of his eighteen years of marriage he has been separated from his wife eleven of them.

"It's all right," he said. "Rather be here than hire me out as a fry cook."

"Fry cooks don't get shot at."

"That's their life. Second day I'm here this time, we land on the hill up there to get this kid. Two of them are bringin' him over to us. Bing! One of 'em goes down and now I got two instead of one. Then a whole load of these bastards come runnin' out of the woods toward us. We shot the hell out of them. We grabbed the two kids and took off. So I got shot at. But I saved a couple of kids. No fry cook can say that to himself."

He sat and looked out at the rain. "Hell, man don't need much here. Appreciate things more. Like last night. Got me a good cold beer last night. Never had one that tasted better."

He closed his eyes and put his head against the side of the ship and took a nap. He felt good. He'd wake up when the pilots came out to take off. He'd wake up and go right to work. Pappy Hilbert likes his job.

The Flight Deck

The *Independence* was 120 miles out through darkness and rain squalls which began when the plane left the drab coastline and ended when the plane flew out of towering clouds and into the bright sun over the carrier, which was moving at 16 knots in 240 feet of light green water.

The gray, angle-decked carrier went into a turn, walking its 80,000 tons through water and into the wind. The fighter planes, darts in the sky overhead, need a 32-knot wind blowing at them when they come onto the deck, their noses pointing to the sky, for landings. Two destroyers, white fountains of water at their bows, followed in file in the wake of the *Independence*.

It was, from the window of a plane coming in to land, the picture of the Navy that has been hanging on the sidewalk outside post offices for twenty-five years.

The *Independence* pulled out of Norfolk, Virginia, last May with 4500 men and 90 planes aboard. Now, 11,000 miles away, it moves through the South China Sea as a reminder of things that are gone.

The *Independence* was put together at the foot of Sands Street in Brooklyn from 1955 to 1958. At that time it was common to say that Brooklyn was the only place of its size in the nation that did not have a daily newspaper, a railroad station, and a left fielder. Now Brooklyn does not have a Navy yard either. The men who built the *Independence* have moved to Philadelphia and Boston. And the way of life which the carrier represents seems to be gone too. The *Independence* is a ship that was built to fight in a war that could be seen and found and somehow understood and then fought to a conclusion. Here in the summer and fall of 1965, the *Independence* is part of a grimy little thing where six men coming out of the water in a rice paddy somewhere constitute an attack.

The *Independence* sends long-nosed, exciting planes called F-4B Phantoms exploding off its deck. The planes race away at 1500 miles an hour and bomb little bridges we would spit at in ordinary war. The *Independence* sends planes known as Skyhawks roaring into the night. They dive from 15,000 feet to fire rockets into fields where a handful of men in black shirts and pants may or may not be hiding. There are no enemy carriers for the *Independence* to destroy, no big factories as we know them, no major bases for its planes to dive from the sky at. There are only clusters of nothing in Viet Nam.

The drip of Asian war comes down on the *Independence*. The carrier has lost four planes. Two of its pilots are prisoners in North Viet Nam. Anti-aircraft fire, modern anti-aircraft fire, high and accurate and heavy, meets the planes over North Viet Nam. When the planes return to hit the gun emplacements, they cannot find them. Or the fire is so heavy it isn't worth the price to go in. Surface-to-air missiles come up from the ground at them. At night, when the rocket boosters look like streetlights, the missiles can be evaded. But in the daytime the missiles are impossible to see. When sites finally are spotted and planes come back to hit them, the planes find only empty ground.

The *Independence* drips down on the Viet Cong too. The carrier planes fly thirteen hours a day, bombing and rocketing, and in North Viet Nam the war is different from what the people there were told it would be. In the South the Viet Cong must remain in small groups and must always be moving and digging holes and getting into them. They are afraid to light fires much of the time. Apparently, malaria sweeps through them. Everybody expected them to come like water under a door in July and August. The jet attacks prevented this. But it all is small. This is a war where you spend a million dollars to fight ten people.

So here is the *Independence,* magnificent and incongruous, lying off the coast of Viet Nam for forty days at a time. The aircraft carrier moves through the light green water as the only way of first-class living and fighting there is.

The captain, John E. Kennedy, was sitting in a high-backed leather chair on the left side of the nearly silent glass-enclosed bridge of the ship. Kennedy was in sunglasses, a blue baseball cap on his square face. His khakis were unwrinkled. He smoked a cigar and had a mug of coffee in front of him.

He asked quietly for another mug and a Marine who had on a white belt with a wide, highly polished brass buckle brought the mug over. A young sailor in denim work clothes ran a waxing machine over the green tiled floor.

Three sailors in white stood in the middle of the bridge, one of them turning the brass wheel of the helm when ordered. Officers in pressed khakis stood at the windows and spoke into intercoms.

A small television receiver was in front of Kennedy.

"It shows landings live and then it plays them back on tape," he said. "It cuts out a lot of arguments about whether the pilot landed right or not. See those little registers on the top of the screen? They show the plane's speed while it is landing. Now if a pilot starts arguing, they just play back the tape for him. We've made a business out of this. Take a look at the planes. Go on any carrier and you won't see paintings of naked girls and nicknames and the like on the planes. That's all gone. The whole attitude here is that it's a business."

An Admiral, James Reedy, a thickset man with gray in his crew-cut hair, was a flight down, sitting in a paneled room that had tan carpeting, easy chairs, and a long brown walnut table with blue chairs at it. The room was set up for President Kennedy, who once used it for a week. Reedy is with the Seventh Fleet. He is in charge of carriers.

"We've lost planes," Reedy said, "too many planes. The anti-aircraft fire can get pretty damn good. And the North Vietnamese are learning how to handle electronics pretty well. Their missiles ride a radar beam to the plane. You've got to read their radar. Then we had one operation accident right on this ship. An officer whose career I've followed since he was on the *Princeton* with me. He came in to land and the ship got out of control and he and the copilot went over the side. We got the bodies. That's all. I watched it right in here on television. I just had to sit here and watch them go right over the side on me. Men I knew."

Through the endless hallways of the carrier, men were going to the dentist, going for religious instruction, going into a carpeted library, or they could be found in paneled sitting rooms, watching the movie *Cleopatra* on a television screen. A lieutenant, Louis Viscomi, who was last seen tending bar in a place called Harvey's in Broad Channel, Long Island, was standing in front of the legal office talking to a seaman who is in trouble with finance companies. The finance companies have been writing the captain of the *Inde-*

pendence about the sailor. Viscomi, whose bartending got him a law degree, helps advise the sailors.

"Only a rat bastard would try and collect money off of you when you're away to a war," the sailor was saying.

"Why don't we sit down and go over the thing? It's always easier to pay," Viscomi said.

The sailor said a very bad word.

Out on the deck, crews in yellow, brown, blue, green, and red sweatshirts clustered around the black-nosed jet planes. All the crew workers had cuts and scars on their hands. The blast from the jets knocks people off their feet and onto the flight deck, which is covered with rough cement-like coating to prevent skidding.

The carrier has three catapults. The planes were wheeled onto the catapult tracks. The first one, a Phantom, sucked in air through two nostrils on its sides and burned it out the back in a stream of fire.

The head of the crew bent down and touched a button. With a crash and with steam billowing up from the catapult tracks and with red flames coming out of the jet's afterburners, the plane disappeared down the deck and into the air. Then they strarted to go from all sides. In seven minutes, the carrier had fifteen planes out in the sky. As the last one was off, the crew turned around and the first plane of an incoming group approached the deck and dropped down onto it, and its hook caught the third of four cables stretched across the deck. The cable pulled the plane to a stop.

Bright jerseys dove under the plane and got the cable off the hook. The plane taxied to the front of the deck as another one landed. When the first plane stopped, the pilot got out and too off his helmet and ran a hand through his wet hair. We walked to a doorway and went downstairs for a cup of coffee in a dining room where white-jacketed Filipino waiters served.

Off in a corner, a bald man in a white shirt and brown slacks sat over coffee. His name is Ellis Bolton. He is a technical representative of North American

Aviation. There are twenty others like him on the ship. If something goes wrong with one of his company's planes, he goes twenty-four hours and more with the project until he likes what he sees. They play a whole game on the *Independence.*

Downstairs, red lights in the dimness of the hangar deck showed white 1000-pound bombs hanging in ceiling racks. Rock-and-roll music screamed out of loudspeakers in the twenty-four-hour cafeterias where non-officers eat whenever they want. Music from hi-fi sets ran through the cubicles where the men sleep in three-decked cots, the gray nozzle of an air-conditioner sticking out over the cot on top. Down another corridor, in a room with high-backed leather chairs, Robert Gormley, a tall, balding man, stood at a lectern and spoke to the pilots in his squadron. They sat in the chairs and drank root beer out of cans. Gormley is a commander. The Navy sent him to Harvard for a year of political-science studies. They seem to have everything handled here. The *Independence* can stay out in the ocean and take care of itself for months.

Its people know what to do. Its planes can knock out a city. But there are no cities to knock out in Viet Nam. There are only these little people moving across empty land who live on cold rice which they carry in a plastic bag. The aircraft carrier does the only job that can be done against them right now. But it is not the kind of war they were thinking of in Brooklyn when they came to work every morning to build the *Independence.*

7

In Which He Sees the Dark Side of Life

Breslin deals in emotions the way some columnists deal in issues. They are the stuff of his writing and his articles gain or lose an audience by how well the public can identify with his private responses to the world. When he and they differ on what is funny, he has written a bad column.

He has a particular aptitude, though, for dealing in tragedy, pathos, and sorrow. A competitor once called him "a male sob-sister," which is somewhere near the truth because he manages to deal with emotions most papers leave to female writers. The difference is that he does his work with an odd mixture of restraint and emotionalism that manages to capture the mood of sorrow in its varying shades.

When President Kennedy was killed, Breslin was on the first jet from New York to Dallas. He knew it was his story. He became so wrapped up in it that, after filing "A Death in Emergency Room One," he went out, re-did all the research that he had gathered in the first place, and tried to file the story again. When he finished covering the Kennedy funeral in Washington he was unable to talk to anyone for several hours.

A Death in Emergency Room One

Dallas

The call bothered Malcolm Perry. "Dr. Tom Shires, STAT," the girl's voice said over the page in the doctors' cafeteria at Parkland Memorial Hospital. The "STAT" meant emergency. Nobody ever called Tom Shires, the hospital's chief resident in surgery, for an emergency. And Shires, Perry's superior, was out of town for the day. Malcolm Perry looked at the salmon croquettes on the plate in front of him. Then he put down his fork and went over to a telephone.

"This is Dr. Perry taking Dr. Shires' page," he said.

"President Kennedy has been shot. STAT," the operator said. "They are bringing him into the emergency room right now."

Perry hung up and walked quickly out of the cafeteria and down a flight of stairs and pushed through a brown door and a nurse pointed to Emergency Room One, and Dr. Perry walked into it. The room is narrow and has gray tiled walls and a cream-colored ceiling. In the middle of it, on an aluminum hospital cart, the President of the United States had been placed on his back and he was dying while a huge lamp glared at his face.

John Kennedy already had been stripped of his jacket, shirt, and T-shirt, and a staff doctor was starting to place a tube called an endotracht down the throat. Oxygen would be forced down the endotracht. Breathing was the first thing to attack. The President was not breathing.

Malcolm Perry unbuttoned his dark blue glen-plaid jacket and threw it onto the floor. He held out his hands while the nurse helped him put on gloves.

The President, Perry thought. He's bigger than I thought he was.

He noticed the tall, dark-haired girl in the plum dress that had her husband's blood all over the front of the skirt. She was standing out of the way, over against the gray tile wall. Her face was tearless and it was set, and it was to stay that way because Jacqueline Kennedy, with a terrible discipline, was not going to take her eyes from her husband's face.

Then Malcolm Perry stepped up to the aluminum hospital cart and took charge of the hopeless job of trying to keep the thirty-fifth President of the United States from death. And now, the enormousness came over him.

Here is the most important man in the world, Perry thought.

The chest was not moving. And there was no apparent heartbeat inside it. The wound in the throat was small and neat. Blood was running out of it. It was running out too fast. The occipitoparietal, which is a part of the back of the head, had a huge flap. The damage a .25-caliber bullet does as it comes out of a person's body is unbelievable. Bleeding from the head wound covered the floor.

There was a mediastinal wound in connection with the bullet hole in the throat. This means air and blood were being packed together in the chest. Perry called for a scalpel. He was going to start a tracheotomy, which is opening the throat and inserting a tube into the windpipe. The incision had to be made below the bullet wound.

"Get me Doctors Clark, McCelland, and Baxter right away," Malcolm Perry said.

Then he started the tracheotomy. There was no anesthesia. John Kennedy could feel nothing now. The wound in the back of the head told Dr. Perry that the President never knew a thing about it when he was shot, either.

While Perry worked on the throat, he said quietly, "Will somebody put a right chest tube in, please."

The tube was to be inserted so it could suction out the blood and air packed in the chest and prevent the lung from collapsing.

These things he was doing took only small minutes,

and other doctors and nurses were in the room and talking and moving, but Perry does not remember them. He saw only the throat and chest, shining under the huge lamp, and when he would look up or move his eyes between motions, he would see this plum dress and the terribly disciplined face standing over against the gray tile wall.

Just as he finished the tracheotomy, Malcolm Perry looked up and Dr. Kemp Clark, chief neurosurgeon in residency at Parkland, came in through the door. Clark was looking at the President of the United States. Then he looked at Malcolm Perry and the look told Malcolm Perry something he already knew. There was no way to save the patient.

"Would you like to leave, ma'am?" Kemp Clark said to Jacqueline Kennedy. "We can make you more comfortable outside."

Just the lips moved. "No," Jacqueline Kennedy said.

Now, Malcolm Perry's long fingers ran over the chest under him and he tried to get a heart beat, and even the suggestion of breathing, and there was nothing. There was only the still body, pale white in the light, and it kept bleeding, and now Malcolm Perry started to call for things and move his hands quickly because it all was running out.

He began to massage the chest. He had to do something to stimulate the heart. There was not time to open the chest and take the heart in his hands, so he had to massage on the surface. The aluminum cart was high. It was too high. Perry was up on his toes so he could have leverage.

"Will somebody please get me a stool," he said.

One was placed under him. He sat on it, and for ten minutes he massaged the chest. Over in the corner of the room, Dr. Kemp Clark kept watching the electrocardiogram for some sign that the massaging was creating action in the President's heart. There was none. Dr. Clark turned his head from the electrocardiogram.

"It's too late, Mac," he said to Malcolm Perry.

The long fingers stopped massaging and they were lifted from the white chest. Perry got off the stool and stepped back.

Dr. M. T. Jenkins, who had been working the oxygen flow, reached down from the head of the aluminum cart. He took the edges of a white sheet in his hands. He pulled the sheet up over the face of John Fitzgerald Kennedy. The IBM clock on the wall said it was 1 p.m. The date was November 22, 1963.

Three policemen were moving down the hall outside Emergency Room One now, and they were calling to everybody to get out of the way. But this was not needed, because everybody stepped out of the way automatically when they saw the priest who was behind the police. His name was the Reverend Oscar Huber, a small seventy-year-old man who was walking quickly.

Malcolm Perry turned to leave the room as Father Huber came in. Perry remembers seeing the priest go by him. And he remembers his eyes seeing that plum dress and that terribly disciplined face for the last time as he walked out of Emergency Room One and slumped into a chair in the hall.

Everything that was inside that room now belonged to Jacqueline Kennedy and Father Oscar Huber and the things in which they believe.

"I'm sorry. You have my deepest sympathies," Father Huber said.

"Thank you," Jacqueline Kennedy said.

Father Huber pulled the white sheet down so he could anoint the forehead of John Fitzgerald Kennedy. Jacqueline Kennedy was standing beside the priest, her head bowed, her hands clasped across the front of the plum dress that was stained with blood which came from her husband's head. Now this old priest held up his right hand and he began the chant that Roman Catholic priests have said over their dead for centuries.

"Si vivis, ego te absolvo a peccatis tuis. In nomine Patris et Filii et Spiritus Sancti, amen."

The prayer said, "If you are living, I absolve you

from your sins. In the name of the Father and of the son and the Holy Ghost, amen."

The priest reached into his pocket and took out a small vial of holy oil. He put the oil on his right thumb and made a cross on President Kennedy's forehead. Then he blessed the body again and started to pray quietly.

"Eternal rest grant unto him, O Lord," Father Huber said.

"And let perpetual light shine upon him," Jacqueline Kennedy answered. She did not cry.

Father Huber prayed like this for fifteen minutes. And for fifteen minutes Jacqueline Kennedy kept praying aloud with him. Her voice did not waver. She did not cry. From the moment a bullet hit her husband in the head and he went down onto his face in the back of the car on the street in Dallas, there was something about this woman that everybody who saw her keeps talking about. She was in shock. But somewhere, down under that shock some place, she seemcd to know that there is a way to act when the President of the United States has been assassinated. She was going to act that way, and the fact that the President was her husband made it more important that she stand and look at him and not cry.

When he was finished praying, Father Huber turned and took her hand. "I am shocked," he said.

"Thank you for taking care of the President," Jacqueline Kennedy said.

"I am convinced that his soul has not left his body," Father Huber said. "This was a valid last sacrament."

"Thank you," she said.

Then he left. He had been eating lunch at his rectory at Holy Trinity Church when he heard the news. He had an assistant drive him to the hospital immediately. After that, everything happened quickly and he did not feel anything until later. He sat behind his desk in the rectory, and the magnitude of what had happened came over him.

"I've been a priest for thirty-two years," Father

Huber said. "The first time I was present at a death? A long time ago. Back in my home in Perryville, Missouri, I attended a lady who was dying of pneumonia. She was in her own bed. But I remember that. But this. This is different. Oh, it isn't the blood. You see, I've anointed so many. Accident victims. I anointed once a boy who was only in pieces. No, it wasn't the blood. It was the enormity of it. I'm just starting to realize it now."

Then Father Huber showed you to the door. He was going to say prayers.

It came the same way to Malcolm Perry. When the day was through, he drove to his home in the Walnut Hills section. When he walked into the house, his daughter, Jolene, six and a half, ran up to him. She had papers from school in her hand.

"Look what I did today in school, Daddy," she said.

She made her father sit down in a chair and look at her schoolwork. The papers were covered with block letters and numbers. Perry looked at them. He thought they were good. He said so, and his daughter chattered happily. Malcolm, his three-year-old son, ran into the room after him, and Perry started to reach for him.

Then it hit him. He dropped the papers with the block numbers and letters and he did not notice his son.

"I'm tired," he said to his wife, Jennine. "I've never been tired like this in my life."

Tired is the only way one felt in Dallas yesterday. Tired and confused and wondering why it was that everything looked so different. This was a bright Texas day with a snap to the air, and there were cars on the streets and people on the sidewalks. But everything seemed unreal.

At 10 a.m. we dodged cars and went out and stood in the middle lane of Elm Street, just before the second street light; right where the road goes down and, twenty yards farther, starts to turn to go under the overpass. It was right at this spot, right where this long crack ran through the gray Texas asphalt, that the bullets reached President Kennedy's car.

Right up the little hill, and towering over you, was the building. Once it was dull red brick. But that was a long time ago when it housed the J. W. Deere Plow Company. It has been sandblasted since and now the bricks are a light rust color. The windows on the first three floors are covered by closed venetian blinds, but the windows on the other floors are bare. Bare and dust-streaked and high. Factory-window high. The ugly kind of factory window. Particularly at the corner window on the sixth floor, the one where this Oswald and his scrambled egg of a mind stood with the rifle so he could kill the President.

You stood and memorized the spot. It is just another roadway in a city, but now it joins Ford's Theatre in the history of this nation.

"R. L. Thornton Freeway. Keep Right," the sign said. "Stemmons Freeway. Keep Right," another sign said. You went back between the cars and stood on a grassy hill which overlooks the road. A red convertible turned onto Elm Street and went down the hill. It went past the spot with the crack in the asphalt and then, with every foot it went, you could see that it was getting out of range of the sixth-floor window of this rust-brick building behind you. A couple of yards. That's all John Kennedy needed on this road Friday.

But he did not get them. So when a little bit after 1 o'clock Friday afternoon the phone rang in the Oneal Funeral Home, 3206 Oak Lawn, Vernon B. Oneal answered.

The voice on the other end spoke quickly. "This is the Secret Service calling from Parkland Hospital," it said. "Please select the best casket in your house and put it in a general coach and arrange for a police escort and bring it here to the hospital as quickly as you humanly can. It is for the President of the United States. Thank you."

The voice went off the phone. Oneal called for Ray Gleason, his bookkeeper, and a workman to help him take a solid bronze casket out of the place and load it onto a hearse. It was for John Fitzgerald Kennedy.

Yesterday, Oneal left his shop early. He said he was too tired to work.

Malcolm Perry was at the hospital. He had on a blue suit and a dark blue striped tie and he sat in a big conference room and looked out the window. He is a tall, reddish-haired thirty-four-year-old, who understands that everything he saw or heard on Friday is a part of history, and he is trying to get down, for the record, everything he knows about the death of the thirty-fifth President of the United States.

"I never saw a President before," he said.

Everybody's Crime

Washington

The Spanish Ambassador was on his knees. The people who were in line behind him walked around him. The coffin was draped with an American flag. But at the bottom, just before the black velvet started, a little bit of the mahogany wood showed. The body of the thirty-fifth President of the United States is inside the wood. Or whatever it is that is left after the .25-caliber bullet that ripped his head apart. You noticed the mahogany wood because it was reflecting the bright, bare light the six television Kleig lights threw onto the floor of the rotunda of the Capitol building.

The place was silent. The people, silent people who had blank faces, moved around the coffin in two orderly lines. They were trying to pick up their feet so their shoes would make as little of the noise of shuffling as possible. The Spanish Ambassador said prayers.

A Negro woman, a black kerchief covering her head, walked around him. A little boy of about three held onto her right hand. The boy had on long pants and an overcoat and a blue cap. He was looking away from the coffin. All the police and soldiers and television lights caught his attention.

The mother yanked his hand. "Look this way, Roger," she whispered. The little head turned and the woman in the black scarf bent over and put her cheek against the boy's. "He's right there under that flag," she whispered. "That's President Kennedy there. Look at it, Roger. Mommy wants you to know about this."

Then she was gone and there was somebody else there. The Spanish Ambassador was on his feet now, and he was walking by too. The place was quiet and unreal, and far above you, up at the top of the dome, shafts of light coming in through the windows crisscrossed each other.

There was a sound in the hallway to the right, the hallway which leads to the Senate offices. The two policemen there moved back. Then you saw what was making the sound. It was an honor guard coming out. There were six of them. They were holding their rifles at carry arms, which means the butt of the rifle is just a little bit off the floor. And they moved imperceptibly. But their heels clicked against the floor in cadence each time they moved, and this was what was making the little noise.

When they got out on the rotunda floor, light from the television Kleig lights sprayed off the bayonets of their guns. Then you noticed the soldiers on duty for the first time. They were at parade rest around the coffin. Six of them. But they had been so motionless that you didn't even notice them before this. You had been seeing only the coffin and the people.

But now you noticed the soldiers. You saw the ones standing so stiffly around the coffin, and the others moving slowly and clicking their heels while the bayonets sparkled. And then everything came over you, and you stood in the rotunda of the Capitol building of the United States of America and looked at a coffin that held the body of a President whose head had been blown off by a gun fired by one of his own people and now you fell apart inside and there was this terrible sense of confusion and inability to understand what was going on. And there were tears; of course there were tears, there have been tears for three days now; and then you started talking out loud.

"Oh, Christ, what are we doing here?" It was a prayer, not a blasphemy.

Dallas. You started to think about Dallas. In Dallas they sat and told you that a Communist shot the President of the United States. They sat and told you that, while everybody in the town with any brains knew that John Fitzgerald Kennedy, the President of the United States, was shot because this is a country that has let the art of hating grow so strong that now we kill our Presidents because of it.

And Dallas does not own hate. Dallas is a collective word and it means Birmingham and Tuscaloosa and, yes, Scarsdale and Bay Ridge and the Bronx too. Dallas means every place where people in this nation stand off with their smugness and their paychecks and their cute little remarks, and run their lives on the basis of hate. Everybody has a piece of this murder. Everybody who ever stood off and said, "That Jew bastard," and everybody who ever said, "I don't want niggers near me," is part of this murder.

It's an Honor

Washington

Clifton Pollard was pretty sure he was going to be working on Sunday, so when he woke up at 9 a.m. in his three-room apartment on Corcoran Street, he put on khaki overalls before going into the kitchen for breakfast. His wife, Nettie, made bacon and eggs for him. Pollard was in the middle of eating them when he received the phone call he had been expecting.

It was from Mazo Kawalchik, who is the foreman of the gravediggers at Arlington National Cemetery, which is where Pollard works for a living. "Polly, could you please be here by eleven o'clock this morning?" Kawalchik asked. "I guess you know what it's for."

Pollard did. He hung up the phone, finished breakfast, and left his apartment so he could spend Sunday digging a grave for John Fitzgerald Kennedy.

When Pollard got to the row of yellow wooden garages where the cemetery equipment is stored, Kawalchik and John Metzler, the cemetery superintendent, were waiting for him.

"Sorry to pull you out like this on a Sunday," Metzler said. "Oh, don't say that," Pollard said. "Why, it's an honor for me to be here."

Pollard got behind the wheel of a machine called a reverse hoe. Gravedigging is not done with men and shovels at Arlington. The reverse hoe is a green machine with a yellow bucket which scoops the earth toward the operator, not away from it as a crane does. At the bottom of the hill in front of the Tomb of the Unknown Soldier, Pollard started the digging.

Leaves covered the grass. When the yellow teeth of the reverse hoe first bit into the ground, the leaves made a threshing sound which could be heard above the motor of the machine. When the bucket came up with its first scoop of dirt, Metzler, the cemetery superintendent, walked over and looked at it.

"That's nice soil," Metzler said.

"I'd like to save a little of it," Pollard said. "The machine made some tracks in the grass over here and I'd like to sort of fill them in and get some good grass growing there, I'd like to have everything, you know, nice."

James Winners, another gravedigger, nodded. He said he would fill a couple of carts with this extra-good soil and take it back to the garage and grow good turf on it.

"He was a good man," Pollard said.

"Yes, he was," Metzler said.

"Now they're going to come and put him right here in this grave I'm making up," Pollard said. "You know, it's an honor just for me to do this."

Pollard is forty-two. He is a slim man with a mustache who was born in Pittsburgh and served as a private in the 352d Engineers battalion in Burma in World War II. He is an equipment operator, grade 10, which means he gets $3.01 an hour. One of the last to serve John Fitzgerald Kennedy, who was the thirty-fifth President of this country, was a working man who earns $3.01 an hour and said it was an honor to dig the grave.

Yesterday morning, at 11:15, Jacqueline Kennedy started walking toward the grave. She came out from under the north portico of the White House and slowly followed the body of her husband, which was in a flag-covered coffin that was strapped with two black leather belts to a black caisson that had polished brass axles. She walked straight and her head was high. She walked down the bluestone and blacktop driveway and through shadows thrown by the branches of seven leafless oak trees. She walked slowly past the sailors who held up flags of the states of this country. She walked past silent people who strained to see her and then, seeing her, dropped their heads and put their hands over their eyes. She walked out the northwest gate and into the middle of Pennsylvania Avenue. She walked with tight steps and her head was high and she followed the body of her murdered husband through the streets of Washington.

Everybody watched her while she walked. She is the mother of two fatherless children and she was walking into the history of this country because she was showing everybody who felt old and helpless and without hope that she had this terrible strength that everybody needed so badly. Even though they had killed her husband and his blood ran onto her lap while he died, she could walk through the streets and to his grave and help us all while she walked.

There was mass, and then the procession to Arlington. When she came up to the grave at the cemetery, the casket already was in place. It was set between brass railings and it was ready to be lowered into the ground. This must be the worst time of all, when a woman sees the coffin with her husband inside and it is in place to be buried under the earth. Now she knows that it is forever. Now there is nothing. There is no casket to kiss or hold with your hands. Nothing material to cling to. But she walked up to the burial area and stood in front of a row of six green-covered chairs and she started to sit down, but then she got up quickly and stood straight because she was not going to sit down until the man directing the funeral told her what seat he wanted her to take.

The ceremonies began, with jet planes roaring overhead and leaves falling from the sky. On this hill behind the coffin, people prayed aloud. They were cameramen and writers and soldiers and Secret Service men and they were saying prayers out loud and choking. In front of the grave, Lyndon Johnson kept his head turned to his right. He is President and he had to remain composed. It was better that he did not look at the casket and grave of John Fitzgerald Kennedy too often.

Then it was over and black limousines rushed under the cemetery trees and out onto the boulevard toward the White House.

"What time is it?" a man standing on the hill was asked. He looked at his watch.

"Twenty minutes past three," he said.

Clifton Pollard wasn't at the funeral. He was over behind the hill, digging graves for $3.01 an hour in another section of the cemetery. He didn't know who the graves were for. He was just digging them and then covering them with boards.

"They'll be used," he said. "We just don't know when."

"I tried to go over to see the grave," he said. "But it was so crowded a soldier told me I couldn't get through. So I just stayed here and worked, sir. But I'll get over there later a little bit. Just sort of look around and see how it is, you know. Like I told you, it's an honor."

At the beginning of 1965, Breslin was planning to go down to Washington to cover President Johnson's first inaugural ball. This elicited the following comment from Art Buchwald, a friend and master needler:

JIM BELLOWS, EDITOR
UNDERSTAND JIMMY BRESLIN COMING DOWN FOR INAUGURATION. IF YOU WILL CHECK MY CONTRACT BRESLIN IS NOT ALLOWED SOUTH OF BALTIMORE WHILE I'M WRITING FROM WASHINGTON. I FEEL THE HERALD TRIBUNE WOULD BE MAKING A MISTAKE SENDING HIM HERE AT THE HEIGHT OF THE SOCIAL SEASON. BRESLIN'S MANNERS AND CLOTHES JUST WOULDN'T FIT IN WITH THE TYPE OF PEOPLE EXPECTED IN WASHINGTON NEXT WEEK, AND I STRONGLY URGE YOU TO PERSUADE HIM AGAINST MAKING WHAT I CONSIDER WOULD BE A GRAVE SOCIAL ERROR. THE GREAT SOCIETY IS NOT EQUIPPED TO TAKE CARE OF PEOPLE LIKE BRESLIN—AT LEAST NOT YET.

Buchwald

To which Breslin sent the following answer in the name of the editor:

ART BUCHWALD, HUMORIST
WASHINGTON BUREAU
THANKS FOR OFFERING US SUCH PROFOUND EDITORIAL ADVICE. I AM CONFERRING WITH BRESLIN, AND WE HOPE SHORTLY TO COME UP WITH A BRESLIN-STYLE COMPROMISE. MEANWHILE, MR. BRESLIN HAS SENT MARVIN THE TORCH AND BAD EDDIE SOUTH TO PERSUADE YOU THAT THE GREAT SOCIETY INCLUDES JIMMY BRESLIN TOO.

Bellows

P.S. JIMMY WANTS TO KNOW WHAT ROUTE YOUR CHILDREN TAKE WHEN THEY GO TO SCHOOL—AND WHAT TIME?

Breslin never got to Washington that time. Winston Churchill, old and ill, was suddenly reported to be dying. To Breslin, as to many others, he was the last of the great wartime triumvirate, a hero beyond any living man, a legend—the stuff of a story. Breslin wanted to go to London immediately.

The problem was that he had no passport, no inoculations, and no clean shirts. David Wise, the *Trib*'s Washington Bureau chief, arranged for the State Department to notify the British Foreign office so that Breslin could get into the country without a passport and obtain one in London from the American Embassy. Dick Wald persuaded Pan American World Airways to take him aboard without any of the normal papers of an international traveler. The proprietor of a men's shop on Queens Boulevard delivered a new shirt and sports jacket to the airport (Breslin ordered them by phone), and he was on his way.

In London he refused to get a smallpox shot required for return to the United States. Whether he ever did or not is a matter of conjecture. He says he didn't. He worked for part of the time with Seymour K. Freidin, the *Trib*'s foreign editor, resident in London.

As usual, his copy from abroad was preceded by a flow of memos abusing the editors in New York—whom he phoned every night "just for the sound of a human voice" —and complaining about whatever was at hand.

NOTE TO JIM BELLOWS:

I AM TELLING YOU WHAT I TOLD FREIDIN. I WOULDN'T OF COME HERE IF I THOUGHT I HAD TO GET THINGS PUT IN MY ARM. IF ANYBODY IS GOING TO PUT SOMETHING INTO MY ARM IT IS GOING TO BE ME AND I AM GOING TO BE MAIN-LINING GOOD HORSE IN THERE, NOT SMALL POX. AS FOR GETTING BACK TO NY, PLEASE BE ADVISED APPROXIMATELY ONE HALF PERSONNEL KENNEDY AIRPORT OWE TABS AT PEPE'S AND WHEN I WALK THRU CUSTOMS YOU'LL THINK DEGAULLE IS ARRIVING.

REGARDS Breslin

BUDDY WEISS:

WHERE WERE YOU WHEN I CALLED BEFORE?

YOU WERE DELIBERATELY DUCKING ME BECAUSE I KNOW YOU WAS DOING SOMETHING BAD TO MY STORY. I WILL FIX YOU FOR THAT. YOU'RE NOT FOOLING ME BY NOT ANSWERING THE PHONE.

Jimmy Breslin

BUDDY WEISS, NEW YORK.

I SEEN WHAT YOU SAID TO FREIDIN. YOU ARE TAKING POT SHOTS AT ME LIKE I WAS A RANK SUCKER. WELL, LET ME TELL YOU, I KNOW WHAT IT IS TO HAVE PEOPLE AGAINST ME AND THINKING BAD THINGS ABOUT ME ALL THE TIME AND I KNOW HOW TO HANDLE IT. SO I JUST SENT A SCHEMEY A CABLEGRAM AND YOU ARE IN FOR IT THIS WEEKEND. WATCH THAT BABCOCK REAL CLOSE. HE IS ABOUT TO PERFORM.

JB

MESSAGE FOR BUDDY WEISS, NEW YORK.

YOU TELL THAT OLD PHONE OPERATOR THAT I AM GOING TO COME BACK AND SET HER HAIR ON FIRE. I CALLED JIM BEFORE AND THEN ASKED THE OPERATOR TO SWITCH ME TO ANOTHER NUMBER IN NEW YORK, SOMETHING WHICH HAS BEEN DONE BY ME A THOUSAND TIMES. SHE SAID WHILE I AM SITTING IN A MISERABLE PHONE BOOTH IN LONDON, THAT SHE CANNOT DO IT BECAUSE SHE HAS A RULE AGAINST IT. I AM NERVOUS AND I HAVE NOTHING TO DO EXCEPT GET UPSET AND AGGRAVATED. WHEN I COME BACK I AM GOING TO FIND OUT PERSONALLY WHAT THIS IS ALL ABOUT.

Jimmy Breslin

There was none of that jollity in the stories he was writing. He had never been in England before and he was trying to convey the sense of an impending death and its meaning in a strange country. The method he chose again, as when he covered the Kennedy funeral and concentrated for a day on the small details that made the life of one of the gravediggers, was to pick out the particular details that could convey a general impression, the individuals who could represent a nation.

The first sentence of his first story from London was about the tangle of black drainpipes on the Churchill home at Hyde Park Gate. The men he quoted were Sergeant Murray and the drinkers at the Crooked Billet. While others kept the vigil in front of the Churchill home, he introduced himself to Lady Cynthia and tried to tell about her way of life, and he went down to Dover to recall the incredible sea-lift that turned Dunkirk from a disaster to a triumph.

'E Was There When 'E Was Needed

London

He was dying in a bedroom on the first floor of a three-story attached brick house that has a tangle of black drainpipes running down its front. His wife stood at the open front window, white curtains blowing in on her while she arranged flowers in a silver bowl.

The house, No. 28 Hyde Park Gate, is on a narrow, treeless street that comes to a dead end and looks up at the streaked kitchen windows and television antennas of the backs of faded apartment houses.

His voice once directed the affairs of continents and his words will move men forever, and he is of history. But only his family and doctors came to him yesterday. At ninety, Sir Winston Churchill is being allowed to die in the understatement and privacy by which his people live.

Sergeant Edmund Murray, of Scotland Yard, stands in front of the black doors and silver handles of No. 28. Murray, Winston Churchill's bodyguard for fifteen years, has a mustache. He stood in the rain yesterday in a black derby hat, gray pinstriped suit and vest, and blue striped tie. His middle bulged against a brown tweed coat. He kept his right hand clamped over a pipe to keep it dry.

"Ups," he said. "What's this now?"

A woman in a raincoat and brown low-heeled shoes started to walk out of the small crowd. Murray's eyebrows went up. The woman stopped and went back.

There were only nine uniformed policemen on the street, and they were unnecessary. A crowd of 150 reporters stood in the street as if they were in church. The rest of the people who came walked down the block in twos and threes and they would stand for a moment at a distance, looking at the brick house, and then they would leave, only to have others take their place. Every few minutes a boy carrying flowers, or a messenger bringing telegrams, would come up to the house.

"Ring the bell," Murray told them. "They'll answer." They pushed the silver bell and the black door opened and a butler in double-breasted jacket and baggy pants opened it, took what they had, nodded thanks, then closed the door. The rest of London stayed away from Hyde Park Gate while Winston Churchill was dying yesterday.

"Why people have respect for tradition and procedure?" Murray was saying. "We're a civilized country. The people won't want to come here. They don't want to be accused of morbid curiosity."

Two houses up, a door opened and a man came out with a black and white cocker spaniel on a leash. He stopped and looked down at the sidewalk. A container of milk had been spilled there and the rain was spreading the milk all over the sidewalk in front of the house.

"Oh Lord," the man said. He shook his head.

Two doors away, one of the great figures in the history of the world was dying. The man turned and walked the other way with the cocker spaniel.

This was Britain's public face yesterday while it waited for Winston Churchill to die. The enormity of England without Churchill, even an ancient Churchill who had only short periods of lucidness each day in his last years, seemed to shake no one at Hyde Park Gate or Fleet Street or Mayfair or any of the other places in this city that are known.

It was different in the Crooked Billet. The Crooked Billet is a pub with three entrances to it on the corner of Cable Street, which is in the East End, and Cable Street is where the dock workers live. Yesterday afternoon, they came in and drank stout and rum and talked about Winston Churchill as they talk about a friend.

The Crooked Billet has a red tin ceiling and a round bar, cut into three separate small bars by ancient frosted glass partitions. In one of the bars, the men were standing in their overcoats at the bar and the old women, kerchiefs and cloth coats, sat at little three-legged tables.

" 'Ow's he now?" a man at the bar said.

"Not good."

"Well, that nyme Churchill is respected everywhere," he said.

"Did you ever meet him?"

" 'E was around," he said. " 'E was around in the raids."

"Did he ever say anything to you?"

"Ask that la-ty," he said. He pointed to a heavy woman who sat at a table alone, her thick legs resting in front of a small gas heater. She had one hand wrapped around a black leather change purse. The other held a pint glass of stout.

"Moad," he said. " 'E wants to ask you somethin'."

"What do you want?" she said.

"Did you ever see Churchill?"

" 'E saved our skins, why wouldn't I have seen 'im?" she said.

" 'E saved our skins for eighteen months," one of the other women said.

"When did you see him?" Moad was asked.

"The Sunday raid," she said. "When else would I see 'im?"

"When was that?"

" 'Ow can I remember that? I've 'ad so much trouble, 'ow can I remember when it was. It was the Sunday raid, that's what it was."

"Was it bad?"

She slammed her glass on the table. "Was it bad? Get away from me, was it bad. There were twenty-six of them dead at one turnin' and one of them was my mother."

"Where?"

"Where?" she snapped. "Under the archway. Right down the street. It was a shelter, only it collapsed and I stood with my three and watched them pull my mother out dead and I was standin' there with my 'usband away and my mother dead and then Churchill came and he told us all. 'E said for every one they dropped 'e'd drop three on them and we knew 'e meant it and 'e was goin' to do what 'e said. And 'e done it. I'll never forget that Sunday morning."

Her hand came out in a fist and she shook it and her face flushed and she told you again, " 'E said 'e'd give them three for every one they dropped and 'e done what 'e said, just like I knew 'e would."

" 'E was there when 'e was needed," another one of the women said.

"We'd a been lost without 'im," the man said.

Then one of the other women said something and so did another one, and the man at the bar started talking and now Moad's fist shook at the air again and here in this little bar, with over twenty years gone since anger was needed, the fire came into them again and now you could see just what kind of job this Winston Churchill did for his own when they needed him.

He lies dying in bed, with the brandy going to waste on a shelf and his mouth unable to hold a cigar and the blood spilling inside his head. And now, for the ages to come, everybody is going to be explaining his life.

I'm right with Moad, who sits in a pub twenty years later with her fist in the air and a snarl coming out of her mouth.

She puts it all together for you.

Dunkirk Recalled

Dover, England

The dull-colored water came from the Channel through an opening in the sea wall, dipping down first, so that seaweed showed on the bottom of a buoy, then coming up high and foaming, and running across the harbor to the stone wall at the foot of the statue. With a slap, it turned to angry cold white. The water drenched the salt-blackened statue.

"What's the statue for?" the guy driving the car was asked.

"That? Oh, that's just a statue they put up for the fishermen who went to Dunkirk that time."

"Oh, that's all?"

"That's all. Just one of those civic things."

"Can you take me someplace where one of those fishermen might be around?"

"Sure."

The car started down the street. White water spilled over the stone wall at one edge of it. On the other side, a wall of white chalk, corrugated with black dirt, climbed out of the ground and went a thousand feet into the air.

The drive was to the Park Inn, a pub across from the gray stone city hall. George Hawkins stood behind the tiny bar.

"Somebody who went to Dunkirk?" Hawkins said. "Now isn't that funny? I haven't heard this brought up in years.

"Now let me see," Hawkins said. He looked up and began to think.

Three people were at the bar and two young kids were off in a hallway, throwing darts at a board. One of them stopped and looked in.

"John Walker," the kid said. "He was there. Tell him to see John Walker."

John Walker was at home, in a two-story tan brick house on a green lane in Temple Ewell, which is a cluster of houses set in the hills behind the white cliffs. And he was surprised too to find somebody who had come to see him about Dunkirk.

"Well now," he said at the front door. "Must be twenty-two, twenty-three years now, isn't it? What was the date? The twenty-seventh of May, something like that, wasn't it?"

It was twenty-five years ago this May, and 335,000 British and French troops were carried off the sands by

1000 ships, most of them only fishing boats. It was Churchill's idea, he called it "Operation Dynamo," and he hoped to save 30,000 troops with it. People like Walker, who came in a cabin cruiser and maneuvered the thing in shallow water as if he were walking on sidewalk, accomplished something that children will be memorizing in school a hundred years from now. He cannot remember the date of it, however.

"Well," Walker said, "why don't you come inside and we'll chat a bit. I hope I can remember enough for you."

"I'm in the shiptending service," he said. "We bring out docking pilots and we do some towing. I can sit home here and wait for a call if something comes up. Now what is it you'd like to know, Dunkirk?"

He looked at the ceiling. "I had a forty-footer, the *Nayland,* its nyme was. It was quite sturdily built then. But a bloody little rifle could have knocked it out. Well, we were commandeered and they said we were going to land some troops at Ramsgate and that was all. Then we were handed some food packages and I asked what that was. 'For the survivors,' they said. Well, of course, then we knew. We traveled all night, my boat only did eight knots, and by dawn we could see all the troops on the sand then, you see.

"You know," Walker said, "it wasn't exactly simple. You had to know water a bit, and there was wreckage all over and you had to watch that it didn't foul your propeller."

"Was that the big worry?"

"Oh, yes," he said. "The bombers, of course. One of the other boats came in and started towin' lifeboats out and I came to help him and a bomber comes over and scores a direct hit and blows them all. We had a little bit of shrapnel from it, too. You had to be more concerned with the overcoats floatin' in the water. If one of them got around your propeller you were in bad trouble. I was more afraid of the bloody overcoats than I was the old bombers."

Out in the car, Walker drove slowly down to the

statue. It is just a short distance. The White Cliffs of Dover, bombs, and the fishermen of Dover who saved the troops at Dunkirk. Churchill dies by fractions of an inch back in a house in London. Here in Dover, on a bone-chilling day, reminders of the era he lived most, the era which made him the most famous man of the century, are all around you.

He stopped at the statue. Seagulls circled it, and then the spray from the ocean hitting the stone wall caused them to fly up, complaining.

"It's a nice statue," he said. "Least they put a fisherman's hat on it, not some big thing nobody around here wears."

The Last Great Statue

London

In the morning rain and mist, the tan pebbles were unlittered in front of No. 28 Hyde Park Gate. A street cleaner moved over to the side to get out of the way of the blue car coming down the street. The old doctor in the front seat was fumbling with the door handle before the car stopped.

Up at the corner, a mother and her daughter, in black derby hats and short tan jackets, sat on white horses and waited for the traffic light on Kensington High Street. When it changed, the horses walked across the street and into Hyde Park. Then the daughter broke her horse into a trot under the leafless trees. The doctor was in the house now, white scarf and overcoat off, looking at the old man in the green bedjacket who was in the first-floor bedroom in the rear.

The rest of London was quiet and empty in the wet Sunday morning. Lord Nelson stood on his spire, high over the black lions and water fountains of Trafalgar Square. The Duke of Wellington glared down at the taxicabs and delivery wagons moving around his plaza. Queen Victoria sat grandly on her throne, surrounded by angels, her back turned on Buckingham Palace.

The water dripped from Gladstone, who was stationed by Saint Clement Danes Church. And at 8:05 a.m., on January 24, 1965, in the rear first-floor bedroom of No. 28 Hyde Park Gate, the old man in the green bed jacket died with the curtains drawn and a lamp turned on and he became England's last great statue.

Sir Winston Spencer Churchill, who saved his nation; saved, perhaps, the entire English-speaking world, stepped into history with its scrolls and statues, and he will be the last who ever will do it as he did because the world never again can survive the things that had to be done in the years he lived.

He died wordlessly. He was a man who put deep brass and powerful strings into words, and then built them up to a drum roll to reach out and grab people and shake them by the shoulders and in their hearts. But he had not uttered a word for ten days when he lay dying in a coma, while his heart throbbed and struggled to throw it off.

There were ten people who watched him die.

"It was strange," one of them who was in the room was saying later. "One moment here was this ancient man, barely breathing. Then the years seemed to come right off his face and he died and he looked just as he did when he was running the country. He simply became younger in death."

A young naval lieutenant was on duty on the sixth floor of the Ministry of Defence building when his phone rang. He picked it up and said, "Sir," when he heard the voice on the other end, and then he reached for a yellow message pad.

"With deep regret," he wrote as the voice over the phone dictated to him, "the Admiralty Board learned today of the death of Sir Winston Churchill. All flags are to be lowered to half staff. The Admiralty Board has today also sent a message of condolences to Lady Churchill."

The lieutenant hung up the phone and signed the message, then put it into a Lamson tube near his desk. The message went through the tube to the fifth-floor communications center and from there it was wired to all commands of Her Majesty's Royal Navy.

Once, in 1939, the message to the fleet read: "Winston is back," and seamen cheered. But that was twenty-six years ago and Churchill was only sixty-four and he was just starting to teach his nation that great wartime lesson in heart. Yesterday the message called him Sir Winston Churchill and the seamen who heard it were too young to have served under him.

David Bruce was having breakfast. His silver hair brushed back, a tie and blue shirt on, he lounged over coffee in the high-ceilinged sitting room of Winfield House, the American Ambassador's residence.

"The phone, sir," somebody said.

He picked it up. It was the duty officer at the embassy telling him that Churchill was dead.

"I'll be in," Bruce said. Bruce has had a three-man group working on details for Churchill's death for some time now. Yesterday, with the death a fact, there was more to do. The United States is to show its respects, as it never has shown them for a foreigner before, at the funeral of Sir Winston Churchill on Saturday.

In a big wooden-floored living room of his apartment on Eaton Place, Sir John Langford-Holt heard the news on the radio and he looked down for a moment and then he told his wife he wanted to go to church immediately.

"I'm almost thankful it is over for him," Langford-Holt said. For the last two years Langford-Holt, a Tory MP, was assigned, by silent agreement, the task of seeing to it that Churchill had help if he needed it when he visited the House of Commons. Churchill was old and gone and he tottered down the gangway, gripping a cane, his arm motioning to people to get back and leave him alone, and Langford-Holt walked with him and all of Commons looked away. They did not want to see, if Winston Churchill ever fell down in their presence.

"I hated it," Langford-Holt was saying. "Here are

we, insignificant people who never led or could hope to lead his life, and we were being patronizing to him. It simply was not right. Now this is no eulogy to the man. He had all the flaws of a human being, he was wrong many times and he was obstinate and temperish, but he was great and we are insignificant and I felt wrong."

He dressed and went to church. Inside, he remembered Churchill, as he always will remember him, the old man sitting on the green leather bench in Commons, holding his cane and tears coming from his eyes.

"They had such difficulty and hardships during the war," Churchill was saying aloud, "and now they are out in the streets worrying about housing and food and money. After all they've done for us. They are heroes and they should live as heroes."

He was crying and talking about the people who had to fight the war he ran.

"He was great because he cared," Langford-Holt was saying. "This is why he was so great. You see, the man cared so very much."

And now, at No. 28 Hyde Park Gate, there was nothing else to do. He was in the hands of history now, history and the carefully planned funeral arrangements which will give London its greatest spectacle in nearly two centuries. And Sergeant Edmund Murray, Scotland Yard, stood in front of the house with nobody to guard any more, and he wasn't sure about what to do.

"I guess I'll go home," he said. "I guess there's nothing else to do but go home." He looked around. "You know, when I'd help him near the end there, I might grab his hand a little too hard and it would press the ring on his finger and he'd give a little growl and say, 'Easy now,' and just for a moment you imagined him back running things again. Well, he's gone now. When the King is dead, you say, 'The King is dead, long live the King.' What do you say now? Who is there to talk of?"

He went home. And in the East End of London the

people came out. He was an aristocrat and he lived with beef and champagne and cigars, but he stood in the streets with these people, stood in the smoke and ruins and watched the bodies being carried out and he bit his cigar and made a V with his fingers and the old ladies screamed at him their cockney and he would growl with them and they would go back and get ready to take another day and night of it.

Trafalgar Square was crowded and there was no more room to stand and people lined the steps of the National Gallery behind it. A group of ministers stood at microphones on the base of the statue of Nelson. They took turns reading prayers to the people. Hundreds of pigeons flew overhead. The people were silent, and only the noise of water spouting in the fountains, and red double-decked buses passing by on the street, mingled with the ministers' prayers. The huge black lions crouched at the bottom of the statue and watched everywhere.

"Oh, God, in all His majesty . . ." a red-robed minister prayed.

8

In Which Erin Goes Blaah

Breslin is about 5 feet 10 inches tall and he weighs about 240 pounds. He has black hair and a face like the ones they used to have on some Paddy mags. He is Irish. He is not, however, a professional Irishman in the usual sense, although he does write about being Irish.

His pride is in the lilt of the words and invention that he marks as being Irish and also in the various madnesses that afflict Irishmen the world over. His disgust is with the way the promise of great words has been denied—as far as he is concerned—by the present generation of Irishmen in this country. For his taste they are too prosaic and too besotted with the Ould Sod to be real Irishmen. Brendan Behan was a real Irishman. The men who keep the IRA going are real Irishmen, and so too are the kids on Sheriff Street in Dublin who live "in houses that have overflowing garbage cans inside the front doors and no baths inside the flats."

The unreal, unpleasant Irish are the new middle class. His complaint really is that they lead such dull lives, they don't do anything, they don't say anything. This attitude produced a steady stream of inventive rhetoric from Irishmen who did not at all agree with the Breslin assessment.

Behan's Book

Brendan Behan probably should be read in a saloon, not in bed. But the modern saloon specializes in juke boxes, shuffleboards, cash registers which crash open, and telephones which never stop ringing. So to examine Behan, it is best to remain home and post a note on the front door to inform the bread man that you will have his hand broken if he rings the bell.

It is not an important book by any means, this new one of Behan's. It is a collection of newspaper columns which ran in the Irish press from 1952 to 1956. Now, most collections of newspaper columns are not worth the paste the author used to get them together for shipment to his editor. But this is a little bit different, because Behan is my set's idea of a real writer. For one thing, he drinks like a writer. The last we heard of the man, he was released from the hospital where he had been taken after being found in the gutter some place with his head bashed in. Although not as bashed as his liver must be.

For another thing, Behan at least tries to write for the entertainment of a reader. He is not some outlandish homosexual trying to sound off on human destiny between paragraphs about his boy friends. Nor is Brendan a hophead of a one-shot novelist who knocks out drivel for some magazine. And he is not a two-dollar bum typewriting non-novels about such as an old friend of mine, John Stompanato. This is Himself, as one should refer to Behan, and when Himself takes to a writing machine it comes out light, and with a little lilt running through much of it, and so what if the material isn't important, and some of the humor is a bit forced? Hold your tongue. For here and there, in *Hold Your Hour and Have Another,* there are these sparing little things about something like the Unemployed Band, which followed a marching column of police through Dublin while serenading them with the lively tune, "Here's the Robbers Passing By."

His lead on the "I'm a British Object, Said the Belfast Man" chapter pretty much sets the tone for the collection. "We were in the little village of Millisle, near Donaghadee in the County Down," Himself reports. "We had gone out there to pass the beautiful day of high summer like true Irishmen, locked in the dark snug of a public house." Now then, and what else would you have the man do?

All the copy in *Hold Your Hour and Have Another*—a title which means exactly what it says: to hell with the train schedule and keep drinking—was written before Behan's *The Quare Fellow* and *Borstal Boy* came out. The book consists of forty-six columns, all of which tell of time spent and poetry recited in various public houses. The literary set would refer to this as Early Behan, and the writer's friends might suspect that the book is out to help Himself pay some of his drinking bills, which run big. But whatever the era of the writing, and whatever the reason for its appearance today, it always is interesting to inspect a fine writer even when he is not making an important effort. For a style is there to examine, and here and there you get these wonderful displays of the complete lock the Irish have on the art of using words to make people smile.

"They looked around and Mick's face lit up with joy and relief," he writes. " 'Praise him,' said he, running over and throwing his arms around it, 'there it is, me lovely coffin.' "

Or, in the fine passage entitled, "The Hot Malt Man and the Bores": " 'Wipe your bayonet, Kinsella, you killed enough.'

" 'Go on,' " says I.

" 'That's genuine,' said Kinsella. That's what Lord Roberts says to me in Blamevontame in 'nought one.' "

This heroic talk came to an end when a bus pulled up to the sidewalk in front of the pub. The bus contained a dangerous-looking "oul' one," the wife of the

Bottle of Stout Man. He fell to the floor like a trained guerrilla.

There were, in Brendan's days in the pubs, great chances for the languge to be used well, and his people did not fail to do so. Here he reports on his singing to an appreciative audience, an old man who was getting stiff with him.

"I struck up, to the air of 'The Rising of the Moon' and with vehemence:

> "They told me, Francis Hinsley,
> They told me you were hung. . . ."

" 'Good on you," said the old man, his hand on his ear, for fear he'd miss one word. 'Ah, your blood's worth bottling,' screeched the old man."

Through it all, with his characters, Mr. Crippen, Mrs. Brennan, and one Brending Behing, and through to Spain and France, one thing keeps hitting you, the music running behind the simple, small-worded sentences Behan writes. He does it with a sparse style—the longest word in the book is "animosity"—and he does it without your noticing it.

Erin Go Blaah!

I struck up, to the air of "The Rising of the Moon" and with vehemence:

> *"They told me, Francis Hinsley,*
> *They told me you were hung . . ."*

"Good on you," said the old man, his hand on his ear, for fear he'd miss one word.

> *"With red protruding eyeballs . . ."*

"More luck to me one son," said the old man, in tears of content.

> *". . . and black protruding tongue."*

"Ah, your blood's worth bottling," screeched the old man.

" 'Wipe your bayonet, Kinsella, you've killed enough.' "

"Go on," says I.

"That's genuine," said Kinsella. "That's what Lord Roberts says to me in Blamevontame in 'nought one. I knew him before, of course, from the time we were in Egg Wiped. 'Shifty Cush!' says Bobs, when he seen me on parade. 'Is that you, Kinsella?' 'It is,' says I, coming smartly to attention. 'Who were you expecting?' "

" 'You've killed enough of Boers,' says Bobs."

"Go on," says I.

They looked around and Mick's face lit up with joy and relief. "Praise him," said he, running over and throwing his arms around it, "there it is, me lovely coffin."

We were with the Doyles—Hurrah Doyle, The Dancer Doyle, Elbow Doyle, the Dandy Doyle and Altarboy Doyle—and there was singing and wound opening, and citizens dying for their country on all sides . . . and I'm the first man that stuck a monkey in a dustbin and came out without a scratch and there's a man there will prove it, that the lie may choke me, and my country's up and me blood is in me knuckles. "I don't care a curse now for you or your queen, but I'll stand by my colour, the harp and the green . . ."

—Little pieces from the pages of Brendan Behan

The above has been typed out and put here so that you can have a small idea of the motion and lilt that goes into words when they are written on paper by somebody who is Irish. They also are put here as the ultimate testimony on what has happened to the Irish since they came to New York City. Now there are many people who say that the best example of what the Irish in New York have become is the fact that on Thursday, Saint Patrick's Day, the vice-chairman of the parade will be a Criminal Courts judge. Lord, to imagine the day when the Irish would honor a man who puts poor human beings into a jailhouse! But having the judge in his black robes at the head of the parade still is not as bad as what the Irish have done with their ability to use the words since settling in this city. For on Thursday, March 17, there will be 100,000 Irishmen, their chests stuck out almost as far as their stomachs, their snub noses as high in the air as a man can get his nose, and they will be marching up Fifth Avenue and you can take all of them and stand them on their heads to get some blood into the skull for thinking, and when you put them back on their feet you will not be able to get an original phrase out of the lot of them. They are Irish and they get the use of words while they take milk from their mothers, and they are residing in the word capital of the world and we find that listed below are two fine passages representing some of the most important Irish writing being done in the City of New York today:

> *Agreement made this second day of March, 1966, by and between John Walsh, residing at 202 Bayview Avenue, Manhasset, here and after called* WALSH, *and George Hoffman, residing at 75 Spruce Street, Roslyn, here and after referred to as* HOFFMAN, *collectively referred to as* BUYERS, *and the Lincoln Corporation, having its principal place of business at . . .*
> —From the selected writings of Brady the Lawyer.

And, of course:

> *In consideration of the provisions and stipulations herein or added hereto and of the premium above specified (or specified in an endorsement attached hereto) this company for term of years shown above from inception date shown above at noon standard time . . .*
> —From the many writings of Walsh the Insurance Man

Beyond these examples of fine, lyrical Irish poetry, months of intense, painstaking research have turned up a nearly complete list of Irish who are writing in New York. The list includes, 8191 members of the Police Department who write traffic tickets and arrest reports, 1112 persons working in credit departments who write strong third-reminder notes, 21,215 Irishmen who write anti-civil rights letters to newspapers, and, of course, the two Celts who sat down and wrote the final strike notice that was mailed to members of the Transport Workers Union.

Oh, there are other Irishmen found around town who are doing other types of writing. But they are so few in number as to be hardly noticed. Besides, such as James Cannon, Robert Considine, Thomas Gallagher, Frank D. Gilroy, Jean Kerr, Walter Kerr, Edwin O'Connor, Walter W. Smith, and Richard J. Whalen hardly can be regarded as typical. Not when you examine the total picture of the Irish and the business of words in New York. For you can walk through floor after floor of newspaper and magazine offices and agencies and television offices and book companies in New York and the only Irishman you will see is the guy operating the elevator, and automation is going to take care of him soon.

"An Irish copywriter?" Julian Koenig, president of Papert, Koenig and Lois, mused the other day. "Well, we have Casey. But he doesn't count. He went to Princeton. Now beyond Casey, let me see. As I recall it, we did have one Irishman writing something here. Oh, yes. Bob Kennedy wrote the last half of one of his campaign ads for us one day."

Mr. Walt Kelly, the foremost expert on the ways of the Irish in New York, was asked to comment on this situation the other afternoon. Mr. Kelly was at the bar of the Orient Room, 200 East End Avenue. He says sitting in the Orient Room helps him think of the Irish. With him was Mr. Raymond Yee. Mr. Yee was born on the banks of the Yangtze River.

"Why aren't there a ton of Irishmen making a living with typewriters today?" Kelly was asked.

"There are," he said.

"Who?"

"Art Buchwald is a great Irish humorist," Kelly said. "Then in book form you have Joe Heller. He's got the real Irish bite."

"Bel Kaufman writes *Up Downstairs* and you gave me the book," Raymond Yee said. "She's a funny Irishwoman."

"That she is," Kelly said. "Of course, all the Irish writers today are Jewish, you know."

"Why?" he was asked.

"The Irish can't write any more since they started getting fed," Kelly said.

"They got fed in the head," Raymond Yee said.

"That's right," Kelly said. "The north end of an Irishman's brain is blocked by a loaf of bread."

Kelly had a Scotch and water. Then he resumed the conversation.

"Did you ever go to a baseball game with P. J. Moriarty?" Kelly asked. "That's one of the great experiences. He went up to see the Yankees play one night. Mantle hit a triple in the first inning. In the fourth inning, Mantle got up and hit another triple. 'Oh, Jazus, they're doing the same thing all over again, let's get out of here and make some money,' P.J. said."

"Irishmen come around and always try to write you out big insurance policies," Raymond Yee said.

"Be thankful for a Jewish arsonist like Marvin the Torch who burns the buildings down," Kelly said. "Anyway, read Art Buchwald. He's about the best Irish writer around today."

There are some people, very anti-Irish people of course, who have had the nerve to suggest a reason why there are so few Irish writers. These people say that since most of the educated Celtic extracts in New York have attended or are attending Catholic schools, and since they come out of these schools unable to write a decent telegram, that something is the matter with Catholic education.

Now this is a total misrepresentation and it should be dealt with harshly.

"Heretics talk like that," Richard J. Whalen said yesterday. He is the author of *The Founding Father,* the biography of Joseph P. Kennedy, which was a best seller for an entire year. He should know what he is talking about because he went to school at Queens College, which is only ten blocks away from St. John's University, the largest Catholic university in the nation. St. John's has 13,052 students enrolled and it has been established for many years and one fellow who once went to the school wrote a novel. His name is Len Giovannitti.

At the present, St. John's has a lingering strike of thirty-one teachers who were fired because they demanded some form of academic freedom. There was one recent morning when one of the striking teachers said, "They have enough Irishmen in there to fill up Dublin, and what are they turning out? Illiterate insurance men. This school has not turned out a writer with impact in its history. What are they doing to these kids who come around with a gift for words? They are ruining them. They put so many strictures on them that they come out so bound up they can't think freely enough to put in a sentence together."

The teacher needed his mouth washed out with soap. For St. John's went to the trouble of mimeographing and releasing to the newspapers a speech alluding to the strike by Archbishop Egidio Vagnozzi, who, as apostolic delegate to the United States, is Pope Paul's spokesman in this country.

Archbishop Vagnozzi said: "It cannot be tolerated that in a Catholic University . . . anything be taught contrary to definitive Catholic tenets. There is here no question of infringing upon a healthy academic freedom, but of preventing an unhealthy license and ultimate chaos."

"There you are," Jean Kerr said the night she read the

speech. "I just knew that this is what the Ecumenical Council was all about. All these other things we have been reading are distortions of fact. This is the truth. Read it. Doesn't it have the ring of truth and common sense to it?"

St. John's is one of the six Catholic institutions of higher learning in the New York area. The schools have a present enrollment of 36,000 students. There are a couple of Catholic colleges where Irish girls go, but they don't count because they come out and start having so many children they can't even read a book, much less try to write one. Now out of the other Catholic colleges in New York, with all the Irishmen who studied there or are studying there, Fordham, enrollment nearly 11,000, proudly reports that the man who wrote *Three Coins in the Fountain* is an alumnus. His name is John Secondari. Manhattan College, which has 4354 in its present student body and has graduated Irishmen for years, came up with two writers. One is the late Howard Breslin. He is no relation. He wrote *Bad Day at Black Rock,* which, after three Jewish screenwriters in Hollywood got through with it, turned out to be a fine movie. The other is William Barrett. He wrote *Lilies of the Field.* Six Jewish screenwriters in Hollywood turned it into a fine movie which starred Sidney Poitier. While both these movies were being filmed, the only important Irishmen on these sets in Hollywood were the electricians and stagehands.

"We must sympathize with our people," Paul O'Dwyer was saying the other day. "The Irish are all so busy helping the civil rights movement that they don't have enough time to sit down and write stories."

"In a way we do get unfair," Walt Kelly says. "The Irish are very active in literary circles. They join clubs to ban indecent literature. It takes a lot of time to do a thing like that, you know. Most of these indecent book dealers run behind the silly First Amendment and you've got to fight them. And then these dopey judges, sometimes they have the nerve to rule that a book isn't indecent at all, when everybody in the indecent book club knows it is. And do you know what I heard the other day? Some stupid guy said he thought the Irish ought to concentrate on producing writers who would fill the market with some real writing, instead of spending all their time at the indecent book club meetings. Did you ever hear of a more stupid thing in your life?"

Kelly was through talking now and he began to call for more drinks, and be off with him, he is just one of those fellows who sits around bars and wastes his time thinking up ideas for cartoons against the John Birch Society and the Ku Klux Klan and what could you expect of a man who spends his life drawing stupid things like the Seven Dwarfs and some comic strip about a talking animal named Pogo? You're better off away from the likes of him because he is a vile influence on the Irish and so are all the rest of them who sit around their publishing houses and newspapers and advertising agencies and television stations and never put an Irishman to work because they have the nerve to tell you that there are no Irishmen around who can use the language. Who cares about these people anyway? You just be on Fifth Avenue on Thursday and you watch them, 100,000 of them coming along, and those that don't have big brass bands out in front of them can start their own. Anybody knows that a real Irish band is one guitar-player and two hundred people whistling. And they all were born with words foaming at the mouth and maybe you don't see much of them put to use now, but that's only because it's very hard to put the mind on writing about some silly thing like civil rights when you are busy countin' the money from the insurance premiums they've paid you.

"Why, I don't know what you're talking about," one Phyllis Noonan was yelling the other day. "Why, look right here, somebody even sat down and took the trouble to write an Irish cookbook and get it published." She waved the book around proudly, all ten recipes in it, three of them for Irish coffee, one of them for Irish whisky cake, and the rest for the food. "It's written very clearly and very well," she said proudly.

Fifty Years After

Dublin

Outside, a fine band, a marvelous type band, was marching down the street to a hotel and they were playing away as if there was no rain coming down onto their heads.

And inside, there was all the tools, stout, Scotch, Paddy's, and brandy, and here was Tom Slater, Matt Connolly, Jim McGibbons, and Tom O'Reilly, who had gone out to buy fish for his wife at 9 a.m. and it was a good thing the day was cold because by now the fish would be rotting on the seat of the car.

And later in the day Terry O'Neill came in with Hand-Me-the-Hook Coile from Cork City, which has one pub for every two hundred people, children of course included, and finally Sam O'Reilly got a drink in his hand and he remembered that in the Irish rebellion of fifty years ago there were only three informers, and they all confessed and said they were very sorry, and then they were killed.

"I was at one court-martial," Sam O'Reilly said. "This fellow had given us away and we all nearly were caught at a meeting. Now we had this fellow sitting at a table with candles on it and his back was to the court-martial judges He never saw them. He never saw the people who gave evidence, either. When it was over, he confessed that he did it. They told him to say an Act of Contrition. When he was finished, they told him to go off."

"Did he think they were letting him off?"

"I don't know what he was thinking. But he wasn't thinking for very long. When he got on the street somebody came right up and shot him in the head."

Sam is one of the old ones, as were nearly all of them in the place. Fifty Easters ago tomorrow, about

1500 of them took up guns, most of them in the General Post Office on O'Connell Street, to start the Easter rising against British rule. Even Irish leaders expected the rebellion to be good for only a couple of hours. But the 1500 fought 20,000 British troops for a week, and at the end of it Ireland was on the way to becoming a country of its own.

So today, on flag-decked O'Connell Street, and at the old Kilmainham Prison, there will be parades and services in honor of 1916.

And for all this week, this little country whose major industry is the export of its people, has been coming back. They are arriving by the planeload from Boston, Chicago, New York, and Liverpool, and many of them are strangers who look for the places their parents or grandparents or great-grandparents were born. It is a fine week for Ireland.

It could be, as anybody with a decent thought in his head will tell you, a better week if some time today or tomorrow there are a couple of explosions or conflagrations up in the North where the lovely British still control six counties. The IRA is still alive in Ireland. It is not as big with everybody in it. It is just a small outlawed movement of young ones who stay clear of the 1916 veterans.

The last IRA venture was the heinous crime of blowing up Lord Nelson's statue which stood on O'Connell Street. The authorities in the North expect the IRA to do something like that today or tomorrow.

All the guards are mobilized for trouble. In Dublin, the ones who would know are silent.

"They wouldn't tell me a thing about what they're doing," Tom O'Reilly said at a gathering of old timers late yesterday.

However, through diligent, proper investigation, certain facts about the IRA and its movements were uncovered yesterday. In its thorough searching of the matter, the New York *Herald Tribune* newspaper has as one of its resources the legwork of Philip Walsh, recently retired chief of New York City detectives. Chief

Walsh, here for his first visit to the Old Country, was found with a whisky sour in the Shelbourne Hotel on Stephen's Green.

In plaid cap and raincoat, Chief Walsh prowled the city and made several findings which he promptly reported. His findings fitted in with other information. All of it points to one man as the perpetrator of the horrible crime of blowing Nelson's statue up. Information also indicates that the same man can be expected today or tomorrow to attempt to somehow disrupt the lovely British in their six countries in the North.

The man is Richard Behal and he is twenty-eight years of age and he is from County Kilkenny. He has a long background of charitable works. In September, in Waterford, Behal and three others were arrested by police for possession of an antitank gun. The police said they ascertained that Behal was in possession of the antitank gun with intent to endanger life. Behal denied this in open court. He said he had the antitank gun because he liked it. Many people on the jury agreed with him.

There have been cases lately where the police do not tell the truth. In Swinlinbar Court recently, Detective Cafferky said on the witness stand that fingerprints had been found in a shop that was broken into by James Joseph Morris. Defendant Morris shouted out, "He's lying, there were no fingerprints. I had socks over both me hands."

The jury in Behal's case was unable to reach a verdict. In the midst of this, on September 10, rifle shots were fired from shore at the British torpedo boat *Brave Borderer,* which was paying a courtesy visit near Waterford. Police rushed to the scene. They found Behal on the shore with a rifle. The police felt this was suspicious. Behal hit one of the police in the face. He was given nine months in Limerick Prison.

Prison authorities kept shifting Behal from cell to cell. They feared more than a break. They feared Behal would blow everybody up. He is a known explosives expert. Still remembered is the fine job he did of blowing out every window in a castle and putting Princess Margaret and her photographer husband under the dinner table during their visit in Ireland in 1964.

On the morning of February 20, a Sunday, a guard made a morning check of Behal's cell at 7 a.m. He found the cell empty, the bars on the window sawed off, and a rope of knotted sheets hanging from the window. The guard ran to the warden. "I think Behal might be missing," he said.

Behal was gone for hours. He had gone down the rope 25 feet to the ground. In the prison yard, he went up a rope ladder which had been thrown over the 30-foot wall by people waiting on the other side.

"How did they get the hacksaw for the bars into the prison?" somebody asked yesterday.

"A guard going to work could have been asked to carry a package in for Richard," the person reported. "The guard could have been happy to take the hacksaw in because he might have been told he would be shot if he didn't."

Behal, all indications are, came out of hiding on March 8. He came into O'Connell Street in Dublin and went into the Lord Nelson Tower. He put a ring of plastic explosives about the lord's neck. Down on the street, young men were stopping all traffic. Cabs were told to stay off O'Connell Street.

"They told me go elsewhere," taxi-driver Thomas Dunne, badge No. 43, testified.

"Did you know the ones who told you to do this?" he was asked.

"Oh, no," he said. "I never seen them in my life. I wouldn't know them if I see them again either."

The explosion took place sooner than planned. At 1:32 a.m., with a cab just passing by and two girls coming out of a dance at the Metropole, Lord Nelson's head came flying down ahead of schedule. Luckily no one was hurt.

Behal disappeared. "I think he has been taking his nourishment in bed so he does not have to walk out of the room," Inspector S. P. Finucane, Guards Station

Kilmainham, reports. The inspector expects no trouble in the Dublin area. He cannot speak for the North. Behal might get out of his bed this morning with his wonderful percussion caps.

Quite ominous is this first page story in the *United Irishman,* the monthly newspaper of the IRA.

"Information received by the Northern Ireland government indicates that the IRA are about to renew their activities and that attacks against selected persons will be made as well as against property and public services," the *United Irishman* pointedly quotes the Minister of Home Affairs for the six counties in the North.

So today while the Irish of Easter 1916 listen to speeches and place wreaths in honor of the past, the new ones might do something to make it an even more wonderful occasion.

"The people at the Great Killeen Border Station, which is brand new and beautiful and bomb-proof but they forgot to build a men's room in it, they best watch sharply when they come out to use field conveniences," somebody said, quite hopefully, last night.

Easter Rising

Dublin

Rain during the night had fallen on the street like a scrubwoman, leaving O'Connell Street washed and shining in the morning sun. New flags hanging everywhere made the street a long swatch of color. By the time the ten-o'clock masses were over, a crowd of about 250,000, probably the largest Dublin has ever seen, crowded on the clean cement to watch the parade which passed General Post Office in celebration of the fiftieth anniversary of the Easter Rising.

The parade was short. There were no speeches. The Irish felt the day was too important to be marred by oratory, of which there could have been very much. There were not even introductions of the people on the reviewing stand. The only words spoken came when old Eamon de Valera, in top hat and black overcoat stood up under a canopy on the post office steps and from behind him came a voice over the loudspeakers. The voice read the proclamation which the rebel Irish Republican leaders had posted when they started their revolt. The absence of speeches before, and the silence that came after, set the words of the proclamation off. The effect on the crowd, because of this, was marked.

"Irishmen and Irishwomen," the voice said. "In the name of God and of the dead generation from which she received her old tradition of nationhood, Ireland, through us, summoned her children to her flag and strikes for her freedom. . . . We place the cause of the Irish Republic under the protection of the Most High God whose blessing we invoke upon our arms, and we pray that no one who serves that cause will dishonor it by cowardice, inhumanity or rapine. In this supreme hour the Irish nation must, by its valor and discipline and by the readiness of its children to sacrifice themselves for the common good, prove itself worthy of the august destiny to which it is called."

The ones still alive who had started the uprising sat in rows on de Valera's left. They all looked alike. Craggy and creased, white hair showing among the deep lines that crisscrossed the backs of their necks, they sat in dark overcoats and they all wore drab hats old enough to have British bullet holes in them.

First man off the reviewing stand was Captain Frank Daly, B. Company, 1st Battalion. Timing his maneuver perfectly and executing it with dispatch, Captain Daly moved from the middle of a row and went down a flight of stairs at the side of the stand. At half past twelve, the legal opening hour, he came through the door of Tower Pub, across from the side entrance to the post office. The barkeep already had pints of stout and halves of whisky set out on the bar ready for the crush. Captain Daly said whisky. The barkeep pushed a half of Paddy's at him.

"Good healt'," the captain said.

"T'ank you and God bless you," one of the mob now in the pub called out.

Daly had four medals from the revolt pinned to the front of his black overcoat. He was asked what each was for.

"Probably for going to jail," he said.

"Oh, the British had you in jail too."

"A many of them."

The pub was packed now, and dark pints of stout were being passed overhead to the ones in the rear rank. Conversation was broken off and the celebration was gathering itself with every pint. It would go on all through the glorious day.

The kids on Sheriff Street had a celebration yesterday too. They scrambled up from the sidewalks where they had been sitting and they came running through the smoke from soft coal and wood which hung in the air, and they surrounded the two strangers in the middle of the street who had just given Christy Costello and Tony O'Driscoll two and six each to go to the show.

"Mister, me; me, mister," they said, hands held out, when they got around the two strangers.

"What's your name?" one of the kids was asked.

"Joe Moore. I'm twelve."

"What's the pin on you for?"

Joe Moore held out his striped shirt and looked down at the small red pin on it.

"It's the pledge in the Choich."

"What pledge?"

"For not to drink."

"Do they drink at home?"

"Me dad drinks. Just one after the job, he says. Keep himself fit. Only he doesn't stop drinkin' until the mother makes him go to bed."

"What does the father do?"

"He woiks odd days."

At first there were only five or six of them. But more kept coming at the two strangers. One of the strangers was Terry O'Neill, who owns two saloons in

New York, and he was handing out the coins. In a matter of seconds he had a crowd of fifty kids around him. They were all ages, four and five and ten and eleven, and they were all dirty and they were all coming off the littered sidewalks in front of these long rows of attached stone houses on the street.

"Me, mister," they kept calling out. Dogs jumped among them. One kid held up a card that said he was a boxer in the Transport Workers' Club.

He wanted a reward for that. Another one, blond and smudged face, with bony, dirty legs sticking out of short pants, pushed close. He was looking up and yelling, "Me, mister," while he put his hands into Terry O'Neill's pocket.

"Get your hands out of there," Terry O'Neill called out. Then he swung his head around to catch the kid who was trying to pick his other pocket. Finally he flung a handful of coins into the air and the kids dove for them in a pack and he ran to the Raven Pub with the stragglers chasing him.

"Me, mister," they shrieked.

The oppression ended fifty years ago. But the product of it still is in Dublin. The kids on Sheriff Street and the blocks and alleys around it live in houses that have overflowing garbage cans inside the front doors and no baths inside the flats. Once a week everybody on the block goes to the Tara Street Public Baths, a couple of blocks away. Last year a movie with Richard Burton in it was filmed on Sheriff Street. The set was of a public bath. When the kids looked out the window and saw it, they streamed out of their filthy houses with towels over their arms and ran at the doors in the set and knocked it over.

"You go home and they talk about Harlem," Terry O'Neill was saying when he got into the Raven Pub.

The parallel is natural. The Irish Rebellion was the first successful ethnic revolt. And it started, the veterans were recalling yesterday, with only a few fighting in the post office and crowds of thousands taking advantage of it to smash into stores and loot everything in Dublin. Watts, then, would seem to have a precedent.

Later in the afternoon more official ceremonies were held in the ugly, cramped courtyard of the Kilmainham Prison, where the British executed sixteen of the Irish leaders. The executions inflamed the Irish and the revolt became successful. The Irish are restoring the prison, the cells included, as a national monument. Great issue is taken with this. Prisons are things men should tear down, not rebuild. So the rest of the day of celebration was spent in the Raven Pub. All afternoon, the kids crowded outside the door and called in, "Me, mister."

9

How He Owns New York

With Breslin, politics is strictly a matter of class, not in the way Karl Marx meant it but the way Norton W. Peppis meant it when he loaned a friend $25 and the friend promptly hailed a cab and offered him a lift: "That fella had class." Breslin secretly thinks that more Democrats than Republicans have class, but he is open-minded on the situation.

He did not think Barry Goldwater had class—at least not political class, "although I got to admire the way he sticks up for his ignorance." He was very worried that the *Herald Tribune*, which had not supported a Democratic candidate in more than a hundred years, was going to endorse Goldwater in the 1964 campaign. It didn't and Breslin promptly sent this telegram to Mr. Whitney:

JOCK WHITNEY
GREENTREE MANHASSET NY
FROM THE START, I HAD SUCH CONFIDENCE IN YOU THAT I DIDN'T EVEN ARRANGE FOR THE LOAN OF A GUN TO PUT IN MY MOUTH IN CASE THE PAPER BACKED GOLDWATER. YOU DID EXACTLY WHAT HAD TO BE DONE TODAY. I MEAN, IF WE LET THESE PEOPLE WITH THEIR IQ OF 95 GET CLOSE TO BEING PRESIDENT, WHY, ALL

MY FRIENDS WILL DESERT ME AND GO INTO POLITICS. AS ONE ALSO CONNECTED WITH THE NEW YORK HERALD TRIBUNE I THINK IT IS TIME I BOUGHT A DRINK AND INTEND TO DO SO THIS WEEK. I'LL BUY YOU 52 OF THEM.

Jimmy Breslin

To which Mr. Whitney replied:

Dear Jimmy:
The only difficult part of the decision was to say it so that our readers would understand the reasons why. And the wonderful part of it is that so many of them do and have taken the time to say so.

It's great that you think it's time for you to buy, but I'd be glad to pick up the tab in exchange for a promise from you that you'll get your copy in on time.

All best,

Sincerely,
Jock

In the column, his political views were usually reserved to portraits such as the following.

Bill O'

Once a year it all comes back for Bill O'Dwyer. Yesterday, with a band playing "Garry Owen" very strong and these young girls from Marymount College parading by and the people all coming around the gray wooden police barriers to shake his hand, Bill O'Dwyer stood on the corner of Fifth Avenue and 65th Street and this was his town again.

He is seventy-four. He returned to New York from Mexico five years ago. He is one of the great personalities in the city's history. Also, as Mayor from 1946 to 1950 and then Ambassador to Mexico, one of the most investigated politicians the nation has had. But now Bill O'Dwyer lives alone in an apartment on 57th Street and he goes through the year almost totally unnoticed. Except for yesterday. Yesterday was the Saint

Patrick's Day parade and he was, as he stood amidst the music and the people on this street corner, anything but an aging man that nobody recognizes.

He was "Mayor O'Dwyer" to everybody and he held a black Homburg hat over his chest while the flag went by; then he put the hat back on and his right hand came out automatically to shake with the uniformed cop.

"You look good," the cop said.

"God's in His heaven," O'Dwyer said.

"I came on the job under you," the cop said.

"Did you? Well, if you did the right thing, the children should be getting married now."

The cop laughed and O'Dwyer looked at the parade.

"How are you, Mayor?" a man in a gray suit said.

"I'm fine," O'Dwyer said. "It's good to see you. How have you been?"

"Fine," the man said.

"My regards to everybody at home," O'Dwyer said.

O'Dwyer watched the man walk away. "Now who is that?" he asked.

"Frank O'Connor," he was told. "The District Attorney in Queens."

"Oh, Frankie, now why didn't I know him right away? I knew him and his people before him. God rest their souls."

Then he began to talk about the town. "It always changes," he said. "When I first came here from Mayo, I worked behind the bar at the Vanderbilt Hotel. I think they used to drink more Alexanders than they do now."

Priests walked by with a Catholic high school band. "I was in a seminary when I was a boy," Bill O' said. "A Jesuit place in Salamanca, Spain. I was there for about a year. Then nature called."

His eyes smiled. "And she was served," he said.

There were a couple of people around him now, and he was enjoying it. They wanted him on the television, and to say something on the radio, and all the time the right hand was out because there was another cop, or another politician, ready to take it. Mention Bill O'Dwyer and a lot of smart people in this city throw the book at him. There was none of this yesterday. Saint Patrick's Day in New York is a time when the spires of concrete and plate glass are here only as a background for the sentiment which slips through the city. And the man who didn't think it was a pleasure to shake hands with Bill O'Dwyer yesterday should have been working overtime on a garbage scow.

"My favorite politician," O'Dwyer said. He thought for a moment. "It would have to be Hymie Schoenstein. From Brooklyn. He was running in a primary and he needed every vote he could get. The Gallaghers, by the waterfront, had twelve of them and Hymie wanted them all. So he went to the Gallaghers and asked for the votes.

" 'What do we get?' they said to Hymie. 'What do you want?' he answers. 'We want seaboots for fishing,' they say. So Hymie says, 'I'll give you twelve left boots now and I'll give you the other twelve boots right after the primary.' They took the contract and Hymie won the primary.

"Hymie Schoenstein was the Commissioner of Records in Brooklyn. Some people sued him in court to get him out of the job because he couldn't read or write. You know what the court found, don't you? The court found that long as the Commissioner of Records did a competent job he didn't have to be able to read and write."

O'Dwyer was beginning to tell another story when a couple of raindrops started falling. Just as Division 6, Ancient Order of Hibernians, Greenpoint, was coming along in the line of march, a man in a gray hat called to O'Dwyer and said they'd better get in the car now.

It was Pat O'Brien, the old movie star. So Bill O' shook hands around one more time and then he started off through the crowd. It had been his day, but now it was starting to rain and it was over. Everybody on the avenue, by the reviewing stand, knew him. But nobody on the street noticed Bill O'Dwyer while he and this old movie star walked away from the Saint Patrick's day parade.

The Bug

Slick Phillips started pushing right away when he saw Richard Nixon in the back of the elevator. Slick Phillips is built like a keg and he came pushing between shoulders, with his right hand out and his big name card from the American Coal Association convention sticking from the breast pocket of his brown jacket.

"Slick Phillips of Charlotte, North Carolina, Mr. Vice President," Slick Phillips said. "I just want to shake your hand and say hello."

"Thank you," Nixon said. "Good to see you. Charlotte's a fine town."

"If you'd a paid us that visit like you were supposed to, you'd a won in the election," Slick Phillips said.

A smile came on Nixon's face. The smile was made of poured concrete. It stayed there until Slick Phillips, with one last wave, got off the elevator at his floor.

"I hear that from fifteen to twenty people when I come to a thing like this," Nixon said. He had just finished giving a luncheon speech to the American Coal Association at the New York Hilton. "Who knows? I did this. If I did that. They're probably right." The smile was gone now.

Then Nixon turned and started kidding a couple of girls from an electrical convention—"Oh, I see, you're turning the lights on, not off, the way President Johnson does"—and everybody else in the elevator was smiling. But Slick Phillips's line hung in the air. You could almost hear it repeating itself, like a record: "If you'd a . . ."

The line is about something that happened four years ago, and yesterday there were a few stray indications that Nixon might just be willing to try something all over again.

In the morning Nixon received a phone call from Nelson Rockefeller. Rockefeller asked Nixon to come out for William Scranton as the Republican nominee for President. Mr. Nixon said he was not about to come out for anybody. He then came into a second-floor ballroom at the hotel, wearing a television shirt, and got up and made a speech about foreign policy. The cameras were there to record it. Nixon, with no script, stood with his hands in his pockets and went, almost by rote, to the lines he used when he ran against John Kennedy in 1960.

"In connection with what happened in the kitchen," he said, "you might be interested in a thing which happened before we got to the kitchen. We went to a supermarket and I remembered that Ambassador Thompson had given me some advice. He told me, 'Remind Khrushchev of the fact that you too have a humble background.' So when we came into this supermarket, an American supermarket with all the food and things like that which you find in a supermarket, I said to Mr. Khrushchev, 'When I was a young boy, I used to work in a little grocery store with my brothers.'

"And Khrushchev said to me, 'All shopkeepers are thieves.' "

The audience laughed and clapped and Nixon smiled and you could almost feel it coming straight out of the man and into the crowded room. Hope. The same hope that every politician has when the word President comes into his mind. The hope was in Madison Square Garden, hanging right out there in the spotlight, the night Barry Goldwater spoke. And the hope was out on the lawn of Governor William Scranton's house last Saturday morning when he came out to go on television. It does not take a political man to feel it. All you have to do is stand there and watch it hit you. And yesterday, while Nixon was speaking about foreign policy and was careful to say nothing, and made sure to play cool about Goldwater and everything else, he was a man just skating for a living and trying to stay skating until San Francisco.

It was different later in the day when Nelson Rockefeller stood in his campaign offices on Fifth Avenue and answered questions from the press. He was finished. A primary campaign with something like $7 million behind it was wrecked. And he looked tired. But he came with a smile and a quip and even the incredible stupidity of some blond show-off of a TV dame did not bother him. This was the third time Rocky has been viewed in defeat in these offices. The place is getting to feel more like Campbell's funeral home than a political headquarters.

"This does it for good, I guess," somebody said to Tom Stephens, who works for Rockefeller.

Stephens shrugged. "Once they get bitten by this bug," he said, "they never get over it. I'm surprised Tom Dewey isn't around right now trying to get the nomination."

The only time he really became involved in the whole course of a campaign, though, was in the last New York Mayoralty race. It was his city and he wanted the best man to win, although he couldn't quite decide who the best man might be.

Messrs Wald and Bellows;

Tomorrow morning, upon arising, I am going to begin writing a piece which I would title:

TELL HIM HE SHOULD SHUT HIS MOUTH

Which is all you hear in the hallways of the Beame and Lindsay headquarters while people in charge scream when somebody says the wrong thing and it gets in the paper.

The piece will be a mood piece. It will attempt to bring to life the last hours of both camps. So far, the political writing in papers on this mayor election has read like baseball stories.

There is Lindsay, orderly, growing confident, sitting in the front seat of the station wagon going uptown, with the phone at his knee and another one in the back.

"I want a sandwich," he says.

Somebody twists around in the back. A tray with a ham and cheese on rye and a container of milk is passed to Lindsay.

There is Beame riding to Brooklyn and the driver doesn't know the address and neither does anybody else in the car and Beame, trying to read, finally has to look up and give orders himself. Then when somebody wants to make a phone call only Beame has the number and he has to go through his jacket for it and Steve Smith, his sense of orderliness offended, shakes his head.

"This guy is supposed to have nothing on his mind but those papers," he says quietly.

And Wagner sits in his office in City Hall, looking old and worn, and he smiles and then laughs about the Johnson endorsement business and he says, "There were so many things they could have done against Lindsay. But they didn't and now it looks like they've lost it."

And Charley Buckley and Stanley Steingut, the old, sitting in their clubhouses and the Lindsay people, the new, in their storefronts.

And I have a thought about good freaking art with it. Two, three pieces. Give these poor bums something they could look at and read.

breslin, esq.

The Elegant Cracker

The more that happens, the more you've got to love the whole country. Anybody who dies a nobody in this country does it on his own. Because this is the easiest place in the history of the whole world to walk out and be a big shot. It's beautiful. All you need is a little nerve. Here's this Robert Shelton sitting in Washington with a whole Congressional committee making a big man out of him. In New York we have Bill Buckley lousing up the big political race for mayor and becoming a big man all of a sudden. And one kid stands up and burns his draft card and the FBI came after him with what looks like more men than they use to chase the Mafia and the kid got his picture in every paper that prints. Beautiful. Go out in the street and take off your clothes and you're an international celebrity.

Look at Shelton. I absolutely guarantee you that he does not carry on a conversation with a nine-year-old and come out a winner. Now here in New York, Shelton would not make it. Everybody has his own place to become big. And Shelton is perfect for Alabama, where public interest in brains centers on what the quarterback for the university is thinking about when it is third down. We're different here. We must have sophistication in New York. A little wit. Which is, of course, where William F. Buckley comes in.

"Has anything surpised you about politics so far?" Somebody was asking Buckley yesterday afternoon.

"Nothing surprises me in politics," he said. "Except honesty."

And all along, his statements and inferences, in New York cuteness, have asked for a little white backlash at the polls.

Mr. Buckley comes out then as nothing more than an Elegant Cracker. But standing at a table in his office yesterday, he had it made. A few months ago, he was just another name. But now he has the political race in New York completely loused up. The Elegant Cracker, just by stepping out and taking a shot at life, has made himself known forever around here. It's great. How are you going to put a knock on any place where it's so easy to succeed?

"I told you," my friend Herbie Sincere, who once wanted to run for mayor, keeps screaming. "I told you that if somebody would have given me enough money just to pay the sign painter I could've raised hell and come out a big man."

He's got it right. Every day, Herbie Sincere sits and hits himself on the head because he didn't keep going and make a splash by running for mayor. Clifton De Berry ought to do that too. He had the Socialist Worker nomination for mayor and he didn't do a thing with it. So now nobody knows who Clifton De Berry is, and it serves him right.

The same with Vito Battista and Eric Haas of the Socialist Labor Party and all people like that.

You see, the way things are today, if you merely do something you surprise people so much that they don't make a move and you can keep going and they won't put a hand on you.

Look at Buckley. Yesterday afternoon, after his formal press conference, he stood around and he said, "I see Mr. Lindsay is going to attack me tomorrow. It'll probably shock everybody. They're not used to Mr. Lindsay saying much of anything at all."

Mr. Buckley, his left hand jammed into his suit jacket pocket the way all the guys from Yale and those schools do it, then said, "*U.S. News and World Report*, by the way, says that one-half of all the registered Republicans are going to vote for me."

The figure probably is wrong. But the fact still remains that by everybody letting Buckley alone he was able to do some good for himself. Like I say, you step out in this country and nobody does anything to stop you. It's beautiful. You got to wake up every morning and fall in love with even the sidewalk. We got the greatest place for a guy taking a shot in the whole world.

On Election Day in New York, people are going to go into the booths and vote for Bill Buckley. That proves it so well you don't even need to discuss it any more. What you need to do is look for a spot, and then run out into the street and get your picture on the first page of the newspaper.

This Is Sincere

After constant urging by his many friends and supporters, Mr. Herbie Sincere today announced that he was the Republican candidate for mayor of New York City. Mr. Sincere has been active politically all his life and he has a strong background for the job. He is a Republican precinct captain in the 7th Election District, 57th Assembly District, Queens. All the people in the district say that Herbie Sincere is so strong during a campaign that he could put Calvin Coolidge over in his district. Through his work, Herbie has built up an impressive list of contacts within the Republican party of this city. He is a very good friend of Representative Seymour Halpern's father, he once was introduced to Vincent Albano at the racetrack, and during the last campaign for mayor he shook hands with Louis Lefkowitz's wife.

Herbie Sincere has his name because he is the sincerest person anybody ever met. This sincerity is bound to swing voters, just as it has affected all who have come in contact with it. "When Herbie Sincere says on the phone that he is going to make a payment on his loan, you can almost feel the money," a collector from Beneficial Finance said last night. And a clerk in Brooklyn Federal Court recalls that when Herbie Sincere went into personal bankruptcy, all his creditors sat in the courtroom and smiled. "They really believed that Herbie was going to make good someday," the clerk says.

In making his announcement for office, Herbie Sincere yesterday said, "I would like very much to live in Gracie Mansion. My mother could sit on the lawn."

His mother, Toni Sincere, is eighty-five and has been a powerful influence in his life. Only last week, Toni Sincere took out her umbrella and attacked Morris the bookmaker when he came around looking for Herbie Sincere.

"Go 'way from here," Toni shouted. "Stop making my son a gambler."

Herbie Sincere's announcement caused all sorts of commotion yesterday. For one thing, it broke up a big deal between Mayor Wagner and Governor Rockefeller. They had agreed that there would be no Republican candidate for mayor this year. And then it had his mother, Toni Sincere, so busy going through closets all day that she didn't have time to watch *As the World Turns.*

"I'm looking for Herbie's civics book from high school," she said. "From 1937, it's been here in the house doing nothing. Now when Herbie needs his civics book to be mayor, I can't find it. Doesn't it always happen?"

Herbie was out explaining to everybody how he was forced into being a candidate. "What was I going to do?" he said. "You see I have this lawsuit going for me. It's the one against Freehold Raceway from the time the roof fell in on me during the third race. So my friends have been saying, 'Herbie, you'll have all the money you need soon. Now you should devote your life to public service.' That's what they say. So I have to do the right thing. I have to be the mayor."

Mr. Sincere was making these observations while Helen the Manicurist was doing his nails in Pat Rosati's barbershop in Queens. From time to time he kept glancing out the window to make sure his car, a blue Cadillac convertible, wasn't being repossessed. The payments on it are $150 a month and Herbie completely forgot to call up the credit people, GMAC, during the last three months.

"I call them up and talk to them very sincerely about my payments and when I finish talking they are so impressed that they put my card back in the file and don't bother me for a long time."

This quality of sincereness has Herbie worried about the damage he is going to do during the campaign, particularly if it gets rough. "If Mayor Wagner says nasty things about me, then I am going to have to say nasty things back," Herbie was saying. "And I am so sincere that the people will believe the nasty things I say and it will give Wagner a very bad name."

"Do you know where it all started?" Herbie said. "In my civics class in James Monroe High School.

Miss Kelly always said, 'Herbie, you should learn more about civics.' So when I came out here I joined the Republican Club and I have been very active politically since. Everybody started asking me to do favors for them and I never turn down anybody. I became very big doing favors."

The favor Herbie does for people is to talk to bill collectors. He sits in your kitchen and handles phone calls from people who want money.

He is so good at this that the place he works for, Pep McGuire's night club, never wants to give him a day off. To get a vacation, Herbie Sincere has to use his political power and get himself on jury duty. But yesterday, like it or not, Herbie took the day off. He was the Republican candidate for mayor of New York and he had to take his mother out shopping.

"I go by the discount house," Toni Sincere said. "I want a new beach chair for the lawn."

The Old Boss

The Old Boss sat at a desk in a bare, windowless room in back of the real-estate office with a comic book in his big hands. He talked of bums who come out of coffee houses to snatch purses from decent citizens. Comic books were stacked all over the rooms of the real-estate office. They are for children, with a letter to parents about school dropouts stapled inside the front cover. Purse-snatchers and kids who leave school are very important issues to the Old Boss these days.

Once you found Carmine De Sapio in ballrooms of huge hotels, and he worried about Averell Harriman becoming governor. Or he talked about Adlai Stevenson as a Presidential candidate. Now, late Friday night, he was sitting in this storefront office on West Eighth Street and at first it was a little bleak to be with him because the prize this time is the Democratic leadership of the 1st Assembly District South, New York City, and this doesn't even sound big.

This soft-spoken guy across from you, with the comic books for kids in his hand and the leaflet with the title *The Mess on MacDougal Street,* on the desk in front of him, was a major figure in national politics. He ran Tammany Hall when it was strong, and even the big ones had to make an appointment to see him. And here, late in the night in this little office, he was back where he started.

De Sapio is in a primary fight for leadership of his district with Edward I. Koch, a lawyer. This kind of thing is roughest of all. Back in 1939, De Sapio made his first move in politics by running against Battery Dan Finn in this same district. Now he is fifty-five and starting all over again, and the primary is just as mean and uncertain as it was twenty-four years ago.

But the bleakness went away as the Old Boss talked. De Sapio spoke to you softly, and as if you were important. The big hands clasped and then spread apart. And he talked of tomorrow, when the mess on MacDougal Street will be gone. This was not some old beaten guy. This was a New York politician running for something and he was covering every step of ground he knew he had to cover.

"When we talk about the mess in these coffee houses in Greenwich Village," De Sapio was saying, "we are not talking about MacDougal Street per se. We mean what happens when MacDougal Street spills over to Washington Square Park. And to Fifth Avenue. We are talking about all these bums coming out of these places to snatch purses and jostle our people.

"Now," he said, and the hands spread in front of him and he leaned forward, "Now, I most certainly am not going to sit here and insult your intelligence by saying these conditions have existed only under the leadership of the people I am running against. What I am saying is that the situation has worsened under these people. And let me emphasize one major point. These bums who are disturbing our citizens are not from this area. They come here for kicks, as they call it. They are not the neighbors' children.

The "neighbors' children" caught you. This is an expression only somebody from the corner of Grand and Sullivan would use. When Carmine De Sapio was dealing politics with an Averell Harriman, the phrase was "vast political knowledge" or "outstanding integrity and experience." The days for this kind of words are gone. De Sapio is back in Greenwich Village now, so he tells you about the "neighbors' children."

He had on an immaculate dark checked suit with a handkerchief in the breast pocket. His sideburns were white against the dark-framed eyeglasses. The hair on the top of his head was in that patent-leather wave which is his trademark.

Then he walked to the front of the headquarters, where seven women were sitting at two long tables, stapling notes to the comic books.

His wife, Teresa, was working at the head of one table. She's a trim, light-haired woman who had on a flowered dress. She smiled and got up when her husband introduced her.

"It doesn't matter what kind of a campaign it is," she said. "You still have to fold things and stuff them into envelopes. I think I've spent my life folding papers."

His daughter, Geraldine, a dark-haired girl of twenty-three, was answering the telephones at the desk. She looked up at the ceiling for a minute and tried to remember the first time she had worked in a campaign.

"She can't remember that," her mother said. "The first time she campaigned she was in a baby carriage."

De Sapio smiled, then walked to the back. "The only thing that bothers me," he said, "is the fact that my opponents, these reformers, abdicated leadership the last time. Mr. James S. Lanigan defeated me as leader in 1961. In exactly one year he quit, and nobody can tell me why to this day. They do not seem to understand that leadership in politics can be changed or improved, but never done away with."

He shook his head. To the old Tammany man, this was the ultimate sin in politics. You never walk away from power.

It was after eleven at night now, and De Sapio was standing and talking to a man about a letter to a registered voter which would be sent out over his name. Then there was a phone call and he went to a desk to take it. And as he took the phone and began to talk, you thought about this night in 1954 in the Biltmore Hotel.

The crowd in the big cluttered grand ballroom went to whisky early because the first returns showed, everybody was saying, that Harriman was going to be elected governor by several hundred thousand.

But down in the front of the room, De Sapio sat at a big bench table and at ten at night he started grabbing telephones and he kept asking everybody to keep quiet because whether anybody understood it or not, they were in a close race. And he was not taking any chances.

He started assigning extra party workers throughout the state to check the counting in counties that were late in reporting.

"Precautions," De Sapio was saying that night. "You must take every precaution on a thing this close."

It was, that night, a master politician at work. He was in a real-estate office Friday night, not a grand ballroom, and he was talking to one voter on the telephone, not a county chairman. But when he hung up he said there was no difference.

"Politics." He smiled. "It is the same on any level."

Outside, West Eighth Street was crowded. De Sapio headquarters sits between a small hotel and a lamp shop. An old-timer named Petey Lock leaned against the fender of a parked car and watched the people in the window of De Sapio's campaign office.

"I don't know what to tell you," he said. "It's a tough race. Carmine has the same story as any successful politician. He has a lot of friends, and a lot of enemies.

The only consistent public show that interests Breslin even more than politics is the game of cops and robbers. His interest is similar—he likes the kind of people who go into it—but more intense. The cops are his kind of people and the robbers are his kind of people gone wrong. It is one thing to be a civic booster and be proud of the police force. It is a foolish thing. It is another and a more sensible thing to know that cops are subject to a few more of the difficulties of life than the rest of us, and they cope with them fairly well. Breslin knows this and he loves them for it.

And, like many cops, he has his own categories of criminals. Bookmakers and embezzlers at banks and big companies are okay. Dope pushers, rapists, and various kinds of sadists are not okay. In the middle are people who get judged on individual merit or lack thereof. He happens to have a wider range of tolerance than most law-abiding citizens but he seldom lets it operate out of the five boroughs of New York. New York cops and New York robbers are the best. After that, it's all New Haven and the hell with it.

> Jim [Bellows]:
>
> I want to get Police Commissioner Murphy and do a long piece under the rough working title, MARY, HAVE DINNER WITH YOUR MOTHER ON SUNDAY.
>
> In Dallas, only 350 cops guarded the President. Here in the big town, we will have, oh, right now, half stiff, I'd say 9000. All will be under Murphy and if you are a cop in New York and you are off on Sunday, forget it. Nobody is off duty when the President comes here. Tell the wife to take the kids to her mother's for the day.
>
> The FBI offices are on the East 60s. But they are amateurs compared to the men Murphy will have on the overpasses. Dawdle a little bit and see what happens around here: "Lady, I don't

care if your baby is only four. Yez'll both be under arrest unless you get a block away from here right away. I got my orders, you know."

With the typical flourish of the Irish when they are given command, one may look for a great show of what is the greatest police force in the world. Go outside this city and you see just how great a thing we have here.

I want to spend the day with Murphy. I mean starting late tonight and going until your Sunday deadline. 2 p.m., or 3, isn't it?

For Monday, I want to stay with Murphy and the cops until they get this guy out of this town and back to bed in Washington.

Meanwhile, I would almost want to see stories on (a) McCormack, (b) Hayden, and (c) Rusk. How did they spend the day? How were they protected? We lose them in a plot and where are we?

Also, a good mood piece about how these great, huge, friendly buildings of ours, with row upon row of glass, all of a sudden disturb you and no matter how tony they are they all look to you like the terrible red brick thing in Dallas. And the warning, built into the story: keep your head the hell away from open windows on Sunday.

I want to show that Murphy, a man from Middle Village, Queens, can take the guys from this town who work as cops and set them up so that we lose no President as did Dallas. And show it dramatically.

If he loses one, then we can forget everything. Monday's paper, apologizing for my story, won't be needed. We will have blown a nation by then.

Oh, yes. Please remember one thing: Johnson, before the funeral, sat in the office and argued with the Secret Service. They said they had the power to make him ride in a car. He said he wanted to walk. They said they would invoke their power. He said he would rather die than show anybody he was afraid to walk. He walked. This mood of the man, plus the mood of this Irishman Murphy, should prevail in all coverage.

I HAVE SPOKEN! BRESLIN X

The Finest Protect the President

Up to the left, maybe half a mile up, this light red brick factory building stood six stories high against the winter sky, and the black limousine carrying Lyndon Baines Johnson, the thirty-sixth President of the United States, was going to pass right under its windows. This was yesterday afternoon, coming into Manhattan on the Long Island Expressway, and for a moment everything became strange and a bad feeling came into your stomach. The same kind of a feeling you had when you first looked up at the light red bricks of the six-story Texas School Book Depository building in Dallas. But now, as the cars moved closer to the building, there was something else. At first it looked like a flagpole on the roof of the building.

Then it moved, and you could see what the object was. It was a patrolman of the Police Department of the City of New York and he was standing on the roof of this light red brick building, the wind blowing the bottom of his overcoat and his hands on his hips, the right hand directly over his gun, and now the bad feeling went away and you knew everything was going to be all right yesterday.

Which it was.

The President of the United States flew into town at 12:40 p.m. yesterday. He flew back to Washington at 2:32 p.m. In the 1 hour and 52 minutes in which he was in this city, the cops of our town, in one of the most tremendous performances they ever have given, threw a navy-blue blanket over Lyndon B. Johnson. They were everywhere.

Look straight up, and there were two helicopters circling Johnson's car. Look at any rooftop, and there was a blue uniform, with the wind blowing at the overcoat. Look at the rows of windows in an office building, any office building, and there was somebody with binoculars, scanning the buildings across the street from him. They were out in Jamaica Bay, off the Idlewild runways, patrolling in boats, and they arrested hunters out there. They were on the streets and up on the overpasses, and none of them looked at the President. The police had their backs to the motorcade and their heads moved back and forth as they checked on crowds and buildings, and anybody who was going to try and take a shot at Lyndon Johnson yesterday was going to run into trouble.

Forget all those books and stories about the FBI and the Secret Service. Yesterday the New York cops, the finest law-enforcement body the nation has known, stepped out and showed everybody how things are done here in the Big Town.

"We are very serious about this," Police Commissioner Michael Murphy was saying just before he went to church in the morning. Mr. Murphy makes understatements. He had everything but field artillery on the streets yesterday.

President Johnson came to New York to attend funeral services for Herbert H. Lehman, New York's former Governor and Senator. The services were held at Temple Emanu-El, 65th Street and Fifth Avenue.

At the end, at 2:27 p.m., Air Force One, its jet whining and throwing a wave of fumes across the landing apron, started to move out and take President Johnson back to Washington. And Michael Murphy, his fingers in his ears to shut out the roar, ducked down behind a green communications car and stayed clear of the wave of kerosene exhaust which would have flattened him if he had been standing up.

At 2:34 p.m., Inspector John Kinsella of the Department's Bureau of Special Services, the undercover group, came trotting over from a parked Port Authority radio car.

"Both planes airborne," he said.

Murphy nodded. "The credit is out there," he said. He pointed to a group of patrolmen. Now usually this type of statement is the essence of corn. But yesterday it seemed the natural thing to say. For after yesterday, when you hear somebody say "New York's Finest," please regard it as something more than a cliché. These fellows who are paid with your money went out yesterday and did the kind of job people write stories about.

"What you don't seem to understand," Murphy said as he went to his car, "is that we guard Presidents all the time. And we guard them like that all the time, too. So I would have to say that today was nothing more than a routine matter. We just took a job and handled it right."

He got into the car and was driven home. He was in plenty of time for dinner.

"How was it?" his wife said when he came into the house.

"All right," he said. "The important thing is how did you do?"

"Roast beef," Kate Murphy said. "Give me a few minutes and it'll be ready."

The Way It Is

At 3:30 a.m. yesterday, Patrolman George Harvey, walking in the darkness on 55th Street, heard a window being smashed on Fifth Avenue. He started running, his right hand reaching under his tunic for his pistol. When Harvey reached Fifth Avenue, a man was standing in the broken glass in front of No. 704, the Peikin Jewelers. Another man was standing inside the broken window. Both of them started running when they saw Harvey. The man in front of the store headed west on 55th Street, toward Sixth Avenue. The other man jumped out of the window and hit the sidewalk on the run and headed downtown on Fifth Avenue. Harvey, running, picked the one going up 55th Street.

He shouted at the man to stop. Nothing happened. The man was flying now. Harvey wouldn't shoot. He figured the man was a junkie. Only narcotics makes a man break into a store on Fifth Avenue. And George Harvey, twenty-five, born and raised on the West Side, was not going to shoot a junkie in the back. He ran out into the street, shouting, and a cab pulled up and stopped for him. Fifty-fifth Street is a westbound block, and the cab, with Harvey crouched in the back with the door half open, tore up the empty block. At Sixth Avenue, Harvey jumped out and ran onto the board-covered street and grabbed the man. The man was exhausted and shaking and he gave no opposition.

"I need a shot," he said. "Can I get one shot before you take me in?"

Harvey handcuffed him and then rode with his prisoner in a squad car to the 18th Precinct. The man gave his name as John Martin McHugh.

"I live uptown," McHugh told the desk lieutenant. Then they locked him up for the night and Harvey went back to his post. It was a routine midtown arrest.

At 3:30 yesterday afternoon, Harvey came up to the third-floor bullpen, a big wire cage crowded with winos and blood-crusted bums, and he motioned for McHugh. The guard opened the door and McHugh, with Harvey at his side, walked down a staircase that has public-school-tiled walls and came through a door and into the second-floor courtroom. "Could I get a shot some place?" he asked Harvey. Harvey didn't answer.

Lawyers, policemen, bail bondsmen, and defendants milled in front of Judge Simon Silver. Harvey waited in a corner with McHugh.

Then a clerk in front of the bench nodded to Harvey, and he brought McHugh across the room and into the crowd milling in front of the judge.

Herman Graber, the Assistant District Attorney, handed the judge some blue-covered warrants, and Bob Ferraro of the Legal Aid Society came to stand alongside McHugh. Harvey stood behind him.

The judge began to open the warrants and thumb through them and a clerk was saying in singsong, "you may stand mute, admit or deny . . ." and McHugh, paying no attention, looked around.

The judge said something to him and McHugh said, "Guilty," and when he was asked if there was any reason why he shouldn't be sentenced he said, "No."

"Is the defendant ready for sentence?" the judge said.

Ferraro, the lawyer, spoke up. "A quick review of the defendant's record reveals a deep-rooted drug problem and a need for medical attention," he said.

The judge nodded. "Eight months in the workhouse," he said. McHugh's neck moved a little bit.

"Put him in, Officer," a court attendant called out and Harvey took McHugh by the arm and started him back to the door leading to the bullpen.

"Listen," McHugh said, "could you do me something?"

Harvey kept walking him.

"Could you please go next door to the women's court and see what happened to my wife? She was being sentenced today and I don't know what's happened to her."

Women's court, one door down, is for prostitutes. It was empty, except for two big Negro hookers, one carrying a baby, who waited for their lawyers. In the office, a woman clerk looked through a sheaf of papers. "McHugh," she said. "McHugh. Here it is. No, he was wrong. She gets sentenced tomorrow. She's in the House of Detention."

That's the way it is. A man uses $50 a day worth of dope. He steals from others to pay for it. His wife gets on the habit too. She goes out and steals from herself.

New York is always the best, in Breslin's way of looking at things. When Princess Margaret and her photographer husband, Antony Armstrong-Jones, came here in 1965, Breslin looked on it as the chance of their lives. At last, he said, they would be seeing New York. They stayed with Mr. Whitney during their time in the city and Breslin gave the official party various kinds of fits by trying to suggest that they should work their passage. "You come to dinner at any self-respecting house in Queens, the wife helps with the dishes," he started shouting in the City Room one day. "What's this dame doing now? She probably don't even make her own bed!"

Mr. Wald:

The New York *Herald Tribune* newspaper this week has a chance to do some good for the entire English-speaking world. If we blow the chance, we all should go up on the Verrazano Bridge and see who is first into a funnel when it passes underneath.

The chance is, of course, to run some pictures of New York scenes, slum scenes undoubtedly, by a fine British photographer who visits New York this week.

Take the pictures from a tugboat at dawn or from in front of the Palms on 125th Street at midnight or from in front of a crowded stoop on East 108th Street. Or from any of the places in this category. And take the art and run it with an elegantly small name line. Except you run the art around eight columns of something on the front of your Sunday newspaper.

With the art, you do a story about the British photographer and his wife going around town at night, away from the same old known places and away from the same old known names.

I say this is an automatic, mandatory move for us to make. The idea has class, taste, and great value. The big asset in carrying it off is informality. As a combination, the art plus a heavy-hitter article on the evening, would give people who read the newspaper something adult and different. The photographer in question also could see his work in a New York newspaper. And I don't care who he is or where he's been, he still is a photographer and everything is Bridgeport compared to having your work run in New York. Hey, we're giving the guy a pretty good shot at it, too. Take the picture at night and see it in a New York newspaper almost the next morning. Also, they would be getting a chance to see things in New York that they never would see. And which will be the things they'll remember the best. Hell, throw everybody into a squad car in Harlem for an hour late on a Friday night and let's go see what's really doing in the world.

Now if I am working elsewhere in New York this week, I am winging and banging away with this idea and Whitney looks up at a cocktail party some place and it's too late; I got the guy in a corner of the room and I got a camera in my hand and I got Fat Thomas and two detectives waiting at the door to give everybody a ride. The fact that I'm working here does not change this situation at all.

This idea is very, very strong for the joint. Which is absolutely all that counts. You give these people who take our paper a chance to read something intelligent on this visit, and with some class and off-beat to it, and to see a couple of fine photographs, and they'll remember it for a long time.

I insist that we take our best shot at this thing. I start by placing this in your very fine hands. Thank you. It is a pleasure to do business with you.

J. Breslin

Nothing happened, but Breslin's furious energy was always applying itself to some aspect of New York and the people who live in it.

A Beautiful Custom

Yesterday afternoon, under a glaring sky which held only the suggestion of clouds, Louis Tomback walked slowly up the concrete ramp from the Brooklyn end of the Williamsburg Bridge and, as he has on every Rosh Hashana for thirty years, he kept going until he reached the middle of the bridge.

When he got there, Tomback turned the empty pockets of his blue suit inside out. Then he looked down at the East River and, with BMT trains drowning out his words, he recited the *tashlikh,* the prayer of purification. Nearly three hundred others, who had come from both Brooklyn and downtown New York, were on the bridge doing the sáme thing.

This is one of the oldest, and easily one of the most beautiful, customs you see in New York. Earlier, Tomback, an Orthodox Jew, had said prayers in the synagogue to ask his God to forgive him for all the sins he had committed in the last year. Now, symbolic of this, he was standing high above the East River and, as he prayed, he was throwing his sins onto the water, which was moving swiftly under this old bridge.

You had a cigarette while the man prayed, and all you could think of was what it would be like if you could throw away everything you'd ever done wrong, and the memories of it too, and throw it into that river and let it go out with the current.

People have been standing on the Williamsburg Bridge on Rosh Hashana and thinking like this for years. Once, the bridge was crowded with thousands of people over the day. All of them came from the downtown East Side and Williamsburg. But both these parts of this town are changing, just like nearly every other part of the city, and yesterday the people who came onto the bridge were only in the hundreds.

"I've done this all my life," Tomback said when he was through with his prayer. "But only the old ones are here now. The young ones, they are all gone. I'm a retired man. I worked at dresses. I still live on Bedford Avenue. But my children, I can't speak for what my children are doing today. They're gone. They're out on Long Island."

"Everything is changing," Tomback was told.

"Changing? Who ever heard of Long Island? Now Long Island is a place where your children go away to when they leave."

Then Tomback started to walk back down the ramp to Williamsburg and a group of others turned and headed toward the downtown East Side. Next year, if they make this trip, there will be even fewer people because the old Jewish people are becoming fewer in these areas.

You could see that any place you went yesterday afternoon. On the Manhattan end of the bridge, Delancey Street was Saturday-empty and gratings were drawn in front of the doors of all the shops because of the holiday.

But off this main street it was different. This was, in recent times, the nation's great Jewish ghetto, these ugly five- and six-story tenements which run for block after block. Originally Germans settled in them; then the Irish came and, after them, the Jews. Today the Puerto Ricans have moved heavily into the area and the Jews, as did the Irish before them, are moving out, and yesterday, on the downtown East Side, Rosh Hashana simply was not that big a holiday.

Stores were open on every block. The tin soft-drink signs all said "Bodega" under them and there were Spanish-American dry-goods stores, and Latin tunes came out of the loudspeakers in the music stores. At one time any Christian kid living at a place like Fourth Street and Avenue C could do pretty well for himself by running up and down tenement stairs and lighting stoves for the Jewish women who could not so much as turn a gas jet on Rosh Hashana.

Yesterday it was all gone. On Sixth Street, between Avenues B and C, for example, there is an old four-story red brick synagogue, Congregation Ahawath Yeshurin Shara Torah. Attached to it is an identical building, the bricks painted gray, which houses the Iglesia de Dios (Lunes . . . Oración, 8 p.m.).

And when the few old men walked out of the synagogue late in the afternoon, the stoop of the tenement next door was crowded with Puerto Rican kids who spoke in this clipped, high-pitched language which must have sounded as strange to the Jewish men as their Yiddish did to the Irish.

The move now, as Tomback noted sadly on the Williamsburg Bridge yesterday, is to places like Long Island, and the young ones who go there all have a valid reason.

"You can't live in the city any more," this fellow Manny Goldberg, who lives in Scarsdale, was saying one night. "You got kids, you got to give them a chance to live. How can you raise a kid in the city? It's impossible."

He comes off Avenue C and slept three in a bed until he was eighteen.

Legit Living

Chickee James was fifteen when she was in a chorus line behind Joe E. Lewis at Ciro's in Miami Beach. She was nineteen when she got her first mink coat and she came out on the floor wearing it for the finale at the Latin Quarter on Broadway. She was a young blond who was married twice and known every place in town. There were chorus lines and a shot in a stage play and a saloon she ran and some B movies, and nothing ever stayed still.

Then it began to get to a lot of them around her. Priscilla Callan, who worked chorus lines with her, became confused and took a bottle of sleeping pills. Whisky belted out another one, Mara Lindsey. Lorna Bolton, a big blonde, dropped dead. A lot of the crowd she knew was in the gambling rackets. The law moved in tight on them. Chickee James started looking around. A couple of years ago, when her son was old enough to start school, she got out.

She bought a thirteen-room house in Merrick, Long Island, and put her boy into the local school. That took care of the night life. Now, at twenty-nine, Chickee James is a daytime girl. Yesterday afternoon she was dickering with a salesman in the cosmetics shop she runs in Merrick. Her shop is on the main street, a couple of blocks of one- and two-story storefront buildings that come to an end, as all these semi-suburban places do, at the Long Island Railroad tracks. Chickee's shop is in a white building. A lawyer's office is upstairs. Her place is decorated in pink and has high stools and a small couch made of red velvet and gold-painted wood. The street outside was hot and empty. The only noise in her shop was the low music from a radio.

"It's square living," she was saying. "I call it legit living. That's the way it's going to be. What am I going to do, be out all night and try to bring up a kid in the city? What's he going to do, ride in the elevator for fun? Suppose I bring him up around a knock-around life. How do I know he's going to be able to make it for himself in a rough and ready? I always knew what to do, but that doesn't mean he will. So I'm bringing up the kid square. He'll have everything, school, music lessons, the whole bit. Just like everybody who lives square."

The other life is all in the past. Once, a district attorney leaned over his desk and pleaded with Chickee, "If you would only open up and tell me things, you'd make me the mayor."

"Mayor?" Chickee told him. "Is that all you think of me? Why, if I sat down with you, I'd make you governor." The guy broke up and she walked out.

Now Chickee goes into Manhattan once a week to buy stock for her shop, and her big move the rest of the time consists of going out to dinner some place. She has run into only one guy from the nighttime crowd. A gambler, he drove out to her shop with his seventeen-year-old girl friend. The girl friend wanted a wig.

"She must be something," Chickee told the guy. "If she needs a wig at seventeen, what's going to happen to her when she's thirty?"

Chickee's main trade is local housewives and high-school and college girls. She doesn't make a big living with her shop, which she calls Silk and Pearl, but she meets the bill. She knows make-up from show-business days, and she gives the women who come in a fair shake. Which was always her reputation.

"I have to do it nice," she was saying, "but I won't let an older woman go out with one of those purple-pink lipsticks. I swing them off it. That's my big thing now. Be nice, but teach them colors."

Chickee looks good. She had on a ruffled white blouse and white skirt and she had a white bow in her hair. Square living agrees with her. But it does have its trouble points.

She has to clean her own house. At first she had a maid, but the maid swung with $4700 in cash and clothes, and Chickee threw up her hands.

"It used to take a Dillinger to rob me," she said. "Now I'm a Long Island housewife and the maid can do it.

"I went to the PTA meeting one night. I sat down, nice and quiet, like any other mother, and the next thing I knew all the husbands are around me and they say they're going to make me a den mother for the Cub Scouts. Christmas, can you see me in one of those blue dresses walking down the street in a Fourth of July parade? Too much. I got myself included out of the PTA."

Whenever any major event hits New York, Breslin sees himself as the central figure. He will praise or blame the official handling given whatever the situation is, but he knows, as most other New Yorkers individually know, that what happens to him is just the most important thing. He also knows that his reaction to anything, and that means his reaction to any of the people involved, is what he really has to write about. Thus the great transit strike of 1966 was made to order for him. He hated or loved Mike Quill, head of the Transport Workers Union, on alternate days, depending on whether Quill was being outrageous (lovable) or demanding (hateful).

With Quill's Byes

For the last fortnight, a distinguished group of twenty transportation trade unionists from Ireland have been in New York to watch the methods, the warking methods of Mr. Michael J. Quill, president, International Transport Workers Union, and while it has been forty years since Mike Quill left Ireland, he goes back every so often to charge the battery and keep friendships growing. Yesterday was the last day that his friends from the unions in Ireland would be around to see him operating. So Mike Quill, sitting there with twenty of them from the Old Country peering right over his shoulders, gave them a grand show for their last day.

At noon Quill called a press conference. He announced he was calling a subway and bus strike for the entire City of New York at 5 a.m. on December 15. His union's contract does not run out until the end of the month. And Mike never has strikes. It's been so long since he was on a picket line that he wouldn't even know which way to turn at the end of the walk. But every other year at this time, with the transit workers' contract coming up, Mike Quill becomes the enemy of the city and anything he says sets everybody off to blathering.

By three o'clock in the afternoon he had the whole city even more upset than it was the day before, which was very upset, and the twenty Irishmen who were watching him had something more to take back with them, and God help the bus company in Dublin. "What else would you have the man do?" they were saying. "This is the way warkers fight for their rights." And then they all took Michael out and threw him a party.

"Will you have a small one?" Jerry Monks of Dublin said while the seating was going on in the restaurant at the Sheraton-Atlantic Hotel.

"It's a little early in the day yet."

"Accardin' to the man," Monks said.

"That makes it too early, then."

"Will you mind if I have a small one?" Monks said.

"I'd be honored if you'd have one without taking it as an insult that I don't have one with you."

"Thank you, thank you," he said. He picked up a bottle from the portable bar set up by the table and he poured enough whisky into the glass to put a housepainter in business.

While Mr. Monks set the tone for the trade unionists from Ireland, Mr. Michael J. Quill sat up at the other end of the table. He was waiting for his pea soup. He had in front of him a soft-covered book, *1913 Jim Larkin and the Dublin Lock-Out,* which is printed by the Workers' Union of Ireland, 29 Parnell Square, Dublin 1, and which contains on its pages this tribute to scabs who went to work for the Dublin Tramway Company during the strike:

You can tell him 'midst a thousand by his cringe and by his crawl,
For of dignity or courage he possesses none at all.
In the aleshop he's a sponger, in the workshop he's a spy;
He's a liar and deceiver with low cunning in his eye.

Sitting next to Michael was Jim Larkin, Jr. It was his father who was involved in the Dublin strike in 1913 and who then came over here and in 1919 was put into Sing Sing prison for four years on charges growing out of union activity. Now this is a long time ago, but it was fresh in everybody's mind yesterday.

"I remember him tellin' me he'd been in jail in probably every state of the country," Jim Larkin, Jr., was saying.

"He probably was, he was arganizing everywhere," Quill said.

And then Larkin got up and as a memento of the visit to this country he gave Mike Quill a plaque and on the plaque was a red hand, O'Neill of the Red Hand, and if you don't know what that stands for let Michael himself, who got up on his feet, explain it to you.

"I've seen the red hand before," he said. "Many years ago, a prince and a fellow both wanted to claim some land and they had a boat race for it and the prince saw he was losing, so he took out his sword and cut off his hand and threw it onto the land and claimed it. And that's the spirit with which warkers fight for their rights everywhere in the world."

Michael then recalled 1913, when he took on the tramways in Dublin. "They told us the chairman of the board of impliers was an English Jew, but he turned out to be a good solid West Cork man named William Martin Murphy and what he didn't kill in Dublin he starved in the streets and of course he went to mass the next day and that made it all right. Kill 'em first and then go to mass. Then the English warkers sent us a boatload of food and they offered to take the children for us and the powers that be told us that they'll all be atheists when they come back. That's what they told us. But we know that the warkers are the same all over the world, boundaries make no differences."

With this spirit, he sat down to his steak and green beans. It is very good that he was lunching, not bargaining with the city's new "implier," John Lindsay, because Quill has had strong thoughts running through his mind for the last two weeks, while he's had the people from Ireland here, and they left last night at 9 p.m. and maybe today things can start straightening out a bit and New York's contract with the transit workers can be handled perhaps a little more easily.

"Have you ever had occasion to meet Lindsay?" he was asked.

Michael reached out for green beans with his fork. He took up a few and put them into his mouth. He chewed on them. Then he put the fork down.

"I've had no occasion to meet Lindsley," he said.

He picked up the fork again. Mr. Quill always has been pictured in the newspapers as some sort of loud mouth. This is fantasy because he is silent Irish who sits and waits and then is very good at answering, which is one of the great arts.

"You called Lindsay a coward. Do you find that language goes further than all these diplomatic terms which everybody has come to use these days?"

This time he reached out for a piece of steak. He cut it and put it into his mouth. Then he put the knife down.

"It does, it does."

"What's the favorite thing you've called people over the years?"

He chewed the steak for a long time. Then his jaw stopped moving.

"Bastard."

Michael reached for the steak again and the twenty trade unionists from Dublin said sure, if a man is a bastard why then you call him a bastard. They all finished lunch and went home last night, which is good because if those men stayed around, the feeling is that the whole city would be walking by New Year's Day.

The Essential Man

Please, if you're not essential to your job, remain at home. Now, I know that every man, when he looks at himself in the mirror when he's shaving in the morning, likes to think of himself as essential. But remember, there are degrees of essentiality.

—John V. Lindsay, addressing the people of the City of New York.

Beautiful. I don't know what you saw when you were shaving this morning, but I know what I saw. I saw the face of Joseph Pulitzer while I was shaving. And I saw it last night and I left the house right away to make sure I'd be the first one the boss saw when he came in this morning. And anybody who doesn't do the same thing is crazy. For now we know what this subway strike, the greatest transportation tie-up in the history of the world, is all about. The Mayor himself told us. This thing is a plot. If you stay at home today, you are admitting that you are not needed. Beautiful. Wait'll you see what they do to you if you don't show today.

Even Mike Quill, who went overboard with most of what he said yesterday, was able to talk sensibly about that point.

"Oh, don't wurra, the impliers will be on the job early Monday," he said. "Oh, yes, all the bosses will be around countin' the warkers' noses. And if your nose doesn't happen to be there, and the implier just happens to notice that the day can go by without you, then he might just ask you to stay home in your hoose permanently."

A lot of smart guys figured this out last night.

"I'm essential, I'm essential, I'm essential, I'm essential," my friend Robert J. Allen kept saying while he walked from Massapequa to Manhattan last night. He wanted to be in the office early and at 9 a.m. he planned to run into the boss's office and shout, "Do you need a match?" to make sure the boss knew that Robert J. Allen was first on board on Monday, January 3, 1966.

And at 8:30 last night my friend Ralphie, who works as a runner in the Stock Exchange, ran into the bathroom of his apartment in Coney Island and looked at himself in the mirror.

"Do you know who you are?" Ralphie said to the mirror. "You're Keith Funston, that's who you are. You're Keith Funston and the whole world counts on you to run a clean operation on Wall Street. You're

Keith Funston and all widows depend on you to protect their money."

You can find Ralphie in the stock market easy this morning. He wore boots when he left Coney Island last night so his ankles wouldn't cave in when he got to downtown Brooklyn and started across the bridge.

"I don't like bothering you at home, but I need some help," Morris, who works as a cutter, said to his boss over the phone last night.

"You didn't have to call me," the boss said. "I know you live way up in the Bronx and you can't get in tomorrow. It's all right. Believe me. I understand."

"It isn't that," Morris said. "I need to know if the janitor has the key to the place. I'm downtown now and want to sleep on one of the couches in the showroom."

"What are you going to do tomorrow?" Danny's wife asked him last night. Danny is a margin clerk at Newburger, Loeb and Company and lives in Bay Ridge.

"Oh, I'm going to make the office," he said. "All the executives got to be in to work."

Now, of course, history shows that one must be realistic during a great emergency. "The level of annoyance is rather high," Cornwallis said at Yorktown. Therefore, looking at life directly, there are some people who are completely unessential to the welfare of the city of New York, and they should stay home in bed all day and not come out of the house even once. These people are: George Sirico, the City Marshal in Brooklyn, who is trying to hit me with a new process; Miss Hyman, the accountant at P. J. Clarke's bar; the shylock whom I was supposed to meet on the corner of 24th Street and Third Avenue at exactly 2:15 p.m. sharp this afternoon; Mrs. Rogers, the lady at the bank who puts down "insufficient funds" on the slip when she mails my checks back to the people I cash them with; Mr. Leary from the finance company; Mr. Peters from the other finance company; and Dick Conlon, whom I owe $100 personal. But everybody else in this entire city should, while shaving, carefully form the words, "The board of directors discussed me last week."

That's the way anybody with any brains was doing it last night. Most of the people who work in New York have jobs in Manhattan. But three-quarters of these people live in the other boroughs. With no subways, the traffic jam on bridges and in tunnels figures to be incredible. But these are things you shouldn't even consider. The big thing is to make sure you're in the office when the boss shows up. Walk it if you have to. Walk ten, fifteen miles. But get there.

The Hitchhikers

This morning, as New York City begins the sixth day of the huge transit strike, Mayor John Lindsay is in the bargaining room at the Americana Hotel. Mayor Lindsay, who intends to stay in the bargaining room until the strike is ended, has at his disposal in the room a television set on which he can view the annual Brown-Cornell football game. While the Mayor deals with the transit union, the incredibly tied-up city thirty-nine floors below him has been forcing the best out of its millions of people.

Most of the forcing is being done by the policemen who stand along Queens Boulevard and at the entrance to the Midtown Tunnel, flagging down cars that are not full and asking the drivers to take some of the hitchhikers who stand in little crowds behind each policeman. This is a fine homey little situation and it enables you to meet a lot of people you never would have had the opportunity to meet.

Early yesterday morning my friend Norby Walters picked me up and we were driving along Queens Boulevard when the traffic backed up. We were sitting in the car, waiting for the traffic to break, when a policeman stuck his head into the car.

"Say, there's a woman here going to Manhattan. Could you fellows give her a lift?"

The woman was at the curb. She was a nice-appearing, well-dressed woman of about forty. She was going to be the first new person I've met this year. I spent all last year fighting with people I've known a long time. Now the cop was giving me a chance to meet a brand-new person.

"We're not going to Manhattan. We're going to Virginia," I told the cop.

"Come on, you take her," he said. He turned and motioned to the woman. When she got up to the car and saw the two of us in it, she looked at the cop.

"Is it all right, officer?" she asked.

"Hey, lady, I don't attack people," I said.

"Come on," the cop said. He opened the back door for her and she got in.

The traffic started moving again and we were off to Manhattan with a guest, a new friend.

"The traffic is terrible," she said. "It must be hard on you driving in it."

"Hey, lady, I don't feel good today. If you don't mind, I don't want to listen to any talk."

"Well then," she said. "I'll just sit back and read my book. Do you know what I'm reading?"

"No, lady."

"I'm reading *In Cold Blood*. That's Truman Capote's new book. Have you read it?"

"My mother hasn't taught me how to do that yet."

"Have you ever heard of the word surly?" she said.

"Stop the car," I told Norby Walters. He pulled the car to the curb in front of a cop. Three men were standing with the cop. "Officer, could we trade this lady for two of those guys you got there?" I asked him.

"We're together," one of the men said.

"Hey, what are you, the Elks Club?" we asked him.

The cop opened the car door and let the lady out and then he waved the three guys into the back of the car. "Be a good fellow and take them all," the cop said.

We started driving along again, and all over Queens you could see the people who use their brains and react properly during an emergency. Here they were, driving their cars through gas stations and cutting across supermarket parking lots so they wouldn't get caught by the cops and have to pick up people.

"Hi, thanks for the lift," one of the three men in the back of our car said. "Yeah, thanks," the one in the middle said. "Sure appreciate it, fellow," the other one said.

What are you going to do when they out-polite you? That's the hell of manners, they break you down. So I decided to try to be nice to them.

"How come you fellas don't have a car of your own?" I said. "What happened, were they all repossessed?"

"Oh, no, we have cars," one of them said. "But we're obeying our Mayor's suggestion to ride only in car pools. We're trying to do the right thing in this situation."

"Yeah, do you do the right thing with your loans and pay them on time?" I said.

"Loans? I don't have any loans," one of them said.

"Oh, you're from out of town," I said.

At the entrance to the Midtown Tunnel, where the traffic jams up, there were cops all over the place.

"Hey, officer," I called out. "Could you get rid of these three in the back? I think one of them has a gun on him."

"Get on, get going and take them into midtown," the cop said. He waved us on and we rode into midtown, and then, the first chance Norby Walters got, he pulled up to the curb and told the three to get out and we were into another day of this strike.

And when the strike was over and the *Trib* printed an editorial praising Mayor Lindsay's handling of the situation, Breslin sent this telegram to the editors:

JOHN IS GOOD
JOHN IS GREAT
AND WE THANK HIM
FOR WHAT WE ATE.

This did not endear him to the editorial writers.

His usual run of stories about the city, however, is fairly laudatory. He likes people and what they do. And he has a knack for finding an upbeat small thing to use in describing any large event.

Clapping for Miss Anderson

A 60-watt bulb on the plaster wall threw a pale light on the small staircase. Marian Anderson was at the foot of it. Her hands were clasped in front of her and her head was cocked so she could listen to the sound coming through the door from the stage. The train of her mink-collared crimson dress was streaked with dust.

Sol Hurok stood in a corner, his cane tapping against a brass fire-extinguisher on the floor.

"One more," Hurok said. "One more."

An usher was at the top of the steps, his hand on the door which leads to the stage. Outside, noise was rising from the floor seats, and falling from the four crowded balconies of Carnegie Hall. The usher looked at Marian Anderson.

"One more," Sol Hurok said.

"No," Marian Anderson said. "It's finished."

Then Marian Anderson turned her back on the stage door and walked over to another staircase and started up to her dressing room. She had just finished what she had announced as the final concert of her career. And now this stately, magnificently formed sixty-year-old woman, perspiration showing through her make-up, her arms filled with roses, climbed the stairs and talked about what it is like to finish a career that began forty years ago in Philadelphia and reached out to the world.

"We wanted that everything would go well," she was saying. "And I'm so glad it did. And now, now I'm going to be a homemaker. A homemaker with a vengeance."

Sol Hurok was behind her on the stairs. Sol Hurok is a promoter of concert singers, and he discovered Marian Anderson. Sol Hurok had just sold out Carnegie Hall, at a $5.95 top, with Marian Anderson. Sol Hurok came up the stairs after Marian Anderson. He held a floppy black hat in his hand. His dark overcoat was unbuttoned. A long white scarf hung around his neck. He stopped halfway up the stairs and looked back at the door leading to the stage. Noise still was coming through it.

"Oh yes, of course," Marian Anderson was saying as Hurok came into the room, "today was special in a way that you can't explain."

"Kiss her, Mr. Hurok," the photographers yelled. He kissed her on the cheek, and the age-lines under Marian Anderson's eyes crinkled into a smile.

Sol Hurok went off to the side. He stood with both hands on the silver head of his cane.

"They're still clapping, Miss Anderson." One of Hurok's staff was at the door of the dressing room, calling to Marian Anderson. She didn't move.

"They're still clapping, Miss Anderson."

"Don' hold her back," Sol Hurok called out. "The public are not going. The public are not leaving."

"Oh, then I had better go down again," Marian Anderson said.

'Don' hold her back," Sol Hurok said.

And, once more, Marian Anderson went down and came out onto the stage at Carnegie Hall and the lights were up and people were shouting over their clapping hands and photographers leaned on top of the stage and took her picture, and her great teeth prodded her face into a smile. Sol Hurok, who was upstairs in the dressing room, had just won the first little tug against Marian Anderson's retirement.

"She should not retire," he was saying. "She must

not stop singing. She cannot do that. She belongs on the boards."

"What would you have her do?" Hurok was asked.

His bald head bucked. His eyes flared behind his thick glasses.

"What would I have her do?" he said. "Huh. An appearance anywhere by Marian Anderson is an event. There are great readings. Lincoln, Benjamin Franklin. Great readings. And then sing spirituals. It would go like a house on fire. No, she must not stop singing."

Marian Anderson, "The Voice Heard Once in a Hundred Years," sang for one hour and twenty-five minutes yesterday afternoon in what the program termed the final concert of her career. She sang with her hands clasped in front of her and her eyes closed and her mouth pursed and her jawbone rippling against her cheeks. She did not, to an untrained ear, sing with the overriding power which was there when she was first heard years ago. But there was some sort of German song midway through the beginning of the concert, and she ended the song with a little low note that ran around through the hall and let everybody know just who was up there on the stage singing for them.

Not that it really was needed. For at three o'clock yesterday afternoon, when Marian Anderson came down the stairs from her dressing room to go to work as a singer, you knew the moment she took her first step what this woman was.

Her right hand held her skirt up. Her left hand rested on the arm of Winston Fitzgerald, a striped-tie member of Sol Hurok's staff. That great woodcarving of a head was held high. Fitzgerald held the banister and started down.

"When she comes down, I hope you won't be smoking," Fitzgerald had said earlier. Nobody was smoking as she came down the stairs.

She smiled at everybody and then looked at the usher who was at the door to the stage.

"I think maybe we can go out now," she said.

"Oh, please wait," the usher said. "They're still being seated."

She walked over to a fire hose that was looped onto a wall rack. She put a package of lozenges, wrapped in a paper tissue, on top of it.

"I'm ready when you are," she said.

The usher opened the door and she came up the steps and went through the door and out onto the stage, and now this old, elegant concert hall shattered into arena noise and people began standing and she walked to the piano and bowed to the crowd and there was something special in every step and every nod. The big ones in life are always like this. It's something that was put into them when they were given their ability and they have it for every day that they live. It does not matter what field they are in. They all come with it, and it is something to see. A few weeks ago Gene Tunney came down the aisle at Madison Square Garden to take a bow in the ring before a prize fight. He is old now, and he is a financier and his world is golf courses and private clubs, but when he came down the aisle at the Garden and came up the stairs and then put that front foot through the ropes and swung himself in, you knew what he was, a champion with the class of a great one all over him.

And yesterday afternoon Marian Anderson came the same way. They didn't even announce her name. They just opened a door and here she was, tall and sweeping, coming out onto the stage, and you knew that her business was singing and that she was one of the great ones.

His Zoo

The water did not seem particularly clean, and crumpled feathers from the geese floated on the surface of the pool in the Children's Zoo at Central Park yesterday. Streaks of silt showed here and there against the blue paint of the bottom of the pool. But these are the kind of things only adults can see. The children saw only the Noah's Ark, and a big wonderous plastic whole. And, of course, the geese. They came boldly out of the water and stood on the edge of the pool and demanded crackers from the children.

It was a raw day, with a threat of snow or rain, so there were not a lot of children out yesterday afternoon in the zoo Herbert H. Lehman donated to this city. But the ones who were there, bundled in snowsuits, kept talking and calling things to their mothers' attention and they were, a Park Department man was saying, just about the way Governor Lehman would have wanted them to be on the day he died.

"The story-telling was called off," Albert Miller, who takes care of the rabbits, said. "But nobody said anything about closing the zoo on account of his death. If you saw the man once, then you would know he would not be the kind to ever have this zoo closed for the children."

Two women came through the entrance gate with their children, and the children, clutching crackers in their hands, immediately ran to the pool to feed the geese.

"Yes," Mrs. Ernest Smith said, "we heard the Governor died. We come here every once in a while, not often, but today we just decided we would come here."

One of the children, Daniel Rosberger, four, moved up to the edge of the pool and tried to short-change the geese with a crumb from one of the crackers. There were a couple of squawks from the geese and then two or three orange bills took a peck at the cuff of Daniel's gray mackinaw.

"Take a big piece," his mother said. "That's too little. Here, Daniel, put your hand right out there."

The boy held a whole cracker out in his hand and, after a fight, one orange bill darted out and gobbled the cracker out of the boy's hand.

"That's it," his mother said. "Here, let's go feed the llamas now. They get hungry too."

They headed for another part of the zoo.

A couple of blocks away, on Park Avenue, people were making arrangements for the funeral of Governor Lehman. But funerals, for three- and four-year-olds, are just like crumpled feathers on top of the water. So Herbert Lehman's zoo was open for the children yesterday, and anybody who knew the man says there would have been hell to pay if anybody thought of closing it.

Mrs. Elaine Levine, who tells stories every day in the Children's Zoo, was talking about this.

"We have suspended the story-telling today in honor of his death," she said, "and of course none of us really feels like telling a story. But you wonder what he would say if he knew there was no story-telling today."

"He was that kind of man," she was told.

"He came one day while we told stories," she said. "He sat with the children and he spent the whole time watching their faces. Then he would do what they would do. When the children smiled, he would smile. If they became tense, he would sit there with his mouth open just as they would. If the children became somber, he would become very somber too. He loved to do that."

"Mrs. Lehman came more often," Gloria Tauza, another story-teller said. "She brought her nephew with her one time I can recall. She would not allow us to introduce her."

"Her husband never wanted anybody to say he was here, either," Mrs. Levine said.

Outside, children ran around the place. Two of them, in new snowsuits, spotted a wet section of the asphalt, so they rushed over and flopped in it. The mothers, of course, yelped.

More than 1.6 million people like this have come to the zoo since Governor Lehman had it erected in 1960. The day it opened he spoke only a word or two to reporters because he said his heart was too full. He died yesterday at eight-five. A man who was in public service for as long as he was must have left a lot of other monuments to himself. There are smart people who can tell you of this. But for just a person around town, you thought that this little zoo for the children, which was open on the day he died, said something about the man.

But the staple of the column was always the New York that no one else seemed to be writing about. It wasn't that he found things no one else would be able to find; it was more that he was interested in situations and places that in general tend to be overlooked. Breslin's New York stretches out to dairy barns in Brooklyn and what it's really like to be on a park bench in the middle of the afternoon.

A Night to Be Jolly

Any place with a bar in it yesterday was packed. They were shaking hands and kissing each other and then taking a drink whether they wanted one or not because everybody drinks before he goes home on Christmas Eve.

Ida Ryan was catching them on the other end, when they came off the train at the el station at Broadway and 31st Street, out in Astoria.

She sat and watched them as they came down the stairs, walking quickly, the whisky showing in their faces, saying "Merry Christmas," and, "Have a good holiday," to each other as they started for home.

One of them came up to the change window, a dollar bill in the hand under the packages.

"Could I get change for the bus?" he said.

Ida took the bill and pushed silver through the window and the hand fumbled from under the packages and picked it up.

"You know, this must be an awful tough night for you to work," the guy said, because he thought that was good to say to somebody working on Christmas Eve.

"Uh huh," Ida said. "Merry Christmas."

She said it automatically, but she was looking down, arranging her change and tokens. It was Christmas for everybody else last night, but to Ida Ryan it was just an eight-hour shift in a change booth.

Her husband, Jimmy Ryan, is in a cell in Attica State Prison. Her son, James Jr., is eighteen and is in the narcotics ward at Manhattan General Hospital. The boy was in grammar school, with report cards that showed honor marks, when the father was sent away in 1957. From then on, the boy slipped in school, and a year ago he came home with his eyes glazed from taking goof balls. Nobody could get him off the habit.

The daughter, Helen, is twelve and Ida has her living with a sister on Long Island now because she can't do much for her at home. A couple of years ago Helen began to have trouble hearing out of the right ear. The condition persisted until the ear went dead altogether. Then the left ear began to go. The doctors look at the ears and say nothing can be done.

"What am I going to do?" Ida said. "Something happens and I guess everybody has to pay for it. Now I have my father down. He's a job all by himself."

"The father? What happened to him?"

"He lost a leg a year ago. Then he had a stroke, and now he's just a patient in bed. He's another patient. That's all we have is patients."

Jimmy Ryan was a first-grade detective in New York. In 1957 he was sentenced to 7½ to 15 years and 2½ to 5 years for burglaries and holdups. He was also hit with a 4-year federal sentence for handling counterfeit money. He was no bargain when they put him away. Gambling had him over his head with money, and he took his gun and instead of protecting people with it he turned it on them. He knew it better than anybody else when he went away: he rated everything he got.

Then, a year ago, Ida Ryan came into the visiting room at Attica and she spoke over a table to her husband and told him that his son was on junk.

"I'll get him, I'll chain him to the bed," Jimmy said. "Let me get my hands on this kid."

"You can't," Ida said. "That's the trouble. You can't do a thing to him. You're here and he's on the street."

Then a guard stepped up and pounded his club on the table. "Time's up," the guard said.

He was locked in his cell for the night at 3:45 p.m. yesterday, just a few minutes after Ida started work in the change booth and all the people came down the stairs with their packages and the whisky in them and saying, "Merry Christmas," to each other.

The stories today all are about Tiny Tim and fat men seeing hungry faces in the windows and stepping out to give them something to eat, and there always is warmth and hope in them, which is why they are fables you tell at Christmas.

She smiled. "Hope, what kind of hope have I got? He's got years to go and his son and daughter are falling into pieces. He comes up for parole in November; if he could get paroled he could start on the federal sentence. But he may not even get paroled this time. I don't know. I just wish I could see a little light. If somebody would come and tell me tonight that I have a chance, that I can see some light, then it would be different. I could hope. Now I just have to sit here and make change."

At a few minutes before midnight somebody came to relieve her and she walked out of the booth and went downstairs to the street and walked up to Saint Rita's for midnight mass.

"I have to make it," she said. "I have more things to talk about in there than anybody else."

Men of Iron

The social event of the season, attended by a smashing crowd of more than two thousand, took place over the weekend in the Promenade Ballroom of Manhattan

Center, 311 West 34th Street. The April in Paris Ball and opening night of the Metropolitan Opera were like evenings spent in a candy store compared to this one. The occasion was the twenty-fourth annual Iron Workers' Ball, sponsored by Local 40, Bridge and Structural Workers' Union of America. Admission was $2.50 per person and there was dancing to a twelve-piece band until 2 a.m. People brought their own whisky, of which there was much.

The Promenade Ballroom at Manhattan Center is a large place. It has a stage, a big dance floor, a wide table area on the ground floor. Upstairs, a theater-type balcony has many tables for drinking.

Usually at the Iron Workers' Ball, a man drinking in the balcony falls over the rail and lands on the main floor like a bomb, disturbing the dancers. That did not happen this year, although, as the evening heightened, many people were falling head over heels down a flight of stairs leading from the balcony to the dance floor.

The tone of the evening was set at eight o'clock when a man named Robbie, who is 5 feet 6 inches and weighs approximately 240 pounds, came into the checkroom wearing a new double-breasted topcoat and carrying in a brown bag two quarts of rye, which he said he intended to drink himself.

The checkroom attendant leaned over the counter and held out his hand to make friends with Robbie.

Robbie stepped away. "I don't shake hands," he said. "I'm not the handshakin' kind."

Everybody else was piling through the doors, carrying whisky. At first the crowd was a bit uncomfortable. Most of the iron workers get their shirts done in Chinese laundries which use a lot of starch in the collar. So iron workers were spending the early part of the evening walking around with fingers hooked onto shirt collars to prevent chafing.

Chick Darrow, master of ceremonies, came onstage to introduce the first of seven acts. When this happened, many iron workers repaired to the bar behind the balcony. At one end of the bar Joe Melcher, aged eighty, an iron worker since 1906, drank beer and showed how Benny Leonard used to box.

"He was a wonder," Joe Melcher said. Mr. Melcher then dug two left hands to the ribs and showed you his right, then wheeled and went back to his beer. Melcher had a saloon with a boxing gymnasium over it in Harlem in 1915 and many fighters, Benny Leonard included, used to train there. The iron workers also used the place as a meeting hall and Melcher spoke fondly of one narrow union election in the early twenties.

"This fella Fredericks and another fella got mad and drew guns on each other," he said. "Fredericks won the argument. He shot the other fella in the rear cnd."

There were several rounds of drinks, with Melcher and his friend Joe, who had a couple of bottom teeth missing and had a lot of class. By now it was 11 p.m. and the entertainment was over. The dance floor was crowded and the iron workers had unbuttoned their collars and were becoming noisy. The Iron Workers' Ball was turning into a complete success.

You knew it was a success when Shaky Sullivan fell off his chair. Shaky Sullivan had been drinking whisky in a glass, with a pitcher of beer for a chaser, and he had been drinking quite a lot of this, and all of a sudden he started to slide off the chair. His friend Bill Carew reached over to grab him, but Shaky fought him off. Shaky Sullivan went down under the table like the *Titanic*. Only his legs stuck out from under the table, and Carew reached down and pushed them underneath, so nobody would trip over them on the way to the dance floor.

"Shaky always goes like this," Carew said. "But he's all right. Over in Staten Island, I fell forty feet into the hole and he was the first man to get to me. When I came to, he had his arms around me and he was dragging me out. Maybe when Shaky walks a beam he wavers a little because he drinks so much, but when there's trouble Shaky is right there."

While Carew spoke, the large blonde wife of an iron worker stood in the aisle and traded insults.

"You're coming to have a drink with me," the redhead said.

"Hell," the blonde said.

The redhead reached out and grabbed the blonde by the arm. The blonde tugged her arm back. The redhead would not budge. Then an iron worker who must have weighed 270 pounds weaved down the aisle and banged into both of them and that broke this one up. But the mood prevailed.

"There's an old guy I owe something to," Carew said. "What I owe him is to hit him in the face with a carnation." By a carnation, Mr. Carew meant a straight right hand to the mush.

The old guy, erect and gray-haired, who looked as if he just might be able to fight, was a table away.

Bill Carew's wife, an exceptionally pretty girl named Jo, put an end to this. "You promised me that if we came you wouldn't get into a fight," she said.

Carew said all right and sat down to have another drink.

The iron workers with him enthusiastically pointed out a man they call the Horse, who was over on one side of the hall. The Horse was wearing a blue serge suit with a belt in the back.

"Somebody bought it for him in Miami Beach in 1928," a guy at the table said. "He wears that and a ten-year-old pair of Thom McAn shoes. He don't buy anything for himself. In the winter he shows up for work with no gloves on and only a shirt. That's why we call him the Horse. He won't buy gloves in the winter, but he goes out and bets $200 on a horse race."

The ball now swung into the "Beer Barrel Polka" and people were stomping on the floor and every place you went somebody put a glass of whisky in your hand, and after a while you tripped a little when you walked and you kept bumping into people like Icebox McNiff and Three-Quarter Worthington. You don't know what bumping into anybody is until you bump into Three-Quarter Worthington.

Anybody who tries to say that Iron Workers' Ball

was not a great one should get punched in the nose. There were no phony dukes around looking for free drinks. Marchionesses were among the missing. These were real people having a real night.

Iron workers go eighty and ninety stories high to earn a day's pay. Or they walk along cables atop such as the Verrazano Bridge. You never hear much about how many of them fall and get killed, but an awful lot of them do. So when they throw a ball, they do not spend a lot of time kissing some old dame's hand.

"The only people we didn't invite tonight were our shylocks," one committee member said proudly.

The thing that kept the evening's activity somewhat in hand, everybody said, was the absence of the Mohawk Indians from the Brooklyn local. The Indians like to fight a lot when they drink. For some reason, only a couple of them showed up, and they were complete gentlemen.

"A friend of mine got stiff with them one Friday and they took him up to the reservation," Bill Carew said over a drink. "On Saturday night they scalped him. When he came back he didn't even need a shave on the top of his head."

But there was some action. In the men's room, late in the evening, a beefy man was bent over the sink, holding a wet handkerchief to his face. When he looked up, he displayed a top lip that had been split open, undoubtedly by a very fine right-hand punch.

"What the hell are you looking at?" the man with the split lip asked.

"Nothing," he was told quickly.

"That's better," he said.

Outside, a soldier walked backward down a flight of stairs with his arms out, so he could catch his father, who was coming down after him. Every second step, the old man would close his eyes and fall forward in one piece. The son would catch him and straighten him out. Then the son would go down a couple more steps and wait for his father to fall again.

"It's easier than carrying him," the soldier explained.

Proceeds from the Iron Workers' Ball go to a college scholarship fund set up in honor of Big Jim Cole, business agent for Local 40. The journal for the Iron Workers' Ball was loaded with ads, and the ads are important because some kid can go to college on them. The finest ad in the book was put in by the Glue Pot Tavern, 6661 Broadway, Peter Magee, proprietor; Pat Moran, head chef; Pete Powers, day manager; Joe Buckley, steward.

The ad said: "Every Saturday Night, 10 p.m., Dancing Girls. Be on Time!"

The Milk Run

The bar is owned by Matrona Wyszynski, and her late husband's name was Benny, so the sign in front of the place says it is Mrs. Benny's Tavern. It is listed that way in the phone book too, although the kids in the neighborhood call her Ma Benny and everybody who goes in there to drink runs the words together and calls the place Mahbenny's. It is on Pitkin Avenue in Ozone Park, right where Queens starts to run into Brooklyn, and Mahbenny's son Henny is in charge of the place from in back of the bar. If you spend an afternoon there, you can learn a lot of things from the people who take care of the milk cows in the barn across the street.

Oh, there are cows by Mahbenny's. There are eight of them, and three new calves, at a place called Balsam's Farm which is really owned by a milk-delivery company called Superior Farm. Each of the eight cows gives twenty quarts of kosher milk a day, which is sold retail to Orthodox Jewish families. They are going to bring twenty more cows to the place soon because business is good. The only trouble with having a lot of cows is that you can't get milkers. New York City would have cows all over the place if there were enough milkers to go around. This is a shame because cows would do an awful lot for the posture of the people in this city. There is an ammonia smell around cows that straightens you out like a stick. Let me put a couple of cows on every block in town and I'll show you more people walking like Marines than you've ever seen.

Because nobody in New York wants to be a milker, Balsam's and Wortman's, a place in Brooklyn which has 140 cows, are the only companies in this whole city that keep cows.

Now these milkers are very important around cows because, as Henny was explaining at the bar, a milker is a man who gets the milk out of the cows. "Some cows don't like milkin' machines, so you got to do it by hand," Henny said. "Steven here knows all about it."

Steve had on a hat and he was drinking blackberry brandy. "You milk cows two times every day," he said. "Four-thirty in the morning, four-thirty in the daytime. You milk them in the barn. You don't graze cows in the city."

"I know one thing about the cows," Henny says. "Bulls are mean. They get born mean."

"One of the calves we have over there is a bull," Dale Speroni, who runs the Superior Farm Company, said.

"Is he mean?"

"He'll hit you," Dale said. He said he would show you the baby bull. So we went out of Mahbenny's and walked across Pitkin Avenue to the cow barn, which is behind the office building, truck garage, and pasteurizing plant. The bulk of the milk in the place comes from upstate.

It was strange to see this barn. Off to the right you could see jets coming up from a runway at Kennedy. Straight ahead was the Belt, clogged with cars. Yet here you were walking through a barnyard and the smell of cows had your nostrils as wide open as a country boy's.

Dale disappeared for a moment, then came back with a small dog, a pug, on a leash. He took the dog up a cement ramp, opened a sliding door, and stepped inside.

There were eight cows lined up side by side in stall-like contraptions made of metal collars hanging from an overhead rail. I don't know what kind of cows they have in some place like Wisconsin, but the cows in Ozone Park, Queens, are big as hell. They are black and white and if one of them steps on your toe it is all over.

There were three small calves resting on some straw.

"Which one is the bull?" we asked Dale.

He was starting to tell us how you tell a bull when the baby bull made himself known. He was a black little thing, and he came off that straw with a swoosh and went right for Dale's pug. The little bull's black head with the floppy ears went down and then came up, just as the big bulls do in an Ernest Hemingway movie. The pug dog jumped back and started barking at the baby bull.

"I'll be damned, this little bum is for real," we said.

We left the bull alone and went back to Mahbenny's. "You see him?" Henny demanded. We told him the bull was something.

The rest of the day was spent in the bar. It was the first time we ever had seen a bull try to butt something and we had seen it on Pitkin Avenue, right across the street from Mahbenny's, which is in New York City.

"We got everything in this city," Henny said.

Park Etiquette

These four women, these four mean, warlike women, came into the park with all their kids, and God bless their kids because the kids are going to need it, and since there was only one empty park bench, the one I was sitting on and trying to read a newspaper on, the four women came right up and sniffed at me and then sat down. And right away it started.

"Hey, lady," I said to the one next to me. She had her head turned away so it would look like she wasn't doing anything. She was shoving me with her fat hip. "Hey, lady, I'm sitting here," I tell her.

"Sheila's pregnant," she says.

"What?" I say.

"Sheila's pregnant," she says. She points to the one down at the end. "Sheila has to stay off her feet."

Now this one next to me starts sliding her fat elbow in between us. I know she is going to really start shoving now. And I'm going to fight.

"If Sheila is pregnant then she belongs home taking care of herself," I say. "She shouldn't be in the park."

The four of them look at me. They look at me with this mean daytime face all women have when they come to the park with their children.

"You're such a smart person, you must have a very large practice," one of them says.

You can win a lot of arguments in this world, but you are not going to beat a dame who even hints that she is pregnant. So I wind up half-sitting on the edge of the park bench and trying to read a newspaper.

I guess there was nothing wrong with these women. They are acting just the way the former Rosemary Dattolico had acted a few minutes earlier, when she put me out of her house because I left a ring on the table with my coffee cup when I got excited watching *Art Linkletter's House Party*. She became very nasty. Women in the daytime in their own element are not like women in the nighttime out with everybody else. These women next to me on the bench showed this.

"Well," the one next to me shouts. They never speak, these women, they shout. "Well, I hope it gets a little cooler tomorrow so I can wear a wool dress. I don't have any more cottons."

"Hey, lady," I say to this one next to me who is shouting in my ear. "Lady, I'm trying to read a newspaper."

"So read!" she says.

She says it with that mean daytime face. It is 3:15 in the afternoon and there are, by rough count, 93 women in the park. They are watching about 141 kids. And this is the real New York. Not the New York with its cute stories of nannies and carriages in Central Park. That's the 1-per-cent New York. This park I am in is the 99-per-cent New York. No nannies or governesses or whatever you call them. Just mean-faced mothers.

"Got a match?" Sheila says. She is sitting there with a cigarette hanging out of her mouth and she looks like she's in the rackets. Being pregnant doesn't do a thing for Sheila.

"Sheila wants a match," the one next to me says. She throws her fat elbow into me. She is digging through this suitcase of a purse she has. She is looking for a match for Sheila.

"Hey, lady," I say to her. "I mean, lady, do you mind?"

"Mind your business," she says.

"What are you looking into her pocketbook for?" one of the others shouts at me.

"I'm not looking into any pocketbook," I say.

"Where's the park man?" Sheila is saying. "I want the park man."

They all start looking around for the park man. And now their strategy is simple. You can almost hear the words.

"Sex offender!" they are shouting to themselves.

"Hey, lady," I say. I say it real loud now. "Hey, lady, I'm just trying to read a newspaper."

This one next to me has her nose in her pocketbook while she is looking for a match for Sheila. I bend my head down so I can look right at her while I am saying this. She pulls her head up quick. I am left with my head bent, looking right into her pocketbook.

"Get out of there, you," she says.

"Hey, lady . . ."

"He's trying to take something out of her purse," Sheila says.

This Sheila, she's so pregnant, you should have seen her come off that park bench. She came off that park bench with the cigarette hanging out of her mouth and her black purse held out so she could take a good swat at me, and she tells me, this Sheila who is supposed to be pregnant, to get away from them.

"I'll call the cops if you bother us again," Sheila says.

I get off the park bench and walk out of the park and go up the block and these four women, these four mean, warlike women, they are sitting on the bench and looking at me through the storm fence and I can haar what they are saying as clearly as if they are screaming at me.

"Purse snatcher!"

"Sex offender!"

10

How He Sold His Heart to the Newspaper Business for a Pot of Message

Breslin is a newspaper writer who has worked for magazines and will probably go on doing so because there is money in it. He also appears on television at various times but he makes sure everyone understands he is a newspaperman appearing on television and not an aspiring television personage. He got his first job on a newspaper when he was seventeen and even when he didn't like it, he loved it.

What he loved at first was the people and then the work. He was always someone who could appreciate the kind of talk that goes on over newspaper bars. He became someone who couldn't go through a week without seeing something that he had written get itself into print. It wasn't egomania, exactly, it was more like the craftsmanship of a good carpenter who gets his real satisfaction from seeing the product of his hands rather than from the money that rings up in the till.

But he didn't really like the newspapers he worked for. "I gotta go for a paper where the owner is around all the time, not for some freakin' plantation where the overseer talks to the freakin' hands." He never really identified with a paper until he came to the *Herald Tribune,* and there he identified all too well. He would argue ferociously about the superiority of its foreign coverage over that of the *Times* without having the vaguest idea which was better. He took every circulation problem as a personal slight. He elected Mr. Whitney to the select pantheon of those who are "all right." And he began to hate the unions.

Through its final years, when the *Trib* was desperately trying to regain its stature, the unions were mounting a huge campaign against the papers of New York. In this city, the history of labor–management on newspapers has usually been abysmal. In the past ten years, it has got even lower. Breslin suspected that the unions would kill the *Trib.*

When he won the Meyer Berger Award he was proud that someone should have thought him worth it, but he wrote his column to try to show what value a newspaper prize really has. He even began to cherish his feud with *The New Yorker.* But his memos and some of his columns became more and more involved in the struggles of the *Trib.*

The Berger Award

The West End, a rectangular bar with many banks of beer taps, sits on the west side of Broadway between 114th and 115th Streets and it is one of the many assets of Columbia University, whose buildings make up most of the real estate in the area. It was filled yesterday afternoon with many college students, all of whom appeared bright and serious except for one man whose blond hair was worn Beatle-style. He was studying in a booth.

Also at the bar was William P. O'Brien. He is not a college student, but the discussion he was conducting was serious and far-reaching. It was about being touted on a race horse. Mr. O'Brien told of a day at "Mammath Park" racetrack when the chief of racetrack security insisted that a filly in the second race could not lose. This surprised Mr. O'Brien because he not only was the breeder and owner of the horse, but also had expert knowledge that the horse could run very well on any day and particularly this one.

Mutchie arrived at the bar a little after 3 p.m. His place of business now is downtown by the Fish Market, and this was farthest north in Manhattan he has been since the twenties, when he operated a still "a stone throw away" from Columbia and did quite well selling out of the bathtub to university professors.

Mutchie had on a dark blue topcoat, a new, well-pressed gray suit which he had bought for "occasions," and a small black hat of the type worn by people from his home town in Italy when they came over here steerage.

Mutchie came uptown yesterday for a tour of the academic facilities and also to attend the Meyer Berger Award ceremonies in the World Room, third floor, Columbia School of Journalism. Mutchie is interested in journalism because so many newspapermen owe him money. He was very interested in the Berger ceremonies because one of the winners, who received $500, was one of Mutchie's prized deadbeats.

"I brought everything with me," Mutchie said.

"What's everything?"

"All your tabs," he said. "One of them here goes back thirteen months."

With Mutchie leading the way, the party proceeded across Broadway and went up a block. Mutchie went to the end of one building, directed everybody with him to go right and then right again at the next corner. He knew the campus quite well because, as he was explaining, he sold a lot of whisky around the place in his time.

"Do you remember Lou Gehrig when he was up here?" Mutchie was asked.

"No, I only sold to the teachers," he said.

The award ceremonies took place in a high-ceilinged room named in honor of Herbert Bayard Swope. It is called the World Room after the late newspaper Swope edited. Chairs had been lined up, theater style, and a table with microphones was in the front of the room.

On the left side of the room a table was set up with several bottles of whisky, glasses, ice, and other things.

"Can we have the whisky now?" Mutchie asked. He was told he had to wait.

Mutchie then was introduced to John Hohenberg, a professor of journalism, and to Dean Richard Baker of Columbia. He said it was his pleasure. He then was introduced to a Mr. Adams and a Mr. Grutzner, of *The Times,* and several young ladies.

The room became partially filled with bright-looking students and people like Bob Harron, of the school's administration. Mutchie took a seat and watched carefully. He clapped his hands together quietly when Dean Baker presented one of the winners with the $500 check.

A top-level panel discussion of journalism followed. A friend of Mutchie's was brought up many times during the course of the discussion.

"He once had a story about a child who fell five stories from an apartment house," a panelist recalled. "He filled the story with quotes from the child about how terrible it was to fall. It was turned back to him when the deskman handling the copy noted that the child was only two and couldn't talk."

The discussion finished, the guests then headed for the whisky. At an appropriate moment, Mutchie made his move. He came through a wall of people as if he were playing football and he caught up with his award winner just as he was attempting to leave the premises.

"Congratulations," Mutchie said.

"It's in a check," the winner said.

Mutchie put his hand in his pocket and produced a large roll of bills. "I'll cash it for you," he said.

He took his $245, put on the black hat which people from his town always wore when arriving here in steerage, then walked out of the Journalism School and onto the Columbia campus he has come to know so well.

Talk of Dubuque

The other day, I received a letter from my old friend Sarah Phillips, whom I have not seen in twenty-seven years, and as I read her cheery words it caused me to think back to the time when I was nine years old and I accompanied my great-aunt to tea in the drawing room of Sir Hubert Arbuthnot's house outside of Delhi, a visit which always was trying for me because I never enjoyed tea at the Arbuthnot house as much as I enjoyed floating wooden sticks in the Ganges River. I remember vividly how I spent the long, sultry afternoon wiggling around in the chair and this so disturbed my great-aunt, who was agitated from the very outset because her teacup had a crack in it, that she asked Darius, the chaprisi *to guide me upstairs so I could spend the remainder of the afternoon sitting at a window and looking out onto Sir Hubert's private compound.*

This is about the way a magazine called *The New Yorker* starts off a lot of its stories. I may be a little off because I have not bought the magazine enough to get that purposely dry Old English style of theirs down. I'm not up on *The New Yorker* because it prints all these stories written by ladies about their childhoods. This is great for little old ladies from Dubuque, although it is not exactly my stick. But I read the magazine when it came out yesterday. It has devoted two pages this week to a parody of a writer named Jimmy Breslin.

Now my first reaction to *The New Yorker* parody was normal. I looked for the name of the person who did the parody. The story was signed J. Q. Purcell. The name has got to be a phony because I never heard of any J. Q. Purcell and neither has anybody else. So, not knowing who wrote the thing, I called Roger Angell, a *New Yorker* editor, and told him that I was going to have him killed and put into a trunk and thrown into Gravesend Bay.

But immediately people in the literary business jumped on me for this attitude.

"Why, it is the ultimate flattery," Sterling Lord, the agent, insisted. "The last time *The New Yorker* ran a parody it was on Arthur Miller and Norman Mailer. This one on you means that you have arrived."

Garson Kanin, the director and producer, said the same thing. Cork Smith, the editor, went even further. "If you didn't owe us money you could retire right now," he said.

But these people operate on a different level from me. They are all smart, high-class fellows and, while I know them quite well, they are not exactly my set. Rather than convince me about this parody business, all they did was make me doubtful. So to get the thing straightened out in my mind, I decided to take the case to my own guys.

Mike the Brain, who was my private lawyer until he got himself disbarred, read the story in the magazine very carefully. He was in ecstasy when he finished.

"We'll bust them out," he said. "Go over and kiss the editor. I'm going to get some stiff out of a law office to front for me and I'll sue these bums in fifty-one states."

"How much can we win?" I asked Mike the Brain.

"A whole magazine," he said.

"What do *you* think?" I asked my other friend, Bobby Seola. He is the president of Bricklayers Union No. 9.

"I'll have ninety guys picketing the joint tomorrow morning," Bobby said. "The people who put out the magazine won't be able to get in to go to work."

Later on, we went downtown to Mutchie's and took the matter up with Joey Brocato, an ex-pug, who was tending bar alone. Mutchie had been out drinking with his girl friend Vivian the night before and he was upstairs, barely breathing.

"Ignore the bums," Joey said. "That's what I done when they used to talk about me at Stillman's. I ignored the bums."

Joey waited for this advice to sink in. Then wrinkles of puzzlement came onto his face.

"The thing that I can't figure out," he said, "is why they would take a shot at you in the *New York Enquirer.*"

Mr. Bellows, Editor:

This matter in the mail reminded me of something I have had nagging at me, but have done nothing about.

I don't want any part of the Guild and intend to do something about it immediately. I die when I think they get money off of me. Six cents is too much. And if they think they are going to have some kind of a strike there will be carnage around here, and this I don't even mouth off. It will come like rain.

So my best move, mentally and sensibly, is to simply tell your accounting people not to touch a cent of my money for the Guild again under any circumstances. Look at this card they send me: DUES CHECKED OFF MONTHLY.

No sonofabitch alive is going to screw with my money like that. It ends today. And I go at them to get every cent they ever took back.

Publishers' Pension Plan.

Freak pensions. I'll make my own pension.

Oliver Pilat, local president. This jerk can't even make a capital letter on a typewriter.

I will do nothing here until I talk to you because some vague thing told me that you locked me in with another one of those promises that I would be good. But I want no part of them and their illiterate freaking notes on a bulletin board and their old bastards getting up and walking out in the middle of handling a story because it is time, under the contract, to go to dinner or something. It is not my stick.

jbreslin, editorial dept.

The Powers What Be

"Joseph," the man sitting at the desk said, "this is what we have to get corrected right away." He made a pencil mark on a proof of a story. "Walk it out to the composing room, will you?"

Joey Goldstein took the sheet of paper and started running. Joey Goldstein, from Second Avenue between 11th and 12th Streets, never walked. Street bums, "air inspectors," they call them on Second Avenue, could walk. But Joey Goldstein was the copy boy in the sports department of the *New York Sun,* and he wanted to be a boss someday, maybe the city editor. He ran with the proof in his hand through the door and into the composing room. It was 7:30 a.m. on January 4, 1950. Outside, Chambers Street and Broadway were bright and cold under the green clock which said, "The Sun Never Sets."

"Look at this," somebody in the composing room said.

Joey Goldstein stopped. A crowd of printers, nearly all the printers in the room, were around one of the tables where they set headlines. Joey pushed through the crowd. The printer at the table held a line of big block type between his hands.

"THE SUN IS SOLD"

"That's the page-one headline," the printer said.

"We're out of business?" Joey Goldstein said.

"That's what it says," another of the printers said.

Joey Goldstein pushed back through the crowd. He ran over and slapped the proof on a table. Then he ran out of the composing room and into the sports department. He did not look left or right. He pulled his coat off a rack and left the building. He had a widowed mother back in the walk-up tenement on Second Avenue, and the landlord was not good at listening to stories about some newspaper that died.

At eight o'clock that night, everybody who used to work for the *New York Sun* was drunk in a place called the Readeway, a block from the office. Joey Goldstein was in the Jamaica Arena, which had a wrestling show going on. He was in the back of the place, standing between the television cameras and a big refrigerator. Each time the cameras started to swing to the refrigerator for the sponsor's commercial, Joey Goldstein raised his hand in a signal and one of the grips would open the refrigerator door for the start of the commercial.

"I couldn't afford to be out of a job even for one day," Joey Goldstein was saying yesterday afternoon. He has a big job at Roosevelt Raceway now and he lives out in the suburbs. But he can tell you everything that happened on the last day of the *New York Sun* because once he thought a newspaper was going to be his life.

The *New York Daily Mirror* went out of this city on October 15, 1963. It was 6:15 p.m. when Selig Adler, the Managing Editor of the paper, walked down one flight of stairs from his office to the paper's composing room. He handed a sheet of white paper to a man named Marty Tanzer, who was in charge of distributing copy to typesetters.

"What's this?" Tanzer said.

Adler took the cigarette out of his mouth. "Get it set in type, and then go get yourself a job," Adler said. The copy began: "The Hearst Corporation announced yesterday that it will cease publication of the *New York Mirror* with the issue of October 16, 1963. . . ."

All last week the people who work on newspapers in New York were talking about when the next one of these announcements was going to be made. For two weeks now, there has been talk that two afternoon papers the *Journal-American* and the *World Telegram and Sun,* will merge. And last Wednesday, the third afternoon paper, the *New York Post,* did not publish. It failed to come out because the manual laborers who print the product refused to allow automation to be used in the composing room.

After a day-long mediation, the *Post's* publisher, Mrs. Dorothy Schiff, and Bertram Powers, the head of the printing union, agreed to introduction of automation for one week's trial. After which, the problem still will have to be faced: the *Post* wants the automation to stay—or the paper, in the face of antique costs, will close up again. And Powers, who regards a newspaper as just another factory job for his men, wants the automation only on his terms, which means virtually no saving for the *Post.*

The automation is done by means of a typewriter keyboard which punches out a tape which is fed into a computer. Powers' union wants its men to handle the whole process. Eight printers at the *Post* were sent to a business school to learn typing. After ten weeks, they now sit at the computer operation and turn out stories more slowly than a linotype and in unintelligible form. One story at the *Post* this week, which was 83 lines long, came out of the computer operation with 43 typographical errors in it. This took a linotype operator 12 minutes to correct. Twelve minutes, for this small amount of work, in comparison to the 12,000 lines of type per hour that typists could produce, is the reason why everybody sat around yesterday and talked about a newspaper in New York folding.

"When a newspaper folds," Theodore H. White, the author, was saying, "we think immediately of the loss of jobs. I think of something much more important. The loss of a voice. This town's major industry is the word business. We make all the ideas for the whole Western world. When the longshoremen threatened to choke the city off as a major port, the state stepped in with a commission to clean it up. Now printers threaten the newspapers, our daily word business.

Words are more important than a waterfront. Somebody must take action."

White was in the living room of his brownstone on East 64th Street. He had a brandy in one hand and a cigarette in the other. A carton, filled with his book, *The Making of the President 1964,* was on a chair, for autographing. The book was written in New York. It was set in type in New Hampshire because New York printing is too expensive even for a monumental best seller.

"Do without a newspaper?" Max Ascoli, the magazine publisher, was saying at breakfast in his apartment on Gramercy Park. "Sure, you can do without a newspaper. Do without this one, do without that one. Pretty soon you find you can do without anything. It is easy to become dull. Then comes a political candidate with the magnetic appeal of a John Kennedy on television and you have a monster. I don't mean Kennedy. I mean somebody with his looks and appeal. With no newspapers, somebody like that could envelop the nation. Do without a newspaper because the mechanics are costing too much? You are dealing with an insane situation."

It is not insane to Bertram Powers, the president of New York Typographical Union No. 6. He is a single-minded man who goes through life as if he had received a late vocation, a thing very common with the Irish. In 1961, after twenty-two years in the union, he became president. He promptly took on the newspaper publishers of New York. This is like beating up hospital patients.

"We will give you 100 per cent of the savings," one management representative, who shook when he even looked at Powers, said.

"I don't care about anything," Powers said one night to a guy who drove him home to Massapequa, Long Island. "There will only be three papers in this city and that's the way it is going to be and I don't care about them."

This has been his theme. And he is about to be responsible for the death of another paper.

Last week the only woman publisher, Mrs. Dorothy Schiff of the *Post,* decided to take a stand against Powers. For one day she closed her paper and sat in her East Side apartment and refused to give in. At nine o'clock at night, she walked into her city room, followed by Powers. Mrs. Schiff stood in a green dress with black print under a greasy fluorescent light held to the ceiling by gold-painted chains with coils of dirt hanging from them. She had bent Powers in the twenty-four hours since she had shut down the plant. The *Post* was reopening with automation. Bad automation, as it turned out all week, but it was in there.

"Of course, I've been a liberal since the nineteen-thirties," Mrs. Schiff was saying yesterday, "and I am against any machine that can put a human being out of a job. But I feel the history of these things always has shown that the more machines there are, the more jobs there are.

"What will happen this week? Well, I hope to continue. I don't want to make any statements. One has to be careful in these matters. I spent yesterday in a meeting with Mr. Powers on this matter. I have faith that it will work out this week."

Other publishers, who are in an association, have done nothing about the man. Most of them find it much easier to bear down on editorial people.

"What do they give you over there?" Norton Peppis, who owns a saloon in Queens, was saying to a reporter on the *World Telegram and Sun* the other night.

"I get $185," the reporter said.

"You get what?" Peppis said. He called over Tippy, one of his bartenders.

"What do you go out of here with?" he asked.

"Over two hundred," Tippy said.

"Throw the typewriter away and start mixing drinks, if that's all they want to give you on a newspaper," Peppis said.

This is the financial end of the daily word business,

which is the newspapers. It goes from poor to bad in all but a couple of papers in town, and it always has been generally bad. But it still is the business of words, and words written by a reporter, whether he makes big money or not, still are far more important in life than is the laborer who prints the words.

Powers, very conscious of cameras since he has gotten into these fights, now feels he is above the words. He says he, a high-school dropout, will set the terms under which these words are gotten to the public in New York. He, and the union behind him.

"I thought I had grown up and the depression was in the past," Paul Sann, the editor of the *Post,* was saying over a drink yesterday. "But I find I am in 1932 all over again. That's all this business reminds me of these days."

Once, and only once, on the day before a strike began, the *Trib* killed one of Breslin's columns. This is the column that never ran:

Immortal Situation

At nine o'clock in the morning, Walter Lippmann sits at his desk in the red-walled second-floor study of his home in Washington. Writing with a pen on white bond paper, he turns out a column for this newspaper. How long does it take him to write the column? As long as it took him to live and acquire an understanding of the things he writes of. He is seventy-five now and he uses the past to help deal with the present. He was at Versailles for President Woodrow Wilson; he regularly saw Roosevelt and Churchill. In 1960 John Kennedy asked his advice on cabinet appointments. And Khrushchev read Lippmann, and spent hours talking to him. Now it is 1965 and Viet Nam is the problem and Lippmann, with the changes of history in his mind, writes of today and tomorrow in Hanoi and Saigon and Peking.

After he has finished writing the column he dictates it into a recording machine. A secretary types it. Lippmann goes over it again, then has it sent to New York. It arrives in the fifth-floor editorial office of the *New York Herald Tribune*. It then is sent down to the fourth floor, the composing room, to be set in type. There, on a machine that was invented in 1880 and has changed very little since, and in a setting of working habits and union procedures that were outmoded when Lippmann was at Versailles, his column about things in 1965 is put into type in an eighty-five-year-old printing process.

On March 31 there is a distinct chance that the members of the New York Typographical Union No. 6, the ones who work under these antiquated procedures and at antiquated machines, will go on strike to keep things basically as they are. Because of this, a man like Lippmann won't be able to be read by people in this city who are interested in what happens now, and could happen tomorrow, in the year 1965.

Here is an incredible, immoral situation in which creative thinking is made subservient to the past. A printer, following the tradition which somehow has been able to exist, can knock out a Walter Lippmann. Anybody who can defend this system ought to be asked to show his second papers. And for a printing union to knock out a Walter Lippmann so it can defend production methods which should have been chased years ago is a walk down Crazy Street.

The printers, for whatever reason, want to preserve the system that has been killing newspapers in this city. They do this by putting shylock prices on any modernization which can save the papers from which they draw their pay. Two years ago the printers, about 2,000 of them, went on strike for 114 days in order to keep the past alive. In the process, the *Daily Mirror* became a place where people used to work. Now, on March 31, the printers are ready to strike again. What it could lead to is anybody's guess. *Fortune* magazine says that three papers in town could fold in a strike.

To compound this, the union seems to have some leadership trouble. There is no logic when men reach for power. Furthermore, Bertram Powers, the head of the New York union, has in the past made a point of saying that he doesn't care about newspapers.

"What if some newspapers fold during this strike?" he was asked by newsmagazine people.

"Oh, if papers fold that's all right with me," Powers said. "The men will go out and print Christmas cards. We don't care."

Yesterday Powers and other union people met with newspaper representatives and continued their struggle to keep the past. In a newspaper composing room, the past consists of a machine called the linotype and it is manually operated at a speed of about one length behind handwriting. An outsider watching it work will make it 8–5 that the machine is breaking down, not operating.

"That isn't a machine, it's an Erector set," a friend of mine, seeing one for the first time, said one night. "Why don't they give the guy a skate key and let him wind the thing up and watch it go?"

The process of getting a story into print this way is as slow as malnutrition and its cost could bust out a couple of savings banks. That the publishers have lived with it for all these years is strong indication that a lot of these people in the front office ought to be sent out to get a whole new set of brains. The production of a newspaper is merely the packaging of an editorial product which the public buys. Packaging, as it took the publishers fifty years to learn, has changed. If food companies packaged their stuff with newspaper methods, we'd all be growing broccoli on the windowsill to get by.

Now that machines finally have been set up to start newspaper composing rooms toward 1965, machines that will not cost one job in the industry, the union heads fight for power, and for the preservation of the past in an industry that depends on what happens today. This suggests a couple of things. One is insanity.

The other is a new law regarding a newspaper strike affecting the interest of the public, not of a man who says he would just as soon print Christmas cards.

When it became clear that the *Herald Tribune* was about to enter a merger with the *World Telegram and Sun* and with the *Journal-American*—in those days the plan was to print a morning paper called the *Herald Tribune* and an afternoon paper called the *World Journal*—Breslin's gloom grew to monumental proportions. It hurt too much to laugh and he was too old to cry. He hated the whole idea that the end of an independent *Herald Tribune* should be dependent on the mechanical unions and not on the reporters in the City Room.

The Headlines

Next Monday three newspapers in New York are going to merge into one company that will put out a morning, evening, and Sunday newspaper. All this week the most important people in the newspaper industry have been squabbling and negotiating over this merger.

The greats of metropolitan journalism have stepped up to take command. First, there is Bertram Powers. He is the great tastemaker in this city. He is the head of the printers' union, and they are the people who have taught New York how to read misspelled words. Powers himself has great creative talent. Cleaning women fight for the doodles of letterheads he leaves on conference-room floors.

Then there is Joseph Baer. He is in charge of the union whose members are the people who drive the trucks that the papers are in. And Joseph Laura, who is the head of the union that wraps the newspapers into bundles to be put on the trucks. These two are acknowledged greats in the communications industry and everybody says you must settle with them first before there are any newspapers, merged, unmerged, emerged, or submerged.

And, too, there is Thomas Murphy. He is the power in charge of the Newspaper Guild. This is a union of elevator operators and accountants which has been kind enough to allow in it a small group of workers who are called reporters and rewrite men and copy editors. These people are only about 30 per cent of the Newspaper Guild and all they do on a newspaper is write what the people read and this is not important at all. They do not fit so well into this Newspaper Guild, so nobody really is worrying about them this week.

You see, the head of the Newspaper Guild, Mr. Murphy, is an ex-bookkeeper. Newspapermen traditionally say the bookkeeper is a two-dollar bum who should be mangled. There also is well-documented evidence that bookkeepers do not know how to make capital letters. But since the newspapermen are only a small item this week, the man trying to govern decisions as to which newspapermen stay and which ones lose jobs in the merger is a bookkeeper.

Which is all right in the end, because the newspapermen had too many worries of their own yesterday to interfere with the greats of journalism above them. The worrying all started when somebody in one City Room dug through records and came up with the fact that no newspapermen will have to go to jail next week because there are no debtor's prisons in this area any more.

To the newspapermen I know in New York, this came as bad news. Most of my people, if they are out of work next week because of the merger, would rather be in jail for non-payment of some simple commercial debt than walking around on the sidewalk where we could be targets for the shylock to drive up on the sidewalk and run us over with his Cadillac.

You see, the newspaper people I know may write about crime or politics, but their real knowledge is in deficit financing. And in true deficit financing there is great danger.

"When I see you, I am going to run the car over you two times, one time forward and one time backward," his personal shylock warned my friend Sam the Rewrite Man late yesterday.

"I'll see you next week," Sam the Rewrite Man told him.

"Next week?" the shylock yelled. "Next week my friend rented your newspaper office to put a dress factory into it."

"We are calling in your loan today," Mr. Peters from the loan company told me yesterday. "If you had a steady job in taxicabs we would deal to you. But you are a newspaperman. Pay the balance by Friday or we will take the couch out of your living room."

This, then, is what has kept New York newspapermen busy this week while the powers of journalism settled the big merger. You could see, just by reading newspaper accounts of the merger, who the big shots are in the Fourth Estate in this city. You read one that says: Bertram Powers says the new merged paper cannot come out because it takes a very long time for him to show his printers how to get to work. And: Thomas Murphy, head of the Newspaper Guild, will not allow the new papers to have separate staffs because then he would have to make out two sets of books to keep their names in.

Nowhere was there a headline which said, "Sam the Rewrite Man Gives Go Ahead to Publishers." Which is the way it should be. Only in those old trench-coat movies do they make newspapermen important on newspapers.

Then it became certain that there was going to be a pre-merger strike and, further, that no one could predict what the outcome of a prolonged strike would be. As it happened, after four months of strike, the *Herald Tribune* died, giving some of its name and a little of its old stuff to a new afternoon newspaper, the *World Journal Tribune*. Nobody knew, in April 1966, that this would happen, but many suspected something like it.

Breslin was all set to write his last column as the most stinging possible diatribe against the unions.

Thanks, Gentles All

I want to thank all the people who had to do so much hard work to get this column out today. I particularly want to thank the printer who went to all the trouble to get this column set into type. He had to come all the way from his house to work at this job. What with his wife stuck home with the children, and all the things around the house needing fixing, he probably belonged at home. But he got up and came all the way in to work and set this column into type and I really want to thank him for his efforts.

A column, after all, is a very hard thing to do. First of all, they hand you sheets of paper with typewriting on them and up in one corner, in pencil, the sheets are marked, "Set two column mutts, 8 on 10." Now this doesn't mean much to you. But it means some load of work for a printer. He has to sit down at his linotype machine and turn a handle to set the width that the type is supposed to be. The width is two columns, and that is double the size of one column.

The word "mutts" is next, and this is a real trouble. It means that at the start and the finish of every line of type, the printer has to tap a special key which makes an indent into the type. It is a lot of work, tapping this key all the time.

After the printer is finished setting the width and getting himself mentally geared up so that his hand will tap that special key all the time, he gets into the heavy work. He has to read the typewriting on the pages in front of him.

All the time he is touching the keys to make letters in type, he has to sit there and read. He reads one word, and then he has to read another word and then another word. And he has to get those same exact words into type on the machine.

But he changed his mind when he had handed in the first page because he had stopped at the desk of Emma

Bugbee. He was furious with the management-to-be of the new corporation. He was furious about an insurance letter on his desk. He was sick about the unions and threatening to go down to the composing room and punch somebody. Then Emma happened to mention what it was like when she started working in 1910. She never used a curse word in public in her life. She maintained more decorum than any other member of her Barnard graduating class no matter if she was in the White House or the midst of rain, riot, or arson. She invited Breslin to come downstairs and have a drink at her going-away party. He said he would as soon as he finished his column. This was his last one for the *Herald Tribune*.

Emma

From somewhere, yesterday morning, from out of one of the 10,000 mornings in the recent past when the newspapers in New York were not able to print, I was remembering a man talking. His words could be heard again clearly. "The New York newspapers. They advise me on inflation. They advise me on agriculture. They advise me on foreign policy. And then they can't get their own *lahnotype* machines to work."

It struck me that the thoughts just might be pertinent. Particularly when I was getting ready to come into the *New York Herald Tribune* newspaper office for what could be the last time. The *Herald Tribune,* you know, is one of the three newspapers that have merged into a new company which planned to start operating Monday with a morning and evening paper. The papers are not expected to appear on Monday because the various labor unions that are certain they are the backbone of the business have decided they are going to strike. In this era, it is impossible to have a clearly written, well-edited newspaper unless the truck drivers and printers feel good.

The president of the new newspaper company, Matt Meyer, immediately said that he thought there was a chance that the *Herald Tribune,* the morning paper, would be killed if there was a long strike. Now, this was the fighting spirit you always look for in newspaper executives. So all the people on the *Herald Tribune* couldn't wait to get to the office yesterday. The *New York Times* office.

So between both sides of this world of newspapers, between the printers who are so invaluable that machines with girls will replace them, and newspaper managements, new and in the past, who were so smart that they let a situation grow to where a laborer can knock out a great publication—between all these people, my big shot at life now is making it as a hard-core welfare case.

So, anyway, into the office we come yesterday. The City Room looks in great shape. Get rid of the desks and put in some cutting tables, put my man Abe Schrader's name on the door, and you have good dresses.

Then on the desk was a highly thoughtful letter from Mr. Andrew Kolis, agency supervisor, Phoenix Mutual Life Insurance Company, Hartford, Connecticut. He writes:

> This letter will not be of any interest to you, if you have not been affected by the imminent merger or disturbed by your industry's difficulties in the past few years. However, if you or your immediate associates have been affected, you may owe it yourselves to investigate our industry. Certainly, it is not an easy one, but to the man possessed of the right talents it is a very rewarding one. It is an industry whereby each man controls his own destiny. You or one of your associates may make one of your better investments by spending 30 minutes with me and exchanging a few ideas about the Life Insurance Business.

Damn if I won't take him up on this. I want to talk to Mr. Kolis about doing some real good life-insurance advertisements for him. I want to do a big ad campaign showing a wife and her two children standing at the coffin and looking at the dead father and, behind them, the man looking sad and saying, "She'll starve because he forgot to pay his last premium to Phoenix

Mutual. You, too, might die today. Don't let this happen to you. Pay Phoenix Mutual!"

Emma Bugbee was sitting at her desk. Emma Bugbee is seventy-seven and she has been on the *Herald Tribune* for fifty-six years. Once, when she was out maneuvering in this business, they sent her to Washington to interview Eleanor Roosevelt. When Emma had done this a few times, she was an overnight house guest in the joint, and the relationship stayed that way over the years. Emma was one of the good ones in this town. When she first came around, women newspapermen used to meet for tea.

"Don't you think Schrafft's is a much better restaurant since they put in bars?" Emma said yesterday.

She had on a flowered hat and a corsage on the shoulder of her blue suit. When she got through the phone calls she was going downstairs to the Artist and Writers for a small farewell luncheon. The other day Emma decided to get out of the business. She heard some kind of talk about people on the merged papers being kept on a seniority basis and she thought there was no sense in anybody putting her on some list if it would mean a younger person got dropped.

"I just thought it was the perfect time to leave the newspaper business," she was saying yesterday. Then she got up and started down to the bar.

"I think I'll have some champagne," she said.

She left and took a part of the business with her.